Living on the Edge in Suburbia

To Chellie

Thank you very
much for your
interest.

Best wishes,

Tiene Lewin Ph.

Living on the Edge in Suburbia

From Welfare to Workfare

Terese Lawinski

Vanderbilt University Press ■ Nashville

© 2010 by Vanderbilt University Press
Nashville, Tennessee 37235
All rights reserved
First printing 2010

This book is printed on acid-free paper.
Manufactured in the United States of America

Library of Congress Cataloging-in-Publication Data

Lawinski, Terese.
Living on the edge in suburbia :
from welfare to workfare / Terese Lawinski.
p. cm.
Includes bibliographical references and index.
ISBN 978-0-8265-1699-2 (cloth : alk. paper)
ISBN 978-0-8265-1700-5 (pbk. : alk. paper)
1. Public welfare—New York (State)—Westchester County.
2. Welfare recipients—New York (State)—Westchester County—
Case studies.   3. Welfare recipients—Employment—
New York (State)—Westchester County—Case studies.
4. Suburbanites—New York (State)—Westchester County—
Economic conditions—Case studies.
I. Title.
HV99.W45L39 2010
362.5'8409747277—dc22
2009028792

In memory of my parents,
Teresa and Victor Lawinski,
and brother, J Russell Law

Contents

Acknowledgments

My relationship with Westchester County began in 1989 shortly after I met Steve Sullivan, when he picked me up from the train station and took me on a sunset driving tour of the village that I would move to a year later. That evening I did not see the poverty in the cities, nor did I imagine that I would come to study poverty in this wealthy county fifteen years hence. My life took twists and turns, as did the lives of the people I came to know who were living close to the edge or below poverty level, as well as those who lived comfortably but experienced a financial downturn. I thank all the women and men who participated in the research upon which this book is based; to protect their identities I do not acknowledge them by name. I am deeply indebted to all the parents who told me about the ups and downs of home life and their experiences at welfare offices and work. I thank the service providers who shared knowledge and who helped with the logistical aspects of recruitment and interviewing. I also thank the people who were not formally research participants but from whom I learned much about issues related to poverty and the social services terrain. I express gratitude to the advocates who alerted and invited me to assorted meetings where I learned about current political and policy matters.

I extend a deeply felt thank-you to Ida Susser for her guidance, encouragement, and unwavering support over many years and for her intellectual insights that helped shape my research and writing. Shirley Lindenbaum's theoretical insights and practical advice energized me. I benefited greatly from Louise Lennihan's enthusiasm for my work. Louise Lamphere's vote of confidence was extremely important to me, and I am especially thankful to her for referring my work to Michael Ames at Vanderbilt University Press.

I extend my appreciation to Michael Ames for seeing the worth of my research and to the anonymous manuscript readers for their reviews and suggestions. I am so grateful for Michael's counsel and patience throughout the publishing process. I value Jessie Hunnicutt's sage editorial guidance, Jeremy Rehwaldt-Alexander's keen copyediting skills, and Sue Havlish's marketing savvy.

I acknowledge Susan M. Barrow and Judith Samuels, each of whom provided a truly flexible work arrangement that accommodated my research and writing. I also acknowledge my many writing seminar cohorts who helped me formulate and organize ideas in the early analysis and writing stage.

Many thanks to my friends Peggy Atkinson, Trudy Gewirtz, Ave M. Kelly, Phyllis Koyner, Fredda Turnof, and Alan Vitolo, who cheered me on during the evolution of this book.

A very special thank-you goes to my family: Charlotte, Zachary, Radnor, and Remington Law; Daniel Buchler; and the Sullivan clan. Lisa Lawinski Buchler's love, wisdom, and laughter help me get through life, and her emotional support was crucial throughout the writing. And a heartfelt thank-you to Steve Sullivan, whose love and music sustain me.

Abbreviations

ADC	Aid to Dependent Children
AFDC	Aid to Families with Dependent Children
DRA	Deficit Reduction Act of 2005
DSS	Department of Social Services
JOBS	Job Opportunities and Basic Skills
NYS	New York State
OTDA	Office of Temporary and Disability Assistance
PRWORA	Personal Responsibility and Work Opportunity Reconciliation Act of 1996
SNA	Safety Net Assistance
SSI	Supplemental Security Income
TANF	Temporary Assistance for Needy Families

1

Introduction

It was a few weeks before the November 2008 elections and the country was in the throes of an economic meltdown. I was seated among a small group of New Yorkers at a community meeting hosted by an anti-poverty advocacy organization. The public was invited to engage in a dialogue with selected state legislative candidates on several issues pertaining to economic security. A meeting goal was to educate and to have the candidates pledge their commitment to the issues, one of which was to raise the amount of New York's welfare grant. The group was informed that New York's basic monthly welfare cash grant had not increased since 1990 and its value had eroded about 50 percent since. For a family of three the monthly grant was $291.[1] A speaker positioned this meager amount against the soaring cost of utilities and consumer goods. For example, the price of a market basket of food items, which cost $37 in 1990, had doubled to $75 by 2008. While the candidates seemed empathetic, they told of New York State's grim economic predicament and its fiscal challenges. Because the state then faced a projected $12.5 billion budget gap for the next fiscal year, I feared that an increase would not be included in next year's state budget and the grant would remain at its insufficient level.

In general, I was familiar with the hardships of many recipients of welfare who told me about the inadequacy of the welfare grant. Several years earlier I had conducted ethnographic research on poverty in affluent Westchester County, New York. My research specifically examined the impact that the 1996 welfare reform law had on families living in suburban Westchester. Throughout the history of the U.S. welfare program, numerous policy changes have had varying effects on families. The Personal Responsibility and Work Opportunity Reconciliation Act of 1996 (PRWORA) unequivocally altered the nature and scope of the U.S. welfare program, favoring the labor market at the expense of impoverished people, especially women. Unsurprisingly, the law has been viewed by many policy makers as a triumph. For example, a decade after President Bill Clinton signed the legislation he reflected on the "great success" of welfare "reform" in quantitative terms, focusing on welfare roll reduction and the labor force participation of recipients:

> Welfare rolls have dropped substantially, from 12.2 million in 1996 to 4.5 million today. At the same time, caseloads declined by 54 percent. Sixty percent of mothers who left welfare found work, far surpassing predictions of experts. Through the Welfare to Work Partnership, which my administration started to speed the transition to employment, more than 20,000 businesses hired 1.1 million former welfare recipients. Welfare reform has proved a great success, and I am grateful to the Democrats and Republicans who had the courage to work together to take bold action. (Clinton 2006)

Some time earlier I met Charlotte Thompson when she and her two children were homeless, living in a family shelter in Westchester County.[2] She had relied on welfare over time and offered her assessment, reflecting the reality of welfare restructuring on the ground.

> I think the idea of welfare reform is great. I believe that nobody should be permanently receiving from the government. But they don't make it plausible for you to get off. I mean, education is everything. . . . Trying to force somebody to go to work, and you're still not able to be self-sufficient . . . doesn't make any sense to me. . . . I feel like I have to leave [Westchester] because I'm not able to support myself. I don't want to have to rely on a man. I don't wanna . . . be in a relationship just so I can survive. I don't understand why they [the government] would rather pay $3,000 a month to [a shelter operator to house us] in [a shelter] rather than [provide me] rent allowance which is like 300 and something dollars for me and two kids a month. And there's no way that you can find an apartment for $300.
>   . . . They say that the first few years of a child's life is very important. You know, that's when their personality is formed and they know that you're supposed to do certain things for a child to make them strong or to give them . . . the foundation that they need to become an independent and viable person in society. . . . If all the experts agree . . . , why doesn't that apply for people on welfare? To me, that would help society, period, if they supported these women. The problem is that, especially with black women

. . . a lot of us have to rely on ourselves. So, they should . . . [help] so you can be self-supportive instead of just trying to put you in a job where you're making $5.50 an hour.

Charlotte had become a single parent after a divorce well over a decade earlier. Some time after her marriage dissolved she fell on hard times and she and her four children moved in with family. But she depleted all her savings helping out kin with whom she was living. Consequently, Charlotte and her children moved into a family shelter. After a few months she relocated to temporary subsidized housing under the auspices of a housing operator. She immediately applied for a Section 8 housing voucher that would enable her to afford permanent housing, though she was aware of the multiyear waiting period.[3] As the years passed, Charlotte raised her children in the apartment, worked in jobs that were usually not permanent, and finished a year of college. But just short of a decade later, when she was still on the Section 8 waitlist, Charlotte's time in "temporary" housing was long expired and she was forced by the housing operator to leave her apartment. Charlotte suspected that an administrative error kept her "at the bottom" of the Section 8 list, but, having no recourse, she and her children moved among family and friends. These doubling-up living arrangements became untenable and eventually Charlotte and her two teens moved to a shelter. By this time Charlotte was in her early forties and had received welfare intermittently for many years when she was unemployed and to augment her low wages when she was employed.

Over the course of a lifetime, impoverished families suffer countless pressures that can destabilize their fragile economic conditions and living situations. Recently, more families accustomed to a middle-class lifestyle have undergone setbacks plunging them into financial straits. Charlotte is one of the forty-two suburban parents I interviewed who told me how they struggled to raise their families. Their stories render a very different portrait of welfare recipients, debunking many racial, class, and welfare image stereotypes. This book sheds light on the dynamics of families' lives, people's need for welfare and other public assistance, their dealings in the welfare system, and their experiences in the workplace. It explores U.S. welfare politics, legislation, program regulations, and bureaucratic machinations, as well as flexible labor practices in low-tier employment.

The U.S. welfare program began as part of the Social Security Act of 1935 and has been amended many times since. Welfare "reform" in President Clinton's administration (1993 to 2001) advanced with the enactment of sweeping welfare legislation in 1996. PRWORA repealed Aid to Families with Dependent Children (AFDC), the federal welfare program that provided cash assistance to poor families with children, replacing it with the Temporary Assistance for Needy Families (TANF) program. The program name change is significant. "Aid" and "dependent" are not in the title. TANF cash "aid" is no longer an entitlement. Cash "assistance" is now "temporary," subject to a federal five-year lifetime limit. Moreover, harsher provisions were imposed in the areas of eligibility and continued receipt.

Access to TANF is hindered in the first place through diversion to other social services and private resources as well as strict eligibility criteria. One example is that most legal immigrants who entered the country after PRWORA became law are subject to a five-year wait period. More generally, recipients I came to know attest to frustrating eligibility approval processes that are sometimes prolonged. It is dispiriting when adults are made to "jump through hoops," doing all that is required of them during the approval process only to receive a denial determination. Such a decision exacerbates a family's extant financial stress.

Once an application is approved, continued eligibility is not secure. Recipients are subject to periodic recertification of benefits as well as ongoing rules in which noncompliance can result in a sanction, a penalty that reduces or discontinues benefits. The combination of life's pressures and a bureaucratic decision that results in a loss of welfare income can have psychological effects. A woman who "had it really hard" lost her benefits due to a sanction. She said, "It's only by the grace of God that I'm sitting here before you sane. Sane. I might be poor but I'm sane." Similarly, a man was at the "point of despair" several months after his benefits were terminated.

A hallmark of the 1996 welfare legislation is devolution, the shifting of responsibility from the federal government to states. But ultimately the responsibility devolves to individuals who are expected to move from welfare to self-sufficiency by working. PRWORA imposed mandatory work requirements. States have to ensure that recipients work or participate in program-approved work activities for a minimum number of hours weekly; this is broadly referred to as workfare. But a number of factors must coalesce for people to achieve economic independence. Generally workers must possess marketable skills and have steady work that pays a living wage for food, housing, health care, child care, education, transportation, and other requisite necessities to raise a growing family, including funds for emergencies. Most of the parents I met were part of the U.S. flexible labor force. A host of structural factors and personal and family circumstance strained or impeded economic security. Many worked in low-tier, unsatisfying, and insecure jobs. When they experienced hardship, they devised different ways to get by that included drawing on resources from a support network of family and friends, private agencies, and the government. They relied on welfare and other government benefits to supplement their paltry income and to provide support during periods of unemployment. For them the U.S. welfare system is also insecure because of welfare grant reductions and case closures for sundry reasons. Parents' stories convincingly illustrate how federal and state welfare policy, rigid welfare bureaucracy, and the flexible, low-wage labor market converge to intensify the insecurity in poor people's lives. I suggest that this interrelationship contributes to U.S. inequality and poverty.

Issues related to welfare and work are revealed primarily from the perspective of forty-two parents who at some time in their lives received welfare and who lived in Westchester County in the early years of the twenty-first century. Westchester County is located north of New York City and is situated between the Hudson River and Long Island Sound. The county is unabashedly suburban and affluent; its median household income of $63,582 in 1999 was significantly higher than median household incomes in New York State ($43,393) and in the United States ($41,994) (U.S. Bureau of the Census 2000a). Westchester is one of the wealthier U.S. counties, ranking twentieth in median household income measurements in 2004 (U.S. Bureau of the Census 2004a). The county is comprised of six cities—Mount Vernon, New Rochelle, Peekskill, Rye, White Plains, and Yonkers—plus numerous towns and villages. The suburban landscape is segregated by class and by racial and ethnic groups. Table 1, depicting U.S. 2000 Census data, shows the distribution of wealth and people within the four largest racial/ethnic groups in the county in select municipalities. Although migration has increasingly altered the racial composition of the population growth, in 2000 whites accounted for 71.3 percent of Westchester's total population of 923,459, down from 79.4 percent a decade earlier (U.S. Bureau of the Census 1990, 2000a). In contrast to the display of wealth, as evidenced by the palatial homes and luxury cars found in some of the more affluent towns and villages, a drive through sections of some cities will reveal the poverty as reflected in the Census

Table 1. The distribution of people and wealth in Westchester County

Municipalities	White (%)	Black or African American (%)	Hispanic or Latino, of any race (%)	Asian (%)	Median household income in 1999 (dollars)	Percentage of families below poverty level
Cities						
Mount Vernon	28.6	59.6	10.4	2.1	41,128	11.8
New Rochelle	67.9	19.2	20.1	3.2	55,513	7.9
Peekskill	57.1	25.5	21.9	2.4	47,177	10.3
Rye	89.6	1.3	4.8	6.5	110,894	1.6
White Plains	64.9	15.9	23.5	4.5	58,545	6.5
Yonkers	60.2	16.6	25.9	4.9	44,663	13.0
Some towns						
Bedford	87.5	7.1	7.6	2.0	100,053	2.4
Mamaroneck	88.9	2.8	10.9	3.1	84,213	2.9
New Castle	91.5	1.4	2.8	5.6	159,691	2.0
Pelham	87.3	4.6	6.0	4.0	91,810	2.2
Pound Ridge	95.5	1.2	2.5	1.7	153,208	0.9
Somers	94.8	1.7	3.0	1.9	89,528	1.2
Yorktown	90.6	3.0	5.8	3.4	83,819	1.9
Some villages						
Bronxville	91.9	1.1	2.9	4.8	144,940	1.7
Dobbs Ferry	80.7	7.4	7.0	7.6	70,333	1.8
Elmsford	55.8	20.3	23.3	9.1	61,685	6.7
Hastings-on-Hudson	89.8	2.4	4.5	4.1	83,188	1.5
Irvington	88.7	1.4	3.8	7.0	96,467	1.2
Larchmont	94.2	0.7	4.5	2.8	123,238	1.6
Pelham Manor	92.2	2.1	4.6	2.8	112,553	3.1
Port Chester	60.7	7.0	46.2	2.1	45,381	10.1
Rye Brook	92.0	1.0	5.4	4.3	98,864	1.8
Scarsdale	84.1	1.5	2.6	12.6	182,792	1.7
Tuckahoe	74.0	10.1	8.8	9.8	60,744	5.7
Westchester County (total)	**71.3**	**14.2**	**15.6**	**4.5**	**63,582**	**6.4**

Source: U.S. Census Bureau 2000a.

data. A disproportionate percentage of impoverished people and blacks and Latinos live in cities and specific municipalities, notably Mount Vernon, Peekskill, Yonkers, Elmsford, and Port Chester.

In 2004, the year I conducted most of my fieldwork, approximately 64 percent of Westchester's occupied housing was owner-occupied (U.S. Bureau of the Census 2004b). The median sale price of a single-family house in the county was $645,000 (Brenner 2005). Poor people are generally limited to apartment living because purchasing a home in Westchester is beyond their financial reach. They are part of the nonpropertied class who live in housing categorized by nomenclature familiar to the poor—rental, subsidized, municipal, emergency, temporary, transitional, and shelter. Obtaining safe, affordable housing is a major concern for low-income and poor people in Westchester. Most families require at least a two-bedroom apartment. According to the National Low Income Housing Coalition's (2004) "Housing Wage" calculation, an income of $24.21 per hour, or $50,360 per year, was necessary to pay for a two-bedroom apartment with a fair market rent of $1,259 in Westchester County in 2004.[4] This wage exceeds minimum wage, which in New York in 2004 was $5.15 an hour. It also exceeds the income of median-income households living in Mount Vernon, Peekskill, Yonkers, and Port Chester, the cities that have the highest percentage of families living below the poverty level (see Table 1). Affordable housing is particularly problematic for families headed by one person who is solely responsible for the rent, such as Charlotte Thompson.

When we met, Charlotte had been living in a shelter for several months; the prospects looked dim for finding affordable housing because there was a freeze on Section 8 vouchers and she could not afford to pay the going rate for the appropriate-sized apartment for her family. Discussing her housing situation Charlotte said, "The average rent for three bedrooms is like $2,000. . . . If I was even making like fifty grand a year, that's about $4,000 a month. So that's still half my rent. I mean half of my income would go towards rent." I asked Charlotte if she ever made $50,000 annually to which she responded "no," elucidating, "the most I ever made was like $22,000."

I met Charlotte and the other parents during my multiyear ethnographic research, which I began in the winter of 2003. I conducted participant observation throughout Westchester, as well as in New York City and Albany. I visited sites that provide services to recipients of welfare and other low-income families, such as welfare offices, workfare programs, employment centers, and soup kitchens. For several years I was a volunteer server at an annual church-hosted holiday community dinner for impoverished residents. At public hearings I heard testimony on issues affecting low-income New Yorkers. I became a member of a few organizations that advocated for poor and low-income people on issues related to welfare, hunger, and housing. Through attendance at meetings, I received timely updates on federal and state legislation, policies and budgets, funding changes, and New York State's labor-market status. With advocates I lobbied twice at the state capitol, where we campaigned on a number of issues associated with poverty. On several occasions I volunteered at a fair hearing support table sponsored by legal advocates in New York City; here aggrieved recipients receive information about the appeal process for disputing public assistance program decisions.

In addition to participatory and observational activities, I conducted fourteen formal interviews and had over two dozen informal meetings and conversations with people employed by agencies serving impoverished people. And I interviewed forty-two people who currently or previously received welfare; I refer to them as "parents." I also refer to them as "women" where my discussion applies only to several or all of the women who participated in my study.

Whenever possible, I use the term "recipients of welfare" when I speak in general about people who obtain benefits. However, at times it was more grammatically appropriate to use the term "welfare recipient." I realize the latter is an aggregate category that risks stereotyping. "Welfare" and the people who receive it have been stigmatized. In public discourse, negative images associated with gender and race, such as "welfare mother" and "welfare queen," have been used to pejoratively portray women who receive welfare. Recently, terms such as "client" and "customer" have been used by welfare system bureaucrats and service providers. In my study, the parents who received welfare did not use these terms to identify themselves.

Most parents were recruited for interviews though flyers that I posted in various places such as service agencies, libraries, and supermarkets. A few agencies sent more than 125 flyers to their clients. Forty-one women and one man completed interviews.[5] At the time their ages ranged from twenty-one to sixty-two. Though they self-identified their race and ethnicity in different ways, their broader racial/ethnic categories were black, Latina, white, and mixed. Their education levels ranged from completion of the sixth grade to graduate school. All of the people cared for at least one child under eighteen years old at the time of the interview. Eight women had one child each, and eleven had two children each. Fifteen parents had three children each. Two women had four children each, two had five children, three had six children, and one woman had nine. Three women were primary caregivers of a grandchild. Most of the parents had a work history, yet during their lives many experienced episodic or persistent economic hardship; many were poor and had been so for a long time. Others described their family life and financial woes within a context that appeared to be middle class. People who were homeless were overrepresented because many recruitment flyers were sent to residents in family shelters.

The interviews with the forty-two parents were conducted in public places such as an eating establishment, a shelter, or the person's home. I usually called those who had phones beforehand to confirm our interview; people frequently cancelled or rescheduled for various reasons—something more pressing came up, the person had forgotten or decided not to go through with the interview or had an emergency. I was stood up about two dozen times, sometimes twice by the same person. Many people were very late for their interviews. I generally waited about an hour; some eventually arrived. When I phoned to reschedule, some never returned my call. After an initial interview most of the people agreed to a ollow-up interview and I conducted several, but this proved difficult to accomplish for most.[6] Cell phones and landlines were often disconnected. People who lived in shelters had moved by the time I tried to reach them. I came to understand lateness, last-minute cancellations, rescheduling, and no-shows after becoming more familiar with the stresses in poor people's lives. In retrospect, this recognition supported one of my central findings that people's lives are replete with pressures, constraints, and crises.

While I expected to hear about people's experiences in the welfare system and labor force, they also disclosed intimate particulars about themselves and others. I used a life-cycle perspective to analyze their narratives.[7] As family members make their transitions through various life stages from childhood to adulthood, personal and family wants and needs change. A life-cycle perspective of a person's family caregiving responsibilities, household provisioning, employment patterns, and stresses aids in our understanding of families' changing economic requirements. Moreover, when a needy family's life is situated within the context of a social service system and the labor market, we see that the interests, aims, and agendas of bureaucracies and employers are often at cross-purposes with those of parents who are struggling to provide for families. A life-cycle perspective was also useful for my examination of a person's welfare and work experiences before and after the 1996 welfare law and helped me to recognize the persistent features carried over from AFDC and to compare how these and new TANF provisions might have affected people's lives. Overall, it was an effective analytic tool to examine how changing welfare policy, welfare bureaucracy, and the labor market might have accommodated families' needs or contributed to their poverty.

2

Living on the Edge in Suburbia

I covered a lot of ground on foot and in my car uncovering poverty in affluent Westchester County. On my drive to see Latrice Parker at her apartment for a follow-up interview, I stopped by the supermarket to pick up a gallon of milk and apple juice as a small hostess gift. She had asked me to call her when I arrived in her neighborhood. I did so, but was told by her sister that she was out looking for an apartment. How to spend my morning? I decided to find someone I had previously interviewed to give the provisions to.

My first choice was Tanisha Moore, whom I had met at lunch at a soup kitchen and talked with afterward at a park while her children played. She told me that a few months earlier her landlord had lost his Section 8 privileges because of violations, thus the housing department withheld direct rental payments to him. He in turn tried to sue Tanisha for about $4,400 for that portion of back rent. On the morning of our meeting Tanisha had been at the courthouse fighting a seventy-two-hour eviction notice. After learning that the landlord had to comply with an "order to show cause," Tanisha was assured not to worry because it was not her fault that her landlord lost Section 8 privileges. A court date was scheduled for five days hence. But the "worst of it" was that Tanisha was also in jeopardy of losing her Section 8 voucher, which she had for two years after being on the waiting list for ten years. This was because three months earlier Tanisha was hospitalized when she gave birth to her daughter and missed her Section 8 recertification meeting. Her recourse was to file and attend a fair hearing, which she did. At the hearing she presented documentation proving her hospitalization and was told a decision would be rendered in ten days. On the day we met it had been almost two months and she still had not yet received a decision.

Recalling her story with the milk and juice in hand, I set out to Tanisha's. Because she did not have a phone, she had given me her address. However, I was unable to find her street that morning, so I proceeded to the home of Celeste Woods, who lived nearby. Upon my arrival, I found myself in the midst of a flurry when one of her children let me in and escorted me to the living room. A group of people were there for a home inspection of her transitional apartment. When Celeste came in the room, I offered her the groceries but it was not an appropriate time to chat, so I left shortly thereafter. In a phone conversation some time after my visit she told me that she had moved and we tentatively arranged a date for me to drive her to a food pantry. I had hoped to talk about her move then, but we never connected.

Some time later when I was at a family shelter, a woman approached me and exclaimed, "I'm the person you interviewed in the park." It was Tanisha! We chatted but never broached the circumstances that led to her shelter stay, though I could have guessed. I had found Tanisha's street on another hunt and discovered a blank space on her vestibule mailbox. I surmised she had been evicted. At our brief encounter at the shelter Tanisha concentrated on her good news—she was about to move out of the shelter and was getting married. She beamed as she flashed the engagement ring on her outstretched hand. After I extended congratulations we parted.

On my way out of the shelter, someone called my name. Turning, I saw Celeste. We hugged. She told me that she had been to her gynecologist and another doctor in the morning and that she had a dental problem. During our short chat Celeste did not say why she was living at the shelter or give the specifics of her medical condition. But when I interviewed her months earlier at her apartment, she had told me about her travails. Her three children are now teens; raising a family that included a child who had multiple physical and mental disabilities since birth had been a challenge. Her own numerous health problems coincided with prolonged unemployment. A couple of years back she lost her job in the food-service industry where she had worked for a few years; she was eligible to receive unemployment insurance. Then, her mother died. Celeste and her children had been living in her mother's house for years and continued to do so after her mother's death. She paid the rent to her brother, but he failed to pay the mortgage and "the house went up for sale." Impoverished and in her late thirties, Celeste became homeless for the first time. Now she was back in a family shelter for reasons unbeknownst to me. I lost contact with Celeste and Tanisha after that day.

When I told some people that I was studying welfare in Westchester County, they would look at me quizzically and ask, "There's poverty in Westchester?" A neighbor was surprised when I told him there was a family shelter nestled among residential homes in a nearby neighborhood. Through the years I came to know about the lives of those living on the edge in suburbia like Tanisha and Celeste, as well as Latrice Parker, Desmond Hughes, Roseanne Tate, and Anita Ramos.

Latrice was one of the first parents that I interviewed. When I arrived at Latrice's spacious two-bedroom apartment, she introduced me to her two children and her cousin, who was there to babysit while Latrice and I talked. Latrice wanted to give me a tour of the apartment and I sensed her pride in establishing a home for her young children. A dinosaur-motif border decorated the walls of her children's bedroom; it hinted of permanency. The colorful sheets suggested comfort and safety. But Latrice's perception of her surroundings was contrary.

> I barely go outside with my kids unless I have somewhere to go. It's dangerous around here. All in front of the building is drugs, crack heads and everything. They'll sniff in your face and everything. I'm serious. It's really bad out here. They don't care. . . . They be all in front of the building. That's why when I leave, I don't stay around the building. I'll go to the store, take them to the store, to the park, to my sister's house. Other than that, I don't be in front of here.

Within the safety of her home, Latrice, an "Afro-American" woman in her early twenties, told me that she lost her mother when she was fifteen.[1] Although her sister retained their mother's house after their mother's death, her sister's "drugging out" made it hard for Latrice to live there. She moved back and forth between her late mother's house and the home of another sister. Latrice said, "They'd get mad and kick me out." Looking back, she said that she would sometimes spend the night with a guy, "You know, just to lay my head somewhere." She recalled riding the subways of Manhattan with her bag: "I just ride the train all day, all day, all day, like that." At some point Latrice applied for government assistance and received aid for about three months, after which she was cut off because the welfare agency required information and paperwork that she did not have at the time. When Latrice was twenty years old, she became pregnant—a difficult situation, since she was sleeping "outside," for she had "nowhere to go." After two months of being homeless, and a few months into her pregnancy, she secured short-term shelter in a crisis center that special-izes in services for youth. Latrice applied for government assistance but encountered bureaucratic obstacles. Three weeks before she gave birth, she reapplied and was able to obtain emergency cash and food stamps. At five and a half months into her pregnancy, Latrice prematurely deliv-ered her fourteen-ounce daughter, who required hospitalization for four months. When her daughter was released from the hospital, they moved into a shelter. Latrice was ill-equipped to care for her sickly infant, and the idea of administering oxygen to her newborn scared her. Some time later, unknowingly pregnant, she fled the shelter with her baby daughter and stayed for several months at her sister's before moving into a shelter in Westchester County. While a resident at the shelter, she gave birth to her son. Latrice received TANF, food stamps, and Supplemental Security Income (SSI, a disability benefit) for her daughter, and she applied for Section 8 housing. Latrice "was so happy" when she obtained a Section 8 voucher after six months and moved into her own apartment.

After relating her trials to me as her two toddlers scurried about, Latrice expressed wonderment: "I'm surprised I'm at where I'm at now. Everything I've been through. I'm surprised I've got kids. Lord have mercy! I guess that was a way of slowing down and getting somewhere. I guess." "Right?" she asked her one-and-a-half-year-old son as though he could confirm her sentiments. Pointing to her children, Latrice said, "Those are my life right there. Then my daughter [when she was an in-fant], she be in the hospital, she had surgery, she was blind, water in the brain, you know, blood transfusion. I'm scared. I don't know what the future's gonna bring for her. Anything could mess up." Irrespective of fi-nancial position, anything could "mess up" a person's life, but the stakes are higher for a woman like Latrice. Her daughter's father denies paternity and provides no support. Latrice said that her son's father is a good dad to both of her children and is involved in their son's life. This father lives with his mother and stepfather and takes his son to live with them two weeks each month. The father's salary from a fast-food restaurant only goes so far; Latrice's son's paternal grandparents provide resources, thus defraying the cost of child rearing for Latrice. When Latrice is low on food before the receipt of biweekly TANF and monthly food stamps, she calls on her sisters. Aside from this small support group, Latrice must rely on the continued aid of the state in order to help raise her two toddlers and maintain a household.

Latrice completed the eleventh grade and her work history totals about a year and a half of babysitting and domestic work. When her son passed his first birthday, the Department of Social Services (DSS) required Latrice to begin a workfare program. Although she has fears leaving her children in a child-care center, she intends to follow her sister's footsteps and secure work as a school bus monitor. "Cause they're hiring a lot where my sister works," she said, noting that "they pay like $8, $9 an hour" and they pay for overtime.

Latrice undoubtedly benefited from the disparate aid—welfare cash, food stamps, rent assistance, and a Section 8 voucher. Her daughter receives $567 a month for SSI benefits and has special education services. When I arrived at Latrice's apartment, her daughter's tutor was just leaving. But given her foreshortened high school education and scant work history, Latrice's options seem limited. It is not difficult to imagine that during Latrice's life she will continue to be assailed with poverty-related stresses.

A month after my visit with Latrice I interviewed Desmond Hughes, an African American man in his late forties. Desmond and I met several times and we corresponded though email because he wanted to keep me abreast of his continuing economic need and interactions with DSS. Desmond's welfare history began in the late 1970s. He became a father when he was nineteen years old and again when he was twenty-five. Around that time Desmond was attending college as a psychology major; his tuition was financed by student loans and a stipend, and he also received welfare. His odd jobs and drug sales contributed to the households of his children's mothers; selling drugs was the reason for his several jail terms. His first incarceration at age twenty-seven was for about a year. Although the incarceration temporarily interrupted his schooling, he was able take part in a postsecondary education program in prison. Upon his release he resumed college and earned a bachelor's degree in the early 1980s. During the ensuing years Desmond had disparate periods on welfare for a variety of reasons. Because employment in the formal economy was irregular, he worked at different jobs and sold marijuana and cocaine to augment his employment and welfare income. But his drug business resulted in his repeated involvement in the criminal justice system. When I asked Desmond what motivated him to sell drugs, he said,

> Mainly because in the community that I was living in, that's basically almost what all the unemployed folks did. . . . I would say that I was basically a victim-slash-participant of my environmental circumstances or my

community environment. Like when in Rome, just do as the Romans do. So instead of being that much of a victim to the drug scene, I tried to capitalize on it. So I proceeded to make a few more dollars and take care of my two kids.

Furthermore, Desmond explained his reason for needing welfare at various intervals.

Mainly because there were times when I just had enough of the drug scene. There were friends that I had who wanted to try to [enlist] my services to help with burglaries or robberies. Rather than be that extreme, all I could do was fall back on the help of social services. It was easier. There was no real pressure on me about being a welfare recipient in spite of the fact that they never even gave you enough to make ends meet. At that time I think my ongoing needs [welfare grant] were like $43 twice a month.

At some point he married Jennifer, his "greatest love." They had a son when he was in his mid-thirties. Desmond moved in and out of Jennifer's household and was on her AFDC grant when they lived together. In the early 1990s, when Jennifer was diagnosed with HIV, they lived together and he supported their household until her death. Desmond found out that he was "immuno-compromised," having also been "inflicted with the AIDS virus." After Jennifer's death, Desmond "spiraled down." Desmond had a history of drug use and dealing and several incarcerations; after Jennifer died he was incarcerated again for a couple of months. During this time Desmond's five-year-old son was sent to stay with his designated guardian, whom Desmond calls his son's godmother, a wealthy woman whom Jennifer befriended. But it troubled Desmond's mother, who was terminally ill, that her grandson was living with people other than family so she decided that it was best if she took over his care. After Desmond was released from prison, he moved in with his mother and son. Because his mother's illness progressed, she was placed in a nursing home and Desmond and his son moved into a family shelter.

With the deaths of his wife and mother happening close together, Desmond "spiraled down" once again and started using drugs. At the shelter, his case manager, drug counselor, parole officer, and a Child Protective Services worker collaborated and devised a detox and rehab plan so as to prevent another incarceration. This was acceptable to Desmond and he received treatment in two residential facilities totaling forty-five days. During this time his son was in the care of his designated guardian. Father and son were reunited at a family shelter after Desmond completed the treatment programs. Since the mid-1990s, Desmond has been the primary caregiver of his son, now a teenager.

Desmond takes his responsibility as primary caregiver seriously despite new setbacks and family disruptions. In the past decade his employment included positions as a recreational consultant, assembly line production assistant, and program director responsible for training and supervising staff. These were multiyear employment stints. But when we met, Desmond had been unemployed for some time. In the face of his illness and the futility of finding steady work, Desmond must appear strong for his son. Though he has ingenuity and a fairly strong support system, Desmond still has to rely on welfare and other government aid. However, these services are often interrupted due to periodic case closures and subsequent eligibility processing delays, which create further economic and emotional stress (see Chapter 4). Nevertheless, Desmond tenaciously negotiates his way through various systems to provide for his family.

Roseanne Tate's life is more typical of what some might think of as a suburban lifestyle. When we sat in the café at Borders, Roseanne, a white woman in her forties, had just finished the workweek and was dressed in smart business attire. She had secured her present job a year earlier. This was after her husband's incarceration triggered a series of events resulting in extreme financial strain.

After Roseanne finished high school she did secretarial work. She married in the late 1980s. Roseanne and her husband "have a beautiful house" in Westchester County. Her husband had his own business. Recalling those earlier times, Roseanne said that it was either "feast or famine. We either had it or we didn't." One time the house was in foreclosure before her husband closed a deal. Roseanne quit work after her first child was born in the early 1990s; she had been making $40,000 annually. But soon afterward when they had "a little bit" of financial difficulty, she resorted to temp work. Nonetheless, her husband did not want her to work after that, calculating that the cost of child care negated the benefits of her working.

At some point one of Roseanne's husband's business deals ensnared him in a lawsuit lasting about ten years. The upshot of this and other legal machinations was that he was incarcerated for a "white-collar" crime. Shortly afterward, Roseanne's financial pressure escalated. She recalled:

The house, of course, was starting to go under again. We tried to sell; we had an offer. He [husband] said, "No, don't sell, let's refinance." His lawyer arranged a refinance, arranged for me to stay in the house so I would keep the kids in a status quo. That money ran out. And that's when . . . I started to try to go back to work. And at that point, I went to apply for benefits because I didn't have the money for child care. I had no money. I had $50,000 worth of credit-card debt. It just left me in a total hole. I couldn't pay the mortgage. . . . So it's in foreclosure now; it's gonna go up for auction but actually we're working that out now.

When Roseanne's money ran out, her family helped her for a couple of months until she was approved and began to receive TANF cash and food stamps. Roseanne found a job a few months later making approximately $35,000 annually. The welfare aid was terminated one month after she started working. However, she continued to receive a child-care subsidy for about nine months at which point all of her government assistance was cut; she made too much money.

While her husband is incarcerated, Roseanne is the sole family provider for her three children and under pressure to maintain her middle-class lifestyle and to pay household expenditures and work expenses that include steep child-care fees. Because the house is in foreclosure, she does not pay the $3,000 monthly mortgage and said, "I don't know what I would do if I had that expense. Then I wouldn't be eating." Roseanne reflected on her experience:

> *RT:* To be living so comfortably all these years with a nice house and never having experienced this, ever. . . . My mother and father married for forty, fifty years, almost fifty years now, . . . they always worked, they always supported us. Never had came from a background of this; neither did he [her husband]. So it was quite an awakening. . . . I've managed to keep my kids, I've managed not to fall apart. It's been difficult and sometimes I feel like I'm not managing. . . . So I guess I have been self-sufficient. But not to my satisfaction, I should say.
>
> *TL:* What is to your satisfaction?
>
> *RT:* I guess I have pretty high standards. . . . We were travelers. But of course my situation doesn't warrant that. I would like to be able to go shopping more. I'd like to be able to go out to dinner. I don't go out. I will go out for a couple of drinks. Basically, I'll have a little appetizer or something. But I don't really go out to eat. I'd like those little extras—

get my hair done, go buy if I see something, or buy the kids clothes. I haven't even had the money to buy my kids clothes that they've grown out of. But the biggest thing is I'm most comfortable when I have enough money in the bank to pay the bills without worry. That I could just write the check and say, "OK, I have enough to pay my fuel bill," . . . that I can balance my check book and there's money in there too, with a little left over to go and get the kids a prime rib once in a while [*laugh*]. That's to my satisfaction.

Months later I began calling Roseanne's cell phone. On repeated attempts I heard the phone service provider's recorded message that the subscriber was unavailable. Failing to make contact, I was unable to ascertain whether she was able to avert foreclosure and the auctioning of her house by means of her salary or by other avenues.

On a late spring afternoon I interviewed Anita Ramos, a Hispanic mother of six who was in her mid-thirties. Seated in a booth at McDonalds, smiling warmly and wearing a stylish sleeveless dress and gold jewelry, Anita revealed her hardships and triumphs. During the 1980s and the early 1990s she gave birth to five children. At some point she began taking drugs and supported herself by making a living on the streets.

Ruminating on her welfare history, Anita said that during her years on the streets, she was not on welfare. However, she did have Medicaid; it paid for her to obtain treatment. She was in many detox and drug rehabilitation facilities during those years. She lost custody of her children at some point. Her two oldest children lived with their father, the next two in age lived with their father, and her youngest was placed in foster care. In the mid-1990s Anita graduated from the last of her treatment programs and "got clean."

At some point during those difficult years, Anita was incarcerated at a state correctional institution, and upon her release she obtained public assistance. She participated in a postincarceration program that set her up in an apartment. As part of that program, she attended support groups and parenting classes and worked with staff who "help[ed] guide you to get your life back together." Eventually Anita was reunited with her three youngest children and was granted sole custody of them in family court. Her two oldest children remained with their father. Welfare aid and food stamps were not enough to support Anita and her three children. She received additional support from the Fellowship of Narcotics Anonymous and relied on other agencies for food and clothing. After the two-year maximum housing stay allowed under the postincarceration program, Anita obtained housing through a community housing foundation where the family lived for three years.

About three years into her recovery, Anita began working as a nurse's aide making $7.00 an hour. The work proved to be unsteady, averaging five to six months of employment throughout the year, thus necessitating the continued support of welfare. Because of her fluctuating income, her welfare grant was changed frequently, complicating her household budgeting (see Chapter 6). When she worked, she was often not eligible for TANF cash because her income exceeded the TANF eligibility test. Anita had a sixth child three years later and married a year hence. Afterward, Anita's husband supported the family, and for a portion of the time they only received food stamps because her husband was employed. He worked on commission and his income was highly unpredictable. Laughing, Anita said they had "good weeks and not-so-good weeks." Nevertheless, his salary paid the rent. But the food stamps were inadequate, lasting only half the month.

Anita's husband, who was "clean" for a decade, relapsed into drug use. Anita figured her only option was to leave him in order to stay away from drugs. When she decided to leave her husband, she resigned from her job and then "went homeless." Going homeless led to another TANF stint. Anita and her children were placed in a family shelter for three months, during which time she obtained a Section 8 voucher and subsequently moved to her own apartment.

Due to the lack of a financial cushion, unforeseen crises generally have an immediate and distressing effect on families who are barely making it. At some point legal action was brought against Anita and her estranged husband. This stemmed from a period when her husband did not report his earnings to DSS when they were receiving government assistance. Although her husband was the head of household when the alleged events occurred, Anita was also implicated and jailed for one day. She was released on her own recognizance because she was employed and had been "clean" many years. The upshot was that the couple was charged with welfare fraud and fined $7,000 with the stipulation that each would pay half. The news was reported in the newspaper, and, as a consequence, Anita's employment at a home health agency was terminated.

Anita also dealt with major family health issues. In the previous year she had had a cancer operation. One of her older children was diagnosed as HIV positive and had not fully accepted the fact. She told her child, "I have a lot of friends that are HIV positive. And they still live." Nevertheless, Anita had already begun looking for a burial plot.

Anita was receiving monthly benefits of $324 welfare cash and $419 in food stamps for her and her four children who were living at home; their ages ranged from three to sixteen. Section 8 and DSS rental assistance paid her monthly rent of $1,700. As she had been unemployed for three months, this aid was essential.

Anita entered adult life in a disadvantaged position due to a sixth-grade education, early pregnancy, long-term substance abuse, making a living on the streets, and incarceration. Nevertheless, the first time she received welfare was at about age twenty-eight; that and other public and private assistance was critical help in her personal transformation. Anita mused,

> A lot of times, when I'm having a real hard day, I think about the person
> that I used to be. And I say to myself, I remember making a promise to
> that judge when I went to go get my kid. And I told him, "You don't ever
> have to worry about me going back to the way I used to live." And I've
> been doing that. Consecutively I have nine years, three months and some
> days. And I still make meetings. I still talk about how I feel—good, bad, or
> indifferent. . . . And I inspire women. Even if they're not an addict, or they
> never had a problem with drugs or just going through domestic violence
> like I went through. You don't have to be a statistic. You don't have to be
> labeled. You can be yourself. You don't have to have a man to validate who
> you are. And it's only through working the twelve steps and the twelve
> traditions of Narcotics Anonymous that I've learned to be the woman who I
> am today. Now I might not have it all together. But just for today I'm happy,
> joyous. . . . So the little problems that might come, I say, "Bring it on."
> But I don't let anything get me down. . . . I tried to live life to the fullest.
> And that's because the way I used to live. I don't ever want to live that way
> again. I don't ever want to go into another penitentiary. And I have to be an
> example, just not for me, but for other women. And also for my children.
> Because my oldest kids [whom she did not raise] are drug addicts.

Anita is an inspiration; I was in awe of her zest for life. But she is in a fragile position. A span of eight years between the youngest two of her six children prolonged Anita's child-rearing years. Moreover, she has fifteen more years to maintain a household until her youngest is eighteen. In the meantime Anita tackles the blows as they come. When we left McDonalds, I drove her to meet a realtor who was showing her an apartment. Anita had been recently told that her apartment building did not pass Section 8 inspection and the Board of Buildings intended to close the house down. Her landlord wanted to break her contract in order for him to do the repairs to become compliant. She had two and a half months to find another apartment. Anita's main concern was finding another place to live and not having to "go homeless."

Latrice's, Desmond's, Roseanne's, and Anita's worlds are different on many accounts, but each is a parent who has suffered one or more setbacks threatening her or his personal and family well-being. They have taken measures to provide for their families by drawing on various resources. One resource was the U.S. welfare system, although their experiences with the system and duration using it varied. And while welfare aid is absolutely essential, conducting business in the welfare bureaucracy can be daunting, as Desmond will later attest. Moreover, various policies and practices in the welfare and labor systems are at variance with parents' capabilities to adequately maintain a family. These and other parents that I came to know have had different work histories. Yet despite employment, they struggled. U.S. recipients of welfare are receiving benefits in a historical moment when federal welfare aid is no longer an entitlement under a welfare model. Under a workfare model assistance is temporary and work is viewed as the panacea. This model abets insecurity in already insecure lives.

3

From Welfare to Workfare

The Crafting of a Stratified and Stigmatized Welfare Program

A woman who lived in an affluent community called me to say that she spotted my flyer on the bulletin board of her neighborhood supermarket and was interested in scheduling an interview. As was my customary gesture to callers, I suggested that we pick a meeting place conveniently located close to her. This woman did not want to meet at her downtown diner or any local venue where someone might eavesdrop on our conversation. She did not want anyone in her community to overhear that she was "on welfare."[1]

Public welfare began in colonial America. Throughout most of U.S. history, the term "relief" was used in reference to the public and private provisions for poor people. The term "welfare" had a positive connotation when it first came into use in the early twentieth century because it differentiated old relief practices (e.g., the poorhouse) from the newly instituted social programs (Katz 1986). Katz notes that it is not clear when the term acquired its contemporary stigma (1986). In the early years from 1911 to 1935, women who received relief from mothers' aid programs (relief programs that predated the Social Security Act) were held in esteem because the programs selected "fit" and "deserving" women. Moreover, the programs were considered prestigious because they set recipients apart from the pauper class (Bell 1965:13). The contemporary meaning of welfare may have been created by the Social Security Act of 1935, which set up a stratified system of provisions (Gordon 1994).

As part of the New Deal, the Social Security Act of 1935 established the U.S. welfare state by federalizing state relief programs and creating two types of benefit programs—social insurance and public assistance programs. From their inception the benefit programs were exclusionary and stratified along lines of gender, race, class, and marital and labor status. The social insurance programs were unemployment insurance and old age insurance (the precursor to the contemporary Social Security program). The benefits were funded through taxation on employment; because of this, during the first half of the twentieth century, the beneficiaries were mostly white males. These programs insured some financial security to those beneficiaries when unemployment and old age resulted in income loss. The public assistance programs were Old Age Assistance (for indigent elderly outside the wage labor market who could not obtain old age insurance), Aid to the Blind, and Aid to Dependent Children (ADC). ADC, which came to be known as "welfare," provided financial aid to needy, dependent children deprived of parental support or care due to the death, continued absence, or incapacity of a parent. That is, children in families headed primarily by widows, as well as divorced, abandoned, or separated mothers.[2]

Overall, the social insurance programs, which were federally administered, were more generous than public assistance programs. In addition, these social insurance programs were based on rights and earnings and respected recipients' privacy, though they also disproportionately served whites, especially adult white men. These federally administered programs had a larger tax base that supported the programs. In contrast, the lower-tier public assistance programs were less supportive because they were state or locally administered, needs-based, and means-tested. They were highly supervised and provided inferior payments; ADC benefited women and children. Locally administered programs were more susceptible to political attacks and a declining tax base (Gordon 1994:5, 11, 294).

The New Deal social programs were influenced by a domestic code, an ideology that flourished in the industrial era when urbanization and the growth and competition of industrialization created a division of labor in which men became the designated wage earner in the public sphere and women were restricted to the home. Women became further subordinated to men, being dependent on their sole wage. In the mid-nineteenth century, motherhood and domesticity were idealized and glorified. Kessler-Harris notes that the domestic ideology "exalted home roles" while it "condemned" women who were forced to take on wage labor—those who worked beyond teen years, free blacks, and immigrants (1982:53). The domestic code, and the fact that it was less costly to maintain poor children in homes than in institutions, led to the establishment of public aid programs that provided assistance to children in their homes (Bell 1965:4). However, women's morality was linked to their eligibility for assistance, and the New Deal policies also selected "deserving" and "fit" mothers to receive financial support to stay home and raise a family, thus dissuading their participation in the labor market (Abramovitz 1996; Gordon 1994). Central to the welfare policies of the early twentieth century was the notion that women's responsibility for children overrode their political and economic rights of citizenship (Mink 1995). Gender roles and gender inequality were inscribed in the New Deal welfare state through the subordination of women's rights to children's welfare in policies affecting mothers.

The ADC program was shaped and influenced by these prevailing ideologies of morality and racial bias, and thus these ideologies were manifest in the exclusionary rules and state policies. States had latitude in developing and administering ADC policies; they determined the standard of need on which ADC payments were based and defined initial and ongoing eligibility criteria. Numerous states instituted a "suitable home" requirement, subjectively defining criteria that created a proper home environment for children.[3] In some states ADC aid was denied to children living in a home headed by an unmarried mother or a mother who gave birth to an "illegitimate" child after receiving welfare. Some rules excluded families who could not exhibit the ability to manage cash. These rules disproportionately excluded African Americans and other nonwhite children from receiving ADC. Statistics show that between 1937 and 1940 blacks only represented from 14 percent to 17 percent of the ADC recipients nationwide. In Georgia, for example, during those years blacks were less than 12 percent of the ADC caseload, although 38 percent of the children in Georgia who were under fifteen years old were black (Bell 1965:34–35). A notorious incident occurred in Louisiana in 1960 after it instituted a suitable homes law whereby approximately twenty-three thousand children were terminated from the state's ADC rolls on the basis of living in unsuitable homes. Although black children constituted 66 percent of the state caseload, 95 percent of the children affected by the law were black (Bell 1965:138). "Man-in-the-house" or "substitute father" rules also denied ADC benefits to the children of women who lived with "able-bodied" men. States justified ADC denial or termination on the assumption that the man, instead of the state, would provide for the family. Also, an "employable mother" rule permitted the termination of ADC to women whose employment was required for seasonal agricultural and domestic work. Black women performed an unequal share of this labor. From the inception of ADC, racially motivated exclusions were endorsed by legislators determined to block aid to agricultural and domestic workers (Gordon 1994:5). Southern conservatives in the Democratic Party opposed the federalization and expansion of the U.S. welfare program, insisting on local control over benefits and program administration in order to maintain "regressive labor-market norms" (Peck 2001:66). Variations of these rules were enforced in many states until the late 1960s when they began to be challenged in court. (For a comprehensive examination of ADC legislative restrictions, see Bell 1965:57–151 and Piven and Cloward 1993:123–46.)

A 1939 amendment to the Social Security Act had significant racial and gender implications. The amendment now extended benefits to the widows and dependants of retired workers under the old age insurance program (i.e., Social Security). The widows were largely white because the occupations covered by the program generally employed white men. Thus, having an alternative, white widow's participation in the ADC program began to decline. Not having that option, divorced, separated, never married, and abandoned women, many of whom were African American, turned to the ADC program and were subjected to eligibility rules and social controls that intensified as the racial composition of the program shifted (Neubeck and Cazenave 2001; Quadagno 1994).

The ADC population remained small until the 1960s, probably as a result of states' slow-paced implementation of the ADC program, racially biased eligibility criteria, lack of information about available programs, intimidation by welfare staff, and women's high labor-force participation during the war years. However, social, political, and economic changes after World War II altered the welfare rolls in terms of overall population, racial composition, and family structure.[4] For instance, mechanized farming, the decline of agricultural markets after World War I, the exclusion of blacks from Southern industries, and Northern industrial expansion precipitated the migration of blacks to Northern and Western cities in search of work.[5] More black women enrolled in ADC for various reasons. Migrating black women were less likely to be disqualified from ADC in the more liberal Northern cities. Moreover, the federal government pressured Southern states to relax discriminatory practices. Women's low pay and unemployment also contributed to their need for ADC.[6] The high unemployment rates for black men in the South and Northern urban areas undermined their ability to support a household or marry.[7] This, plus the increase in fertility rates and changes in marriage, divorce, and childbearing patterns, contributed to a trend in single-mother status among women and the increase in the number of black women applying for ADC. In 1939, 61 percent of the mothers who received ADC were widows; by 1961 the majority were separated, divorced, and unmarried women (Abramovitz 1996:319–21; Bell 1965:54–55; Neubeck and Cazenave 2001:62–63; Piven and Cloward 1993:194; Valentine 1983).

In the 1960s, following local-level activism, a national welfare rights movement formed. Promoting the concept of welfare rights through activism and litigation, the movement encouraged poor people and minorities to apply for welfare and challenged states' laws restricting welfare eligibility (Abramovitz 2000; Mink 2002; for histories of the welfare rights movement see Piven and Cloward 1979 and West 1981). The Supreme Court decided numerous cases pertaining to welfare between the late 1960s and mid-1970 and invalidated many of the restrictive rules. For example, in *King v. Smith* (1968) Alabama's "substitute father" regulation was unanimously struck down by the Supreme Court. The welfare program itself became more liberal; for example, some two-parent households were eligible for aid. In 1962 the program was renamed Aid to Families with Dependent Children (AFDC).

As a result of a confluence of these and other factors and events, in the 1960s national welfare rolls increased substantially (for comprehensive explanations of the "welfare explosion" see Piven and Cloward 1993:183–99). Between 1965 and 1970 AFDC rolls rose from 4.3 million to 8.4 million recipients (U.S. Department of Health and Human Services 2000). In the 1960s, the combination of blacks and Latinos receiving AFDC constituted a majority of recipients, though almost 42 percent were white. By 1970 African American families made up approximately 45 percent of the families receiving AFDC (Neubeck and Cazenave 2001:121; Abramovitz 1996:321).

The mid-1960s saw the start of a political backlash to the civil rights movement. Neubeck and Cazenave point out that "the white backlash" is typically depicted as a single historical event and erroneously portrayed as a brief reaction to the violence and the militant "black power" phase of the civil rights movement. Taking a historical view and noting three other major white backlashes in the twentieth century, they perceive white backlash as a process of racial control that restores white racial hegemony when it is threatened. They argue that "the white backlash that emerged in the 1960s left a *legacy* of racialized politics that, consistent with a process approach to racism, was kept in motion by an organizational base of racial state actors and other political elites." The ensuing attacks on welfare are part of that legacy (2001:118). As welfare rolls increased, "culture of poverty" rhetoric influenced public opinion and legislators (Lewis 1966). Moynihan (1965) provided statistics about black female-headed households and traced what he saw as welfare dependency to the lack of fathers, passed down through the generations from slavery in a "tangle of pathology."[8] Negative images of women on welfare were incorporated in the Republican Party platform; Ronald Reagan made pejorative and erroneous comments about a woman he referred to as a "welfare queen" in his presidential primary speech in 1976. He said, "She has 80 names, 30 addresses, 12 Social Security cards and is collecting veterans' benefits on four nonexisting deceased husbands. . . . She's collecting Social Security on her cards. She's got Medicaid, getting food stamps and she is collecting welfare under each of her names. Her tax-free cash alone is over $150,000" ("'Welfare Queen' Becomes Issue in Reagan Campaign," *New York Times*, February 15, 1976, cited in Neubeck and Cazenave 2001:127). Poor single mothers receiving welfare, especially black mothers, were stereotyped and vilified. The media portrayed women who received welfare as deviant and seldom presented a counter-image, fueling the stereotyping that shaped public consciousness (Williams 1995). Sidel writes, "Systematic stereotyping and stigmatizing of 'welfare mothers' was necessary in order to dehumanize them in the eyes of other Americans before the harsh and tenuous lifeline of Aid to Families with Dependent Children (AFDC) and the other bare-bones social programs could be shredded" (1996:490).

Indeed, toward the end of the 1960s the AFDC program began to shred. In response to a number of pressures that included the white backlash and claims of entitlement by recipients, Congress enacted in 1967 the Work Incentive Program (WIN), a nascent workfare program.[9] In 1974 Old Age Assistance, Aid to the Blind, and Aid to the Permanently and Totally Disabled (created in 1956) were consolidated into the Supplemental Security Income (SSI) program, a federal income-support program categorized as social insurance. Consequently, the only program that remained in the inferior public assistance category was AFDC. Unsurprisingly, the stigma of the public assistance category worsened (Gordon 1994).

Shift from Welfare to Workfare

The U.S. welfare state expanded during the postwar economic boom until the early 1970s economic crisis triggered global restructuring of financial systems, technologies, markets, labor processes, and the welfare state. What emerged was an era characterized by deindustrialization, growth in the service economy, and flexible production and labor processes. A resolution to the worldwide economic crisis entailed policies and practices that have been labeled as neoliberalism, which emphasizes economic growth through unregulated markets, privatization, and minimal state intervention. The latter is facilitated by devolving responsibilities from the federal government to states, private agencies, and individuals; by slashing social service expenditures; and by dismantling national welfare programs. Welfare "reform," a probusiness political strategy, contributed to the shrinking of the welfare state and movement toward a workfare state. Policies and practices emphasized a shift from welfare to employment; poor women were targeted as sources of cheap labor for the growing service sector in the flexible labor market (Piven 1998; Susser 1997; see also Goode and Maskovsky 2001; Kingfisher 2002). According to Harvey (1990), the structure of the flexible labor market consists of a "core" of full-time, permanent, educated, skilled workers who reap the benefits of high salaries and perquisites and a "periphery" of lower echelon full-time employees as well as part-time, fixed-term, contract, subcontract, and public-subsidy workers.

An ideological shift toward neoliberalism resulted in more punitive AFDC program changes. President Ronald Reagan crusaded against big government by deregulating myriad industries, cutting budgets for social service programs, and making changes to AFDC. In the aftermath of the 1960s and 1970s court rulings that challenged eligibility rules and other discriminatory practices, there was a movement toward federal government centralization of authority and consistency in the administration of the AFDC program. But this began to reverse during the Reagan administration (1981–1989). President Reagan drew on federalist traditions and his agenda aimed to restore power, autonomy, and funding to the states. States were allowed to waive AFDC provisions and experiment with program changes. This was an early move toward devolution, the shifting of responsibility from the federal government to the states. New legislation strengthened the work initiatives under the WIN Program enacted in

1967. The Omnibus Budget Reconciliation Act of 1981 established stricter work rules and states acquired the authority to design their individual WIN programs; some states experimented with welfare-to-work programs. Selected programs became targets for research (Gueron and Pauly 1991), the results of which promoted bipartisan support for moving recipients into work. The Family Support Act of 1988 created the Job Opportunities and Basic Skills Training (JOBS) program. JOBS replaced the WIN program, which became largely a registration requirement. JOBS obligated women, whose youngest child was at least three years old (or younger, if a state opted), to participate in a JOBS activity (e.g., job search, job skills training, work). The Family Support Act commenced operation in the late 1980s and coincided with a national recession during which increasing welfare caseloads, the rising cost of Medicaid, and the demand for prison expansion resulted in declining state revenues. This impeded states from matching federal funds, allocating resources for employment training and other resources, and achieving participation goals. Moreover, states liberally exempted recipients from JOBS participation. In 1992, 7 percent of all adult AFDC recipients participated in the JOBS program; some states reached about 15 percent of their recipients (Bane and Ellwood 1994:23–25; Blank and Blum 1997). Nevertheless, these early programs were coercive measures that began moving impoverished women with young children into low-wage labor.

Despite these efforts to mandate work, the programs were relatively ineffective in moving massive numbers of women from AFDC into the labor force. And the public's disdain for the AFDC program continued. Conservatives blamed AFDC "incentives" (Murray 1984) for the rise in female-headed households and welfare dependency. By 1994, 79 percent of Americans perceived AFDC as not working well and fewer than 20 percent believed that most recipients deserved benefits (in Rogers-Dillon 2004:60). That same year the national AFDC rolls peaked at 14.2 million recipients (U.S. Department of Health and Human Services 2000). By this time, Bill Clinton, whose 1992 presidential campaign included welfare "reform," was in office.

The 1990s marked an era of aggressive welfare program restructuring. In his acceptance speech to the Democratic National Convention on July 16, 1992, then presidential candidate Bill Clinton proclaimed that a new approach to government was needed, calling the approach the "New Covenant." This was to be an agreement between the government and the American people that entailed a number of "visions" in which the people were asked to "do your part," "pay it back," "pay their fair share," and "be responsible." The visions included the creation of "millions of new jobs and dozens of new industries," and "more incentives and more opportunity" for entrepreneurs and businesspeople to develop workers' skills and create jobs and wealth. It promised the opportunity for people to "borrow money to go to college" and to "make health care affordable for every family." Clinton's New Covenant was also about welfare reform: "An America where we end welfare as we know it. We will say to those on welfare: You will have, and you deserve, the opportunity, through training and education, through child care and medical coverage, to liberate yourself. But then, when you can, you must work, because welfare should be a second chance, not a way of life" (Clinton 1992). Clinton's vision was more sanguine than that of the Republicans. Shortly before the 1994 midterm elections in which Republicans would gain control of Congress, they introduced their "Contract with America," which framed ten legislative acts. The action pertaining to welfare reform read: "THE PERSONAL RESPONSIBILITY ACT: Discourage illegitimacy and teen pregnancy by prohibiting welfare to minor mothers and denying increased AFDC for additional children while on welfare, cut spending for welfare programs, and enact a tough two-years-and-out provision with work requirements to promote individual responsibility" (Republican Members of the House of Representatives 1994).

Initially, President Clinton's changes to the AFDC program involved an expansion of the waiver program.[10] During the first few years of the Clinton administration, although states were implementing welfare reform, federal movement was sluggish. President Clinton proposed a plan in 1994 that limited assistance to two years after which subsidized work would be available to those recipients who failed to find employment in the private sector. And the plan allowed for liberal exemptions to the time limit. Conversely, the 1995 House Republican plan terminated benefits after five years and denied benefits to women who had children out of wedlock. Clinton vetoed the plan twice, prompting Republicans to shift the goal from discouraging aid to single-headed families to enforcing work requirements.[11] Ultimately, President Clinton signed the Personal Responsibility and Work Opportunity Reconciliation Act of 1996 (PRWORA) on August 22, 1996. This radical welfare legislation constitutes a U.S. welfare program overhaul. It dismantled the federal safety net for poor families that had begun in 1935. The act repealed the AFDC and JOBS programs and replaced them with Temporary Assistance for Needy Families (TANF). The part of PRWORA public law that defines the purpose of TANF reads:

> (a) IN GENERAL.—The purpose of this part is to increase the flexibility of States in operating a program designed to—
>
> (1) provide assistance to needy families so that children may be cared for in their own homes or in the homes of relatives;
>
> (2) end the dependence of needy parents on government benefits by promoting job preparation, work, and marriage;
>
> (3) prevent and reduce the incidence of out-of-wedlock pregnancies and establish annual numerical goals for preventing and reducing the incidence of these pregnancies; and
>
> (4) encourage the formation and maintenance of two-parent families.
>
> (b) NO INDIVIDUAL ENTITLEMENT.—This part shall not be interpreted to entitle any individual or family to assistance under any State program funded under this part.
>
> (U.S. Congress, Public Law 104–193—Aug. 22, 1996)

This language clearly abolished the entitlement aspect of AFDC.[12] Federal funding for the TANF program is a single, capped block grant of $16.5 billion annually. Funding is allocated to states primarily to meet TANF program goals, which are ostensibly to provide basic assistance payments to needy families and to promote work and marriage; funds may also be allocated for other related uses such as child care. The funding is fixed regardless of a decrease or increase in caseloads (federal matching funding for AFDC was open-ended and responsive to rising caseloads). The law increased states' flexibility; thus, the design and administration of TANF programs and services has devolved to the states. Consequently, this resulted in diverse state TANF programs nationwide. However, although seemingly more autonomous, the program is constrained by federal guidelines and disciplines. The law established strict mandatory work requirements for states and recipients. States may not use federal TANF funding beyond five years to pay for TANF benefits; hence, a five-year federal lifetime limit is imposed on recipients. Nor can states use TANF funds to assist unwed mothers under eighteen years old unless they reside in an adult-supervised setting. PRWORA is highly complex legislation. These are only a few of the myriad provisions that created a harsher environment for recipients, contributed to the unprecedented reduction of welfare rolls, and increased family insecurity under a workfare model.

Although many residual features remain, numerous aspects of the welfare system have been transformed—its structure, ideological principles, discourse, program purpose, and duration, as well as social relations between welfare bureaucracy and recipients. Because of welfare reform, the U.S. welfare program has evolved from a welfare model to a workfare model. Under the welfare model the program was a federal entitlement-based program. States had limited discretion and the program allowed voluntary or limited participation of recipients in work-related programs and wage labor. A workfare model, on the other hand, involves state-designed programs in which states have broad flexibility and recipients are subjected to inculcation of work values, behavior modification techniques, mandatory program and work requirements, work enforcement, and strict penalties for noncompliance. In the PRWORA era, "welfare-to-work" and "work-first" are core principles and have also become catchphrases that connote the essence of today's welfare programs. Initially "workfare" was terminology for welfare recipients to "work off" or "work for" welfare benefits in lieu of wages. While the term still applies to such activities today, the meaning of workfare has expanded, encompassing a wide range of work-related policies, welfare-to-work programs, and other activities under a workfare model (Peck 2001).[13]

Poor women have historically provided inexpensive labor when they were systematically excluded from the welfare system; so have recipients of welfare when they augmented wage labor with welfare payments (Bell 1965; Piven and Cloward 1993). But PRWORA fundamentally accommodates the flexible labor force because it legislates and regulates welfare recipients' labor and imposes strict sanctions for noncompliance. To be sure, PRWORA propelled millions of women into the "periphery" group of flexible, service-sector employees. Having educational deficits and little opportunity to enhance or acquire skills for jobs that pay a wage sufficient to support a family, they now compete in large numbers with other candidates for lower-tiered jobs in the insecure labor market, thus driving down wages (Piven 1998). Quantitatively, the 1996 welfare legislation has resulted in a significant reduction of the welfare rolls.

When I began interviewing welfare recipients in January 2004, the TANF rolls were down to 4.8 million recipients and 1.9 million families (U.S. Department of Health and Human Services 2004a). Legislators and lawmakers had begun proclaiming the success of welfare reform based on the decline in welfare rolls and, by extension, former recipients' work participation. An October 7, 2004, U.S. Department of Health and Human

Services news release reported that since the enactment of PRWORA, the federal welfare rolls had dropped 60.7 percent for individuals and 54.7 percent for families, reducing the rolls to a 1970 level of fewer than two million families in the first quarter of 2004. Secretary Tommy G. Thompson concluded, "Welfare reform is working because former welfare recipients are working."[14] Wade Horn, Assistant Secretary, similarly claimed, "This is an extraordinary milestone in the Bush Administration's effort to help families leave public assistance and escape poverty. . . . As our economy continues to grow, more Americans are leaving welfare, entering the workforce and becoming part of the economic mainstream" (U.S. Department of Health and Human Services 2004b). But such proclamations of success overlooked the realities of workers' struggles in the low-wage flexible labor market (see Chapter 6) and disregarded publicly available data that indicated the rise in poverty and unemployment rates.[15]

Despite the insecure lives of people who receive TANF and other public assistance benefits, and in spite of the so-called success of welfare reform, welfare restructuring continues. For example, in February 2006 TANF was reauthorized by President George W. Bush as part of the Deficit Reduction Act of 2005; federal funding that had expired was reauthorized and a number of changes, especially related to work requirements, were made to the TANF program. I completed my interviews and analysis before the changes resulting from the legislation became effective (2006 interim rules were superseded by final rules in 2008). My research does not cover states' responses in terms of policy changes or the impact of this legislation on recipients. Nonetheless, I would expect that as a matter of course workfare pressures will bear down on recipients so that states can meet federal mandates and avoid penalties.

4

The Business of Welfare

Welfare Governance

In New York the business of welfare is primarily conducted within the Department of Social Services (DSS) in the counties. Poor people meet staff to apply for public assistance benefits, deliver requested documentation for eligibility and status changes, recertify for continued benefits, and conduct other related business. At a DSS Service Center (welfare office) a typical scene is of people waiting. Some queue to speak to DSS staff at a counter. Some sit for a long time waiting to meet with a caseworker located in the offices beyond the waiting area. Some wait to speak with someone via a phone installed in the waiting room. People do not wander too far to avoid missing their turn. The welfare offices that I visited in Westchester County varied in their proximity to the commercial district and neighborhoods, and they differed in the waiting room size, ambiance, noise intensity, and comfort level.

When I was conducting fieldwork, the Yonkers DSS Service Center was located on an industrial strip along the Hudson River waterfront; it has since moved. Parking was not available close by. A common sight was of mothers walking slowly up or down a long, steep hill with children in tow or in a stroller. The building was located on a county bus line and many people traveled that way, but for some it may not have been ideal. Thus, a steady taxi flow discharged and picked up families and individuals in front—a costly transportation expense for poor people. The large Yonkers welfare office waiting room was flanked by two numbered-window counters that separated DSS staff from the streams of poor people with myriad issues. In the center of the room people sat on wooden, backless benches. About forty-five minutes of sitting on them was my limit before my back and posterior felt discomfort. The most coveted benches were those against the wall, where people could lean for back support. The recitation of people's names over the public address system punctuated the incessant radio. A baby's wailing might compete with these sounds. People filled out multipage applications or milled about. Some conversed; others quietly sat alone or with others. It was not unusual to witness angry people ranting. Most people kept their coats or jackets on as if they would be called any minute. Not so.

In DSS offices a security guard surveys the crowd. I concur with Davis's (2006) assessment of the spatial design of an upstate New York welfare office. She views the class dichotomy evident in the separation of poor people from frontline workers and the location of an on-site sheriff's office in terms of a "design of discipline" (69). One summer day I spent over an hour sitting in the Yonkers office; it was lunchtime so there was a sparse crowd, not much movement, and, in the background, an insipid "smooth jazz" commercial radio broadcast blared. A group of women were sitting on the bench along the back wall. They chatted with a husky security guard. Though he looked friendly, the guard appeared to represent authority ready to dispense discipline.

Desmond Hughes recollected a time when a multimonth public assistance application process necessitated repeated meetings with caseworkers (described later).[1] He had been told by other recipients that "sometimes you have to raise a little hell" to get things done, but he had never done so because it was not his "demeanor." One day after waiting hours to meet with his caseworker, Desmond witnessed an irate woman proclaiming to DSS staff that she would not leave the window until she saw the person she came to see, even if they called security or the police. She succeeded in meeting with the person she sought. Desmond assessed the situation:

> I had a mind to do exactly what she did. But I don't doubt that they would deal with a man a little bit differently. And having just returned from being incarcerated, I don't doubt that they'd [security] come at me in a more physical manner in a way that I might find a little frustrating and aggravating and that I might find repulsive. And I would respond to in such a way that wouldn't give me anything.

The threat of discipline is a constant presence in the welfare office and beyond (e.g., sanctions). Disciplinary measures are in place to establish compliance. The system is designed so that if people's waits had been futile or business was not resolved in one day, they returned again. Poor people are practiced at waiting, operating on institutional time, a requirement that creates unequal power relations between poor people and service providers (Susser 1996:418). Some people like Desmond, who resist being "the loudest wheel that gets the oil," sometimes wait until day's end without seeing a caseworker. Others take a risk and "raise a little hell."

Regulatory aspects of welfare have long been recognized (Bell 1965; Abramovitz 1996; Piven and Cloward 1993; cf. Susser 1982; Davis 2006).[2] Piven and Cloward (1993) argue that public assistance programs are ancillary to the economic system and primarily function to regulate labor. In periods of mass unemployment that gave rise to social instability, relief was expanded to quash turmoil; it contracted during periods of economic stability and social order. And the principle of "less eligibility" is intended to keep relief payments lower than labor market wages and thus influence people to choose employment (36). In the postindustrial economy the relationship between the relief system and the labor market is a specific "regime of regulation" that, among other things, interprets PRWORA provisions, imposes discipline, and regulates flexible labor (Peck 2001:56).

In my examination of a *local* "regime of regulation" and TANF processes, Foucault proves useful, as governance entails discipline and punishment about which he writes. Foucault wrote that "'discipline' . . . is a type of power, a modality for its exercise, comprising a whole set of instruments, techniques, procedures, levels of application, targets" (1984:206). Historically, the targets of discipline in the U.S. social service system have been poor people who apply for the stigmatized public assistance benefits (as opposed to social insurance programs such as Social Security and unemployment insurance). More recently, as the middle class shrinks, the target encompasses an array of flexible workers. In the welfare system manifestations of the theme of "panopticon"—surveillance, observation, security, and documenting knowledge about individuals—prevail as "concrete forms of the exercise of power" (217). Foucault also posited that "the systems of punishment are to be situated in a certain 'political economy'" (172).

As the business of welfare has become more decentralized, the layers of bureaucracy having a hand in governing recipients have increased. John Clarke's insights on welfare governance today are fitting. Clarke sees a shift in the governing of welfare from integrated to dispersed. He writes, "At the core of this is a view of *dispersal* as a set of flows from the state to other agents and agencies that have become engaged in the tasks of governing. This process of dispersal involves divergent strategies of reform and generates new sets of tensions, contradictions and potential instabilities" (2004:116). In today's political economy, where neoliberal strategies such as devolution and privatization shift welfare provisioning and services away from the federal government, the business of welfare is carried out by the state, but social service provisioning extends to private and not-for-profit organizations (e.g., housing/shelter operators, workfare training providers) who collaborate to promote (and capitalize on) the ideology of personal responsibility. Consequently, impoverished people become enmeshed in disjointed bureaucracies in public and private support enterprises. Recipients of services must negotiate their way through a fragmented system undergirded by legislation and rules where they are just as likely to meet people who obstruct their way or create bureaucratic snares as those who are highly supportive. Poor people confront myriad agents who are undoubtedly charged with meeting agency program goals, some of which may not necessarily be in sync with their own interests or with the realities of living in poverty. Moreover, it is particularly problematic when recipients' endeavors to receive aid entail governance and compliance with state and nonstate rules that have been foisted upon them. Noncompliance can result in punishment. Indeed, the system is rife with regulations and attendant governance, tensions, contradictions, and dysfunctional processes that can create destabilizing moments for people in need.

Governance through Shifting Ideology

A persistent feature of the U.S. welfare system has been its rules and regulations that are grounded in historically shifting ideologies in particular political economies.[3] And these prevailing ideologies, as well as extant economic conditions, have influenced caseworkers who historically have exercised personal judgments in local rule enforcement. Through the years, recipients' "dependency" has been racialized, feminized, and pathologized (Fraser and Gordon 1996), and thus recipients are stereotyped and vilified (see Chapter 2). Hence, they experience poor treatment, degradation, and punishment when they do not comply with rules.

In the early twentieth century the prevailing maternalist ideology inspired the notion that "mothering" and "homemaking" had an economic and social value, and that children should not be deprived of a home life. It also served to protect patriarchy and the family wage by excluding some women from the mainstream labor force. Morality has also been a constant guiding principle. Eligibility criteria for early mothers' aid programs and AFDC selected for a preponderance of "fit" and "deserving" white mothers without male partners (Abramovitz 1996; Gordon 1994, 2002). Caseworkers were guided by state statutes, some of which were more specific than others in what constituted "suitable homes" and physical, mental, and moral "fitness." They also relied on intelligence tests and information from recipients' social networks, but ultimately the decision rested on the "judgment, prejudices, and perception of the investigators [caseworkers]" (Bell 1964:10). In the early welfare programs even deserving mothers were subject to continuous direction, monitoring, and investigation. Some programs were designed for poor women, mostly white immigrants, who could be educated and assimilated into American culture (Mink 1995).

In the PRWORA era TANF caseworkers' actions are informed by the neoliberal agenda of devolution, privatization, reduction of welfare dependency, promotion of self-sufficiency, and mandated labor. The ideology of self-sufficiency is the disciplining ideology that compels welfare bureaucrats to refashion the remnants of AFDC and enact and implement new procedures, such as time limits and more stringent workfare and sanction measures. Morgen found in her study of Oregon welfare workers that "the single most important way that welfare reform has changed the work of welfare is that caseworkers must now combine eligibility determination (for benefits) with assisting their clients to move toward self-sufficiency" (2001:750). Oregon case managers, as active agents of a neoliberal agenda, "embraced the *value* of self-sufficiency," yet their individual interpretations were subject to a cluster of other values that influenced implementation and the extent of local policy enforcement (751).

The valorization of work informs current welfare policy and caseworkers' determination of the "deserving" recipients. TANF recipients are no longer just chronically poor and low-income people but, as the middle class shrinks, also include those who experienced a financial crisis. Many TANF recipients are workers who resort to TANF after their unemployment insurance benefits expired. Today, impoverished people move from a constructed category of "deserving" to "undeserving" during prolonged unemployment, as they move from the socially accepted unemployment insurance program to the stigmatized TANF program. But because the *worker* has subsumed the *fit mother* as the model of deserving recipient, a person receiving TANF might be considered "deserving" only if aid is thought to be temporary and if she or he proves to be actively seeking work or is employed. In reality, work does not ensure self-sufficiency and low wages and flexible labor increase the risk of recurrent unemployment, thus necessitating reliance on TANF.

Governance through Complex Rules

The 1996 welfare legislation granted states the flexibility to design and administer TANF policy in exchange for federal funding and accountability of program goals. Although states could set a cash grant amount under AFDC, PRWORA gave states greater latitude in deciding who could receive TANF cash and other noncash supports and in determining the requirements for eligibility and continuation of aid. States can decide on the extent of their support for moving welfare recipients into the labor force and whether they will provide postemployment services. They can establish the criteria and benefit level of child care and the strategies to encourage marriage and discourage childbirth outside of marriage. States can also choose how much of the TANF block grant they will spend, save, or transfer to other programs (Weil and Finegold 2002:xviii).

Because of devolution, the U.S. welfare program no longer exists as an entity. We have instead a complex pattern of state rules and regulations; there are dissimilarities in welfare policy nationwide, as well as some minor variations within states. Weil and Finegold posit that devolution has some benefits—states can experiment with welfare policies to determine what works best and tailor policies for specific populations, local values, and preferences. Yet, it is also problematic because two children in an identical situation would be handled differently in different states (2002:xviii–xix). Still, many states adopted the same punitive provisions. Schram (2000) points out the irony of devolution. When states tighten restrictions, other states feel compelled to follow suit, fearing that more liberal benefits might attract welfare recipients. He argues that, instead of fifty states experimenting innovatively to devise programs to meet the needs of public assistance recipients, "devolution may have sown the seeds of conformism" (108). Many states "follow the pack," similarly imposing stricter restrictions than the federal standard (108).

Rules and regulations are the foundation for governance and are now enforced in a workfare model that includes residues from the past. Keeping track of variations within states and among states is an enormous feat and it was never an aim of mine to do so. Nor was it ever my intention to analyze New York State TANF policies in depth or to compare state policies for efficacy. But here I briefly cover a few broad categories of rules to illustrate the devolutionary aspect of TANF, program complexity, nationwide variation, and, conversely, the conformity of states to impose punitive regulations on TANF recipients. The rules also provide an insight into the formidable regulatory nature of the welfare programs. I draw on the Urban Institute's *Welfare Rules Databook: State TANF Policies as of July 2003* (Rowe with Versteeg 2005). The publication compares and summarizes TANF policies across fifty states and the District of Columbia, covering an array of rules that were in place in 2003, the year I began fieldwork.[4] The rules are related to initial eligibility assessment procedures, welfare benefits, recipient requirements, and ongoing eligibility. The *Databook* also charts some changes to state policies at set time intervals between 1996 and 2003. Periodic changes add to the complexity of state programs. Reading about welfare rules pales in comparison to the lived experience of a financially desperate applicant or recipient whose emotional state has been frayed by dealings in a confusing, punitive, and trap-laden welfare system. For many recipients, abiding by the rules or being accused of not complying adds undue stress on their families' lives. And those who make interstate moves and must apply for TANF in the new state must become familiar with a new set of rules and regulations.

ELIGIBILITY RULES

All states set procedures to determine an applicant's initial eligibility for TANF cash assistance. Over half of the states have formal diversion programs whereby families may choose to receive a one-time cash payment for a financial emergency, but this typically will disqualify them from receiving ongoing TANF cash benefits for a time. In almost all states, when a family applies for both diversion payments and TANF benefits, they must pass nonfinancial tests (based on demographic and family composition characteristics) and financial tests (based on income and assets available to the family). For example, if a family's total assets exceed the state-determined amount, a family is deemed ineligible. Some states' asset limits are as low as $1,000; Hawaii's limit, for example, is $5,000. States also impose income tests and have the flexibility to set the portion of income (e.g., gross or net), the type of earned and unearned income that is counted, and whose income will count. Nationwide, for a family of three the maximum income allowed for initial eligibility ranged from approximately $200 to $1,300 per month (Rowe with Versteeg 2005:15–17, 22–23, 52, 58, 64–65).

All states require that a family must include a child, or in some states a pregnant woman, to be eligible for TANF. In nineteen states a pregnant woman with no other children is ineligible for cash benefits. States that do provide benefits have established the month of pregnancy when benefits begin, ranging from the first to the ninth month. A never-married minor parent is subject to specific rules. Unless exempt due to a good cause, in nearly all states a never-married minor parent would be ineligible to receive TANF unless the person lives with a parent or in an approved setting (Rowe with Versteeg 2005:17–19, 38–39, 42–43).

PRWORA created a "qualified alien" category that narrowly defined distinct groups of immigrants as TANF eligible, and it established disparate rules and exemptions for specific groups. Qualified aliens who entered the United States before the PRWORA enactment date in 1996 are potentially eligible to receive aid without a waiting period; those who entered after PRWORA are subject to a five-year ban. States have some flexibility, and state decisions vary widely regarding eligibility requirements for post-PRWORA entrants (Rowe with Versteeg 2005:20–22).

REQUIREMENT RULES

States set many behavioral requirements for individual family members as a TANF eligibility condition and for continued receipt. These requirements attempt to influence or alter behavior; some relate to activities in the areas of school, immunization, health screening, and drug testing. For example, thirty-four states impose school requirements on dependent children; these could include requirements associated with school attendance, minimum grade point average achievement, and involvement of parents in children's education (Rowe with Versteeg 2005:85–86, 90–91).

As a result of the 1996 welfare legislation, states are obliged to meet an annual work participation rate, that is, the percentage of a state's caseload that must be engaged in work activities. And they must ensure that recipients engage in work or work activities for a minimum number of hours each week as soon as the state determines that the person is able to work or after two years of benefit receipt, whichever is sooner.[5] However, there is great variation among states in terms of who must work, when work requirements begin, the type and amount of work activities allowed, and minimum hours required. Though states are not required to do so, they may exempt individuals or certain groups from work obligations. About a dozen states do not exempt a head of household over twenty years old from work requirements even if she or he is ill, incapacitated, or caring for an ill or incapacitated person. Some states do not exempt a pregnant woman from working. States can impose a sanction, a financial penalty, when an individual does not comply with work requirements. States vary in determining conditions of noncompliance and the severity and duration of the sanctions. A sanction can range from the noncompliant individual's benefit portion being suspended, reduced by a percentage, or cut completely to the entire family's benefits being terminated. The severity is based on the number of times a person is noncompliant and the duration of noncompliance (Rowe with Versteeg 2005:87–89, 92–93).

CASH BENEFITS AND ONGOING ELIGIBILITY

In July 2003 the maximum monthly benefit level for a family of three with no income ranged from $164 in Alabama to $923 in Alaska. However, the national mean was $418, and the median was $396. These levels were calculated for an adult and two children who are not subject to a family cap, have no special needs, pay for shelter, and live in the state's most populated area (Rowe with Versteeg 2005:80–81, 167).

Throughout the duration of a benefit period, states continue to impose asset and income tests and nonfinancial rules. For instance, nearly half of the states impose some type of family cap, that is, they prevent or limit an increase in TANF cash when another child is born during the time when the family receives benefits. Additionally, PRWORA legislation imposed a sixty-month lifetime limit on federal cash assistance. However, states have the authority to set the type and duration of limits. Consequently, some states have imposed shorter limits while others extend welfare benefits using state funds (Rowe with Versteeg 2005:107–15, 128–31).

This cursory overview of some welfare rules nationwide is devoid of specificity, nuances, and exemptions. Yet it shows the complexity and severity of rules, and the paltry benefit amounts ought to dispel a popular misconception that welfare benefits are generous. Importantly, these are only a few of the requirements that make eligibility and ongoing receipt of TANF a challenge. And rules change due to continuing welfare restructuring. Some of the rules that were in place in 2003, most notably the ones pertaining to work activities, will have changed due to the TANF program changes made by the federal government resulting from the Deficit Reduction Act of 2005; final TANF rules took effect in late 2008.

Local "Regime of Regulation"

By comparison, New York is more progressive in some areas than other states because it is obliged by the state constitution to provide care for the needy.[6] The state's Temporary Assistance program consists of two main programs that provide assistance for general living expenses: the Family Assistance program and the Safety Net Assistance program. Additionally, a few other programs cover emergency needs. The Family Assistance program is the TANF-funded program; aid is limited to sixty months. The state's Safety Net Assistance program provides benefits to individuals and families who do not qualify for the Family Assistance or other federal temporary assistance programs. Among those who may qualify for Safety Net Assistance are families who exceeded the sixty-month TANF limit.[7] Even understanding local welfare program rules is a frustrating feat. Some of the parents I interviewed were confounded by the complexity of the rules and regulations of the New York State welfare program, while others were quite astute interpreters. Some who were accustomed to the old rules learned about the new regulations when they were in the midst of solving an issue that threatened their benefits.

I found myself in the confounded category and referred to documentation on the website of the New York State Office of Temporary and Disability Assistance (OTDA), including the approximately six-hundred-page *Temporary Assistance Source Book* (2005b) and *Policy Directives*, which contains administrative directives, informational letters, and local commissioner memorandums from 1990 to the present that provide periodically updated information on policy and procedures (2007).[8] I spent hours reading through these documents, attempting to familiarize myself with New York's welfare program. I found the documentation, which was apparently written for state and local district staff, far too technical and thorny. It was never my aim to analyze discrete rules and point out contradictions to the rules in parent's stories and I have not done so. My aim was to relate what happened to people and depict the welfare system from *their* perspectives. Nonetheless, on those occasions when I tried to resolve inconsistencies, it was often fruitless because of the complexity of the rules, changes over time, and the dense documentation. It is doubtful that recipients of welfare refer to these specialized documents. But even information booklets designed for their use and their notifications from the state can be confusing. College-educated Desmond Hughes and I had trouble interpreting exactly what was required of him when we read the decision notice denying him public assistance. For individuals with educational deficits and learning disabilities, this can be problematic. Thus, it became apparent how recipients became mired in convoluted problem-solving situations and were caught in the system's traps owing to multifaceted rules, exceptions, exemptions, and the interpretation by layers of bureaucrats and the recipients themselves. The complexity of the system hinders recipients' ability to know and understand their rights and to negotiate or contest deleterious actions that jeopardize their benefits and thus their livelihood. Furthermore, enforcement is often uneven and contradictory. Applicants and recipients are subject to the scrutiny and judgment of many people within the social service system and within private agencies from which they seek aid or at which they are mandated to attend programs.

Applying for Benefits

In New York State the eligibility process for temporary assistance begins with the completion and submission of an application and an in-person meeting with one or more DSS staff members. The sixteen-page New York State application used during my fieldwork allowed for a person to apply for Temporary Assistance (TANF and Safety Net), Medical Assistance, Medicare Savings Program, food stamp benefits, and services including foster care and child-care assistance. An applicant is required to provide basic demographic information about everyone who lives with her or him, even if those residents are not applying. Some services require the disclosure of immigration status. Temporary Assistance applicants must provide information to help obtain child support. Sources of income for the applicant and all household residents must be specified within twenty-nine discrete categories; information about assets must be furnished. The application asks who in a household pays child support, alimony, child and dependent care, and tuition. Cash giveaways and the sale or transfer of certain assets within a specific number of years by the applicant or spouse, regardless of a spouse's domicile, must be reported. Medical questions including ones about receiving treatment in drug abuse and alcohol programs and inability to work due to disability or illness must be answered. Details on education and employment history, including current participation in a strike or migrant/seasonal labor, are required. Shelter expenses and landlord's contact information must be supplied. Lastly, there are potentially incriminating questions about the applicant and other household members. Questions ask if anyone in the household, and if so who, has been found guilty or disqualified for Temporary Assistance or food stamps because of fraud or intentional program violation, received unentitled benefits that have not been repaid, been convicted of making a fraudulent statement or representation of residence to receive Temporary Assistance in two or more states, or violated probation or parole. The applicant is instructed to read three pages of "important information" and sign the application. The signature entails acknowledgment that the applicant read and understands the notices; understands and agrees to the assignments, authorizations, and consents; and under penalties of perjury swears or affirms that the information is correct (New York State Office of Temporary and Disability Assistance 2003). Not only is the application lengthy, but the applicant is also required to submit specific documentation. Initial and additional requests for documentation within a specific time frame can pose obstacles for applicants; failure to submit documentation on time results in cases being denied and closed.

A comparison of the application for welfare and unemployment insurance reveals the two-tiered class disparity in the U.S. social service system. Unlike an application for public assistance, an application for unemployment insurance benefits can be made via telephone or the Internet. The demographic information required is minimal; most questions are employment related. None are invasive. Certainly, there are regulations associated with applying, claiming, and maintaining eligibility for time-limited unemployment benefits of twenty-six weeks. A person must seek employment, keep job search records, and claim weekly benefits. The latter can be done by answering a few questions via the New York State Department of Labor's computerized telephone claim certification system or on their website. Applying for and claiming weekly unemployment insurance benefits is generally uncomplicated and unproblematic.

In contrast, public assistance applicants must expend a disproportionate amount of time, energy, and money compared to those who apply for unemployment insurance benefits. They are subjected to intense scrutiny about themselves and those living with them. Inscribed in their application is the notion that they are undeserving and even fraudulent. Furthermore, the application form is merely the first step; additional time, energy, and expense is required during the eligibility determination period in which applicants are subjected to more intense scrutiny, judgment and governance.

Caseworkers: Personal Judgments, Unpredictable Outcomes

Recipients of welfare interact with DSS staff members that include, but are not limited to, caseworkers. Because the people that I interviewed spanned the class spectrum, some people had more experience applying for and obtaining government benefits than others and thus had more dealings with DSS personnel over time. They had sundry opinions and commentary about their interactions and relationships with caseworkers. Obtaining welfare and other benefits has been variously described to me as ranging from unremarkable and hassle-free to frustrating, laborious, daunting, degrading, and demoralizing. A person's assessment of the eligibility process is weighed against disparate factors that can include an applicant's gravity of need, relationship with DSS caseworker, caseworker's attitude, hassles encountered, time and energy expended, stress level and coping mechanisms, DSS determination of approval or denial, and the extent and amount of benefits received. Melba Jackson said that many years ago one of her caseworkers was a "real good friend" who suggested to her that it might be easier for Melba to stop working and take care of her children and grandchild while she received AFDC benefits. (This suggestion would not be made today.) Latrice Parker was impressed with a previous caseworker in the PRWORA era who facilitated getting her birth certificate "and everything," thus accelerating her application and approval for a Section 8 housing voucher after living in a shelter for a six months. Latrice contrasted him with her present caseworker who requires her to "do a whole lot of stuff" and who threatened to cut her benefits if she did not comply.

A persistent aspect of welfare is that relationships between caseworkers and recipients are based on inequalities of power. And it appears from parent's narratives that caseworkers drew on old and new ideologies as well as stereotypes based on gender, race, class, and personal characteristics. Roseanne Tate, a white, middle-class homemaker, applied for TANF and other benefits when her finances deteriorated in the aftermath of her husband's incarceration. Having but one experience on welfare, she told about her interaction with the personnel.

> They were very nice. And some of the people in there were like, they told me like, "You are totally out of your league here." . . . It was hard. It was not a good experience sitting there. . . . The caseworker I was assigned, he was actually very nice. He wasn't a nasty; he was very helpful and he told me, "You're the person that this was designed for. . . . You're not living on this. . . . You need a hand." [*laugh*] So he was very helpful, . . . he got me the benefits I needed. He was very available.

Although Roseanne said the caseworker was "nice," she was subjected to his evaluation based on longstanding welfare ideology insinuating that she is the deserving type—a white, abandoned mother in a financial bind who requires temporary aid.

Mercedes Montgomery, a white woman, commented on a meeting she had with a caseworker in the PRWORA era: "Like telling me, why do I need to go on welfare, I can't find a boyfriend, you know, to help me? Yes. They said that to me, 'You can't find anyone? You were a flight attendant, you can't get another job? I mean come on.' I'm like, 'No. I can't. If I could, wouldn't I have one? You think I want to be here?'" Faint remnants of a patriarchal ethos blend with neoliberal ideology as Mercedes' caseworker attempted to shift welfare provisioning from the public sector to the private sector and the private realm—a "double privatization" (Clarke 2004:122).

Eligibility Process: Layers of Bureaucracy and Investigation

Another persistent feature in the welfare program is that even when people are ostensibly eligible due to their financial need, some are denied not only cash but food stamps and other benefits because of seemingly benign but insidious traps (see also Kingfisher 1996; Susser 1982; Susser and Kreniske 1987). Many recipients of welfare experience bureaucratic difficulties. They work hard to obtain benefits in the stigmatized public assistance program. Stall tactics are common. Such delays and denial of welfare and other government benefits have different consequences for people depending on their class location, present circumstances, and personal safety net of kin and friends. In New York receipt of Temporary Assistance benefits is based on initial eligibility approval, periodic recertification, and compliance with myriad requirements, notably employment enforcement. Unless they are exempt, recipients must work or participate in work activities.[9]

After a person files an application, she or he must be told if the application is approved or denied within thirty days for Family Assistance (TANF) and forty-five days for Safety Net Assistance. An applicant might also have to meet with someone from the Front End Detection System (FEDS), an additional investigative process aimed to identify fraudulent or incorrect information. Even if state welfare offices make good on these decision-making deadlines much of the time, many people can attest to prolonged eligibility determination. Some had their cases closed in the process, necessitating reapplication or an appeal, thus protracting bureaucratic procedures and interaction. For many this caused hardship.

Monique Butler, a black woman in her late thirties, had moved from a Southern state to New York. At her FEDS appointment she brought what she thought was the requisite paperwork. Upon presentation, she was directed to submit additional documentation to her caseworker and casework supervisor. It took close to three months for a determination. Monique viewed the layers of personnel as a hindrance to timely decision making. Added layers hold the potential for imposing new demands. In comparison to many others Monique appeared to have had more resources. While she was awaiting the decision, she was also waiting for her New York license to practice respiratory therapy and relied on family in New York and in the South to help her get by during that time. She recalled, "If it wasn't for family support, I don't know what I would have done. . . . I probably would have been practically on the side[walk], I would have been homeless." Obviously, her personal safety net was intact. Her cousin was her "major support system." She and her teen daughter doubled up with him; not an ideal housing situation, but it reduced her expenses. Monique has an associate's degree and was able to pick up some substitute teaching. Her chances for employment after she received her license were good. In fact, she secured full-time work one month after receiving TANF.

Eligibility Process: System Incompetence, Laxity, and Inflexibility

After her employment termination, Mercedes Montgomery's job search, in the post–September 11 airline industry during a recession and jobless recovery, had been futile; thus, she had a series of short-term, low-income jobs. At one point, having exhausted her unemployment benefits, she experienced financial distress after she broke up with her partner, and she then applied for TANF and other government assistance. She was eligible to receive rental assistance for back rent. However, several sequential checks were made out to the wrong person; she could not cash them nor could the landlord. Each administrative error necessitated a return visit to the welfare office and more hours of waiting. The matter was still unresolved when Mercedes received her income tax refund check. Frustrated with the bureaucracy, she decided to pay the back rent with the tax refund and returned the error-laden checks to DSS. For all her effort, Mercedes said, "In the end. Nothing. Honestly, nothing. Nada."

At some point Mercedes finally secured a full-time job that grossed approximately $400 per week; she was also able to obtain subsidized child care. As described in detail in Chapter 6, DSS failed to pay the child-care provider who subsequently harassed Mercedes for delinquent payments and eventually requested that Mercedes remove her child from the day-care center. Under duress and lacking child care, Mercedes quit her job and once again her finances plummeted. Hence she applied for TANF and food stamps. She was deemed ineligible for TANF. But her food stamp application was proceeding through the DSS maze and Mercedes was required to produce certain documents for eligibility determination. She did, but not within the required timeframe, and thus her application was closed. Stalwart, she reapplied. Three months later Mercedes was required to produce within one week's time her marriage and divorce certificates. This was the first time in her welfare system experience that she was asked for these documents. She did not understand "why all of a sudden are they making everything so difficult?" A one-week window within which to produce the documents became problematic because Mercedes' ex-husband, the keeper of the documents, was out of the country. Fearing a case closure if she did not meet the deadline, Mercedes frantically attempted to speak to DSS staff. I met with Mercedes during the week of the DSS deadline. She complained:

> And this week too. I made another call. You just never get a call back. I left my number. I have a machine. No call. From four people. A total of eight times I called now. It is just ridiculous. The same thing happened with child care. The same issue. I'm just asking for food stamps. . . . I'm not asking for anything else. Just to help. Cause I had no food. And just recently, a miracle

happened. I got my income tax. So that was really good, like $800. . . . I've been stretching it for food.

When Mercedes' ex-husband returned from his vacation, he sent her some documents, but not the marriage certificate. So she turned in what she had. Some time later Mercedes left me a voicemail saying she received a letter of denial for food stamps.

It is not unusual that applicants and recipients are penalized for bureaucratic laxity and incompetence. In the first episode Mercedes resolved the bureaucratic rigmarole by returning the error-laden checks rather than wasting more of her time; hence, she received no aid. The child-care non-payment fiasco caused her to quit a job, after which she suffered financial decline that caused her to seek public assistance. Then she was denied benefits due to system inflexibility. Although Mercedes' personal safety net is fragile, her professional work history and education are buffers. Typical of low-wage single mothers, she cycled between government benefits and work (cf. Edin and Lein 1997), although her employment was at a somewhat higher level in the formal economy. She was also able to receive unemployment insurance. At one point a student loan carried her for several months. Because she had some employment, an income tax refund check was a well-timed financial Band-Aid.

Eligibility Process: Excessive Governance

Desmond Hughes was no newcomer to welfare; he first applied in the mid-1970s and received benefits on and off since then. When we first met, he had been living in temporary housing for five years and caring for his teenaged son. A few months later Desmond was incarcerated for several months during which time his government benefits ceased. During Desmond's incarceration, his son lived with Desmond's sister. A month before his release from prison, Desmond's application for Temporary Assistance was faxed to DSS. That fax initiated a public assistance eligibility process. After several months, Desmond's frustration compelled him to telephone me to vent his exasperation. We scheduled an appointment to meet so he could impart the details of the multimonth ordeal.

Desmond and I met in a meeting room at his local library—a comfortable and convenient place for us to meet. While setting up my tape recorder, he extracted from his briefcase a pile of documentation that consisted of correspondence, fax cover pages, time-stamped fax transmittal proofs, and DSS forms. Although these twenty-four pages were only some of the documentation that traced his ordeal, it produced a paper trail that aided in Desmond's narration. To simplify my chronicle and to preserve anonymity, I have changed the names of social service staff and omitted exact dates; instead I describe his activities in roughly one-month intervals. My attempt at a precise reconstruction of Desmond's ordeal was arduous because his recollection of dates did not always match the exact date on the documentation, and he undoubtedly left out some particulars. Nonetheless, his narrative of events and the paper trail convinced me his application process was punitive and fraught with delay tactics.

MONTH 1

On the application he made from prison, Desmond applied for Temporary Assistance, Medical Assistance, and food stamp benefits for himself only. He requested money for rental arrears and future rental assistance. A month after applying for aid Desmond was released from jail.

MONTH 2

Desmond moved back into his apartment; his son remained with Desmond's sister for an additional month. Since it was expected that Desmond's son would move back home soon, Desmond was required to reapply for public assistance for himself and his son. He did so and produced what he thought was all the necessary documentation for his son's data to be calculated into the budget.

MONTH 3

In the middle of the month Desmond met with Ms. Hardcastle, his caseworker, who advised him that she did not have all his documentation. She reviewed with him the outstanding documents and formalized her request on a "Documentation Requirements" form on which appeared a check next to the three "eligibility factors" and the deadline by which he was required to produce the three requested documents. Those documents were proof of his son's Social Security benefits, proof that his son is in school, and a letter from Desmond's sister verifying that his son is back in his household. The deadline was ten days hence. Desmond remembered phoning Ms. Hardcastle on the day before the deadline, telling her of his intent to deliver the documents. She responded by telling him that it was not necessary because his case was closed. In fact it was closed two weeks earlier, on the day of their meeting. Desmond was confounded. This turn of events prompted Desmond to communicate his frustration to Ms. Hardcastle's supervisor, Ms. DeLay, and explain to her what exactly had taken place. Desmond expressed how he felt.

> In essence I had kinda felt stonewalled and that she [Ms. DeLay] stood behind everything that the worker [Ms. Hardcastle] said, even though I had related and intimated [to Ms. DeLay] that the worker said that she miscalculated when I was to bring those documents in to her.
> . . . I was under the impression and suspicion that somewhere out on the line somebody was either losing documents or trying to recompile a whole new case folder on me. Because somewhere along the line also documents were either lost, misplaced, misused or maybe they were just making me jump through these hoops because they could. Because as I see it, that's what the Department of Social Services does. I'm not saying that they are a bad agency. . . . I know in the past that times when I might have needed treatment from my therapy program which involved an outpatient program because of my drug history, the case would have been opened almost immediately. But at this time, because I believe this is not the case, they seem to be either dragging their feet or giving me a hard time or maybe I'm just one of those cases that they're just having a little difficulty with. I don't know. Cause I don't want to take their side. I don't want anybody to lend any more credence to my situation than ought to be and just understand that all I'm simply trying to do is open my case for my son and myself so we can have, however temporary, assistance that most people apply for when they seek public assistance.

Subsequently Ms. Hardcastle was removed from his case and Desmond was assigned a temporary caseworker, Ms. Block. Because his case was closed, Desmond had to fill out a third application, which he did. Ms. Block did not provide a written request but told him to bring in the outstanding documents because she did not have them. Attempting to simplify matters, on the third application Desmond applied only for himself. But about a week later Ms. Block indicated that applicants were no longer permitted to do that and directed him to fill out a fourth application that included his son. Desmond met with Ms. Block and received a form letter with handwritten instructions to attend a meeting with an employment counselor and thereupon provide verification of his attendance. He was also instructed to meet with an Eligibility Examiner from the Bureau of Case Review. The deadline for completion was five business days hence. If he did not comply, the case might be denied or closed.

MONTH 4

At the employment meeting, Desmond met with a counselor for about ten minutes, during which time he was given a letter mandating him to participate in an approved employment activity, specifying the vocational training program and scheduled date. It stated that without documentation of "good cause" a person must comply with the program requirements. He was administered a basic education aptitude test that took him about a half an hour to complete; he never saw the results of the test. He left the meeting laden with a booklet and other documents regarding employment.

The appointment with the Eligibility Examiner from the Bureau of Case Review resulted in yet another request for documents—this time a list of *ten* items (in contrast to the *three* outstanding documents requested by his DSS caseworkers). Desmond was perplexed why some requests were made in the first place, presuming that many of them should have been in his file for years. He explained:

> My folder is at least three inches thick. And I don't doubt that the
> documents which they already have range from birth certificates, to marriage
> certificates, school letters, letters from Social Security, letters from my
> landlord, shelter verifications, all types of documents which there should
> be no question [about] because my position with all of these organizations
> and agencies are still the same—with my landlord, with my son's school,
> with Social Security. . . . But yet for each application, I've been made to
> understand, and I could be wrong because it seems like they have one of
> those crayon rule books that they just write the rules as they go along. Again
> I'm just trying to be humorous about this to keep from pulling my hair
> out. Which I don't have any [*laugh*]. But I try to comply as best I possibly
> can. . . . I try to handle myself in a manner which they can clearly see that

all I'm trying to do is get certain services. And if I comply with them, they'll comply with me. Or they'll give me what I'm asking for once I comply. But this isn't always the case.

At various points throughout this ordeal Desmond attempted to get resolution by escalating his complaints to higher management levels within DSS. He spoke with the supervisor, Ms. DeLay, whom he said was "nasty." She suggested that he file for a fair hearing. Frustrated, Desmond made a trek to the commissioner's office where a receptionist intervened and relayed to him the commissioner's advice—to go back to his local office and exhaust all avenues there. He thought he had already done that by leaving voicemails or speaking to other higher-level staff by phone. But he made continued attempts and was ultimately directed to speak to Ms. DeLay, the supervisor to whom he initially spoke. Desmond said,

> Which to me seemed pretty much like a vicious circle that they are running me through. Or whatever, fiery hoop or whatever it is that people have to do. I did [contact] them all numerous times. That next day after I didn't get any satisfaction from [local DSS management] I went back . . . and I spoke to the commissioner. . . . She told me that before coming out she spoke with [one of the managers] and Ms. Block and that it was suggested that before my case could be opened, and these are her words verbatim and I quote, "Fax to Ms. Block a letter from the Social Security Administration and the school letter from my son's school and my case would be open."

Fax transmission verification reports indicated that Desmond faxed the two documents necessary to open the case. However, a week later he received a notice of decision denying his request for public assistance and food stamps; a separate decision for medical assistance would be forthcoming. The denial indicated that he failed to provide two pieces of information related to his marital status. They were different from the two documents he was instructed to fax! Other convoluted and confusing language containing a series of double negatives mentioned proof of recent expenses; it was unclear to me whether substantiating documents for this were required.

Requests for different documents by various DSS staff along the way made the application process confusing, laborious, and delayed. And it had severe ramifications for Desmond. Approximately 110 days transpired from the faxing of the first application to the date of the DSS rejection decision, during which time Desmond received no cash, food stamps, or medical benefits. It seems as though Desmond was caught, to borrow a phrase from Moynihan (1965), in a bureaucratic "tangle of pathology."

Desmond filed a request for a fair hearing soon after he received the notification of denial. I had not seen Desmond since the meeting where he told of this fiasco, but he kept in touch by email for a while. Six months later he wrote to say that things were not going well for him. Apparently he had obtained benefits because he indicated that they had been terminated. He wrote months later to say that he was without benefits for three months, his rent was $5,000 in arrears, and he had just received a utility turn-off notice. The following month he wrote that he went to two fair hearings and was at the "point of despair." A month after that, we were scheduled to meet so he could update me on his situation. I worried when he failed to arrive after an hour, as he was always prompt. Three days later he wrote to tell me he was evicted and "subjected to minor hell." He and his son spent a few nights in a homeless shelter and then were sleeping with whomever they could. A few days after that he received a date for a fair hearing two weeks hence and hoped for a decision reversal that would result in seven months' retroactive rent assistance. A month later he had not yet received a decision. Apparently Desmond had been reinstated in his apartment, because five months later he wrote to say that he was being evicted again because Social Services refused to continue his case.

Desmond has the advantage of a bachelor's degree but is disadvantaged by a poor work history, multiple incarcerations, and a drug history. His son benefits from the caregiving support of Desmond's sister and the son's "godmother." About his son's godmother, apparently a wealthy woman, Desmond said, "Nothing for him is too much for her. The price is no object." Desmond's role as father and caregiver is an advantage because singles and single homeless men are treated far worse than women in the welfare and homeless systems as a result of laws and cultural attitudes (Passaro 1996). Desmond's reluctance to "raise a little hell" at the welfare office was influenced by his gender assumptions that the repercussions for such action would be worse for men. Yet, as a single parent Desmond shares similar problems with women. Delays, case closures, denials, and sanctions can have a severe impact on a family's finances, stability, health, and emotional state. Even if benefits are reinstated and retroactive payments are made, parents must deal with the interim anxiety and uncertainty about their future.

Continued Benefits, Continued Governance

Once an application is approved, continued eligibility is not secure. Recipients must comply with welfare program rules while receiving benefits and must periodically recertify for continuation. Noncompliance with rules can result in a sanction. As the self-sufficiency ideology intensified and stricter work enforcement evolved through the neoliberal years, so did the severity of sanctions. Sanctions are financial penalties for violation of a welfare program regulation or mandate that results in a benefit reduction or elimination. They appear to be designed to govern, motivate, manipulate, and alter recipients' behavior and to punish them for their transgressions as well as for bureaucratic errors.

In the pre-PRWORA era some states reduced the AFDC benefits of those recipients who failed to participate in the JOBS training program initiated in 1988. In the 1990s many states believed that the penalty was too lenient to influence compliance with work participation; thus, some states applied for and received waivers to impose more severe sanctions. In 1996 PRWORA legislation required states to impose at minimum a "pro rata" grant reduction for noncompliance, but the law's flexibility allows states to inflict greater penalties. State sanctions differ in type, amount, duration, remedies, and measures for repeated noncompliance. The most common sanctions are partial and full family; a full family sanction means that the entire family's benefits are terminated, either gradually or immediately (Pavetti et al. 2004:2–3). New York State imposes a partial sanction, that is, the welfare grant is reduced by the noncompliant adult's share.

I interviewed attorney Randy Nash, who said that people are sanctioned usually for one of two reasons—for not complying with work requirements and for not following through with a drug or alcohol treatment plan. Randy explained how the workfare mandates operate in the PRWORA era.

> And if you don't show up to anything, even the first appointment, they'll
> sanction you. And for people who they say that they're unemployable
> because of drugs or alcohol, they make you go through a treatment program.
> And then if you don't comply with the treatment program, even one session,
> they can sanction you. And the only way you can get out of that mess is if
> you have very good reason for missing it. If you don't have a good reason,
> basically the law says yes, they're gonna sanction you. And then they are
> sanctioned. The average person who doesn't feel well, if [they] wake up with

a stomachache and nauseous, they'll just call in sick. But these people have to go to a doctor. If they don't go to a doctor and get a note that says this person's sick on this day, they will be sanctioned.

Some parents I interviewed were never sanctioned; many others were. Some were sanctioned many times over the years. Their welfare histories show that generally a missed appointment was the principal violation resulting in a sanction; this usually applied to a routine or workfare meeting, but it could also have been a drug treatment program session. Additionally, a sanction can be imposed for not complying with myriad work-related and other program requirements, such as cooperating with DSS to obtain child support. When I met Chandra Alexander, she was living in a family shelter. She complained to me about a sanction that stemmed from an alleged failure to notify her caseworker of her new $7.00 per hour employment. In fact, she could not get in touch with her caseworker in person to advise him, so she left him a memo in his mailbox. Subsequently Chandra received a sanction notice and consequently her welfare grant was cut by $52 a month, reducing her monthly aid to $164 a month for her and her daughter. She expected the grant to remain at this amount for several months. She felt the sanction was particularly unfair because her employment only lasted seven weeks; she quit her job at a drugstore because "there was discrimination going on there heavily." Chandra said, "It just gets to me because I know to them it's a little bit of money. But it takes its toll, you know. Especially when you don't have. What little you [do have] don't seem like you even have."

Sanctions are an absolute threat to all who seek or obtain TANF because of workfare mandates. Because states must comply with federal work requirements, the pressure bears downward on the individual to comply. Recall that Desmond Hughes received a letter instructing him to attend a workfare program. The letter stated, "As an employable customer you are mandated to participate in an approved employment activity to remain eligible for Public Assistance."[10] It indicated the specific vocational training and followed with, "Failure to meet the program requirements without documentation of good cause may result in a closing or reduction in your Public Assistance and/or Food Stamp benefits." The letter enumerated some conditions of "full compliance": keeping DSS appointments, attending assigned classroom activities, and completing training program assignments.

Many people, like Lorna Webster, complied with mandates. When she was required to attend a workfare program she rationalized her attendance: "Well you had to do something. And when I was looking for a job, it wasn't going too well. And if you don't show them that you're trying to do something, they're quick to like sanction you or whatever. So I just went and took the class 'cause it was hard to find me a job." Yet some people missed appointments because they forgot, or the appointments conflicted with other government assistance related meetings, personal commitments, or even their work schedules. After Lorna was evicted and placed in a homeless shelter she had an appointment scheduled for a month later. But she forgot—an easy thing to do considering her families' displacement and trauma. She remembered her emotional state.

> Yeah, they tried to sanction me because when I had first went to [the shelter] . . . I had forgot about my appointment [scheduled for a] month later 'cause I was hysterical when I first lost my apartment. . . . So when I got there, I'm like going crazy 'cause I didn't know what to do. I didn't have any money . . . 'cause I lost my job and I lived six months off my bank accounts and stuff like that. And I really didn't have anything when I went there [to the shelter]. And I totally forgot about the appointment. And they sent me a letter like they're gonna kick me out of a homeless shelter because I missed an appointment. If I'm already homeless, how are you gonna kick me out of a homeless shelter? That was really stupid I think.

Lorna contacted her shelter caseworker, who intervened and "got everything straightened out" in three or four days.

People also miss appointments because they never received notifications. This can happen for various reasons. Poor people often move frequently or abruptly and their mail might not have been forwarded, or notices were never sent by DSS because of a technical problem or human oversight. Unaware of the appointment, people do not comply and a sanction might be imposed. While Amber Hamilton lived at a family shelter for a year, she was sanctioned twice. After she first moved in, a notice was sent to the shelter instructing her to attend a mandated workfare program. Amber never looked in her shelter mailbox because no one told her she had one. Furthermore, she had been accustomed to retrieving mail from her U.S. post-office box. Consequently, she missed the appointment and was sanctioned. Amber sought the help of her shelter caseworker, who during the course of his intervention discovered that the workfare program, run by a private agency, had been canceled due to lack of funding. Despite the cancellation, he still had to advocate on her behalf for DSS to lift the sanction.

Some time later Amber received a second sanction alleging that she "refused" to attend a meeting and sign an affidavit that would have initiated court proceedings for child support collection from her sons' father. She said she never received the paperwork. Her shelter caseworker interceded. Before he succeeded in getting the sanction lifted, her benefits were cut for a month. I asked Amber how much she lost and the implications. She said, "And by me not doing that, they took away part of my food stamps and stuff. Like a hundred and some dollars. . . . I was only left with $130 for the month." When I asked how it affected her and if she struggled, she replied, "Yeah. I had to wash clothes out by hand and stuff. . . . We was eating things like little packs of soup noodles and stuff like that. We wasn't eating like we used to eat. . . . Always eating sandwiches and soup. . . . And they took away my part of the cash too. They didn't take my kids' food stamps and my kids' cash." Fortunately for Amber and other New York welfare recipients, Governor Pataki's attempts to legislate full family sanctions during his administration were thwarted. Yet a sanction eliminating her portion was bad enough.

> We was just really, really poor. . . . Yeah. I didn't even have the money to get on the bus to go somewhere where my family was to get some food out of their refrigerator. I couldn't even do that. I was stuck here [at the shelter] until my mother came and got me. . . . She gets off at eleven at night so she came down here right after work to come get me. It was like twelve something. And that's after curfew. They [shelter staff] didn't want me to leave. But I was not staying here [at the shelter] another night starving and stuff. I would not. So I left. I don't know if I got written up for it. I don't know what happened but I had to go.

Commenting on the welfare system in general, attorney Randy Nash said that singles are treated worse than families "because of the long line of law that says when the children are involved, you have to treat them a little bit better." Randy also indicated that "sanctions are bad for anyone because that'll mean that your rent won't be paid. So a sanction can lead to a person being evicted." Homeless shelters are an option for some evicted individuals and families, if they are deemed eligible. But there residents must comply with shelter rules in addition to DSS regulations, and thus they are at further risk for transgressions and penalties. Mothers and fathers living in a family shelter often conduct their "parenting in public" and therefore are routinely scrutinized (Friedman with Clark 2000). Parents must be especially diligent to avoid situations that could jeopardize their housing and their family well-being. In institutional settings such as shelters, impoverished parents are at greater risk of being reported to child welfare authorities by someone. The upshot of investigations for suspected child abuse or maltreatment can range from a determination that the allegation is unfounded to one that involves removing children from the family.

Shayleen Vaughn, a young mother living at a shelter for a year with her baby, said it is "not easy" living there. She is "tired of being in an environment where it's like I'm constantly being watched." So she keeps to herself. She explained, "I don't associate; none of that. I go to school. I come home. That way I don't get into any trouble. . . . You get into any kind of altercation with anybody, they're calling the police, they're writing my name down. And that's all I need for my probation officer to see. And I don't need it. So I pretty much stay out of everybody's way." Furthermore, Shayleen understands the consequences of not following shelter regulations. She was once evicted from a shelter for single women for not following rules. She subsequently decided to go "AWOL" from the system and lived on the street where she sold drugs to make a living. But after becoming a mother Shayleen held a different attitude; she had a son to raise and protect. She abides by shelter rules, some of which she says are, "You gotta sign in and out every day. You can't be out of [the shelter] for more than twenty-four hours." Shayleen is also compliant with welfare program rules, saying, "Oh, no. I don't get sanctioned. You know what I'm saying? Sanction is a form of incompetence. . . . You're not gonna cut me off. It's like this is what I need for my son. Not even me. If it was just me, I wouldn't be on this. I'd be in the street. But it's for my son. That's why I don't fuck around. They're not gonna cut me off."

Tina Brown expressed a similar sentiment. She has a long welfare history and was sanctioned several times. I asked her if she was sanctioned recently while living for the past several months in a shelter.

> *TB:* No. I did what I had to do. You know what I'm saying? Especially when I got my kids with me. I have to. I'm in that predicament where I got to do what I got to do.

TL: How do you know what you have to do?

TB: When you're mandated to do something by them, they send you a letter. And you either do it or they sanction you. As far as that, I have to do what I have to do to make sure my kids are all right and they have a roof over their heads. I can't just [*laugh*] let them take my kids like that. I'm mommy, I'm the head of household. . . . They [children] don't have a worry in the world right now. Not a worry. I'm the one that do all the worrying.

Indeed, parents have cause to worry about the implications of a sanction, therefore many comply. Their recourse is to accept the sanction, attempt to resolve the problem at the local DSS office, or request a fair hearing.

The Fair Hearing Process

Recipients of public assistance have the right to challenge DSS actions or determinations in a fair hearing—a formal procedure overseen by an administrative law judge from the New York State Office of Temporary and Disability Assistance (OTDA). A person might request a fair hearing when she or he is experiencing a prolonged eligibility determination; disagrees with a determination and reason for denial or discontinuation of cash, medical assistance, food stamps, or other service; challenges the amount or reduction of benefit payment; opposes an evaluation that she or he is able to work; or a host of other grievances. When making a request, the aggrieved person can request "aid continuing," that is, the continuation of existing benefits while waiting for a fair hearing decision. People who receive a notice of intent, decision, or denial of benefits have a specific timeframe associated with different services within which to make a request for a hearing. For example, there are sixty days to request a fair hearing for TANF/Safety Net or Medicaid, and ninety days for food stamps. Emergency hearings can be expedited. Between the time of the request and the fair hearing, attempts can be made to resolve the problem locally. If the problem was solved, an appearance at the hearing is not required. If the problem remains unresolved and the person does not attend the hearing, she or he will lose the case if rescheduling is not initiated. People can represent themselves or have legal counsel or another advocate represent them; they can also bring another person to support them (New York State Office of Temporary and Disability Assistance n.d.b.).

Given the effort involved in fair hearing preparation, presentation, and waiting for a decision, some people do not bother to apply for a fair hearing. Several parents indicated to me that they filed for and attended a fair hearing at some time. Some even enlisted the services of legal aid. Yet, an attorney told me that overall very few people seek out free legal counsel when they have a welfare problem of any sort. Several women said that they did not even contest a determination. For example, Chandra thought that the reduction in her benefits was unfair since she did the right thing by informing her caseworker (see above). But when I asked if she filed for a fair hearing, she said, "I should have did that, gone to a fair hearing, because it's not like I was trying to beat the system or try to take advantage of the system in a negative way. . . . I didn't have the energy."

Desmond's multimonth administrative fiasco (detailed above) was not the first time that he was involved in a drawn-out process to obtain public assistance. Desmond told me about another incident that illustrates how much time, energy, and angst is involved in appealing a determination. It is even more galling when a sanction or case closure is triggered by a bureaucratic mistake, as in this case.

Two months prior to our initial interview Desmond received a notice of decision that his public assistance would be discontinued; it stated that his gross monthly income of nearly $3,000 was more than the $748.33 limit. When I read aloud that part of the notice, Desmond exclaimed, "I wish that were the case." He had been unemployed for a long time and could not afford a termination of benefits. Shortly after he received the notice, he filed a request for a fair hearing with "aid continuing."

Desmond was granted a hearing date. In order to prove the DSS error he had to investigate the matter and piece together facts. It was a fact that earlier in the year Desmond was in a workfare program at a nonprofit agency and his job search led him to a firm that helped people set up their own fragrance shop. Desmond reported his workfare activity to his job counselor at the agency who advised him to attend a subsequent group interview. Even though Desmond was not interested in the operation, he complied and arrived at the appointed time, but was sent home by staff at the firm. Desmond was suspicious, believing the firm to be a sham or a shell company. Subsequently, the job counselor erroneously sent paperwork to DSS indicating that Desmond became employed by the firm. This triggered a public assistance budget recalculation on the inaccurate salary, which made him ineligible for assistance, and all benefits were scheduled to be discontinued shortly after he received the notice. While conducting his investigative work for the fair hearing, Desmond learned that the agency lost its workfare funding and that program became defunct. This disadvantaged Desmond because the job counselor was unavailable to corroborate his facts and provide evidence of his mistake.

At the fair hearing Desmond presented his case in front of an administrative law judge. He suspected that the judge had heard about these types of "fly-by-night places" because the judge postponed his decision and instructed Desmond to write a certified letter with return receipt to the firm asking for verification that he was not an employee. The judge also instructed him to try to find the job counselor. Allowing ample time for the accomplishment of these tasks, the judge set a future date for a second hearing.

My initial interview with Desmond was between his first and second fair hearing. Sensing his anxiety during his narration, I asked Desmond how he felt about the situation.

> I would have to feel like my whole existence really hinges on what their decision is going to be. Because I could lose my apartment and I might have to go into a shelter system again until they see fit that I can reapply for assistance. Everything that I have up to this point could be lost, which I am sure will do damage on my spirits. But I will still have to move ahead to keep my son from seeing that I'm going to be all broke up about it. I basically have to be strong for myself as well as for my son.

A month later I met Desmond at a café. Amid a noisy lunch crowd Desmond shared the good news that he won his fair hearing and his benefits. He said that at the second hearing he submitted to the judge his letter to the firm, which had been returned to him unopened with no forwarding address. The judge found that to be sufficient and declared the DSS decision to be unfounded.

To be sure, the fair hearing is a means of recourse in an inflexible system. For some people, their time, energy, and research pays off when they win the hearing, thus preserving benefits. However, it is often an arduous and punitive exercise. In an era of dispersed governance the onus is on recipients not only to challenge unfair decisions but also to rectify the mistakes of state and nonstate actors.

"It's Way Stricter and Harder"

Close to three-quarters of the parents I interviewed who received welfare did so in the years both before and after the enactment of PRWORA, receiving benefits from both AFDC and TANF; many assessed various aspects of PRWORA changes. Nellie Blake, a thirty-four-year-old woman who has a high school equivalency diploma and a long welfare history, gave her assessment:

> It's all the same. The system never changed. Nothing changed. And they're making it harder with less resources. . . . Like they'll tell you, "Go find a job." And basically after that, they try to close your case. And I'm like, "You're telling me to go get a job, but you lack skills. Can you help me? 'Cause, you know, you're not ready to give an education to get a good job." They wouldn't do that; they cut that.

Nellie's contradictory response is typical of those who perceive the welfare system as a static bureaucracy. It is understandable why people view the system as unchanging because conceptually it is more of the same—incessant waiting and disregard for poor people's time, caseworker discretionary powers, invasive and laborious eligibility procedures, catch-22s and procedural traps, and regulatory aspects. Yet their narratives tell of a transformation. Even Nellie's statement covers several PRWORA changes—stricter workfare mandates, ending entitlement to welfare, and limiting access to education. Although many facets are enduring, parent's narratives described how they "definitely got worse" or said "it's way stricter and harder." It is stricter and harder after the 1996 legislation because of the ideology of self-sufficiency, regulations, and especially work mandates and sanctions.

An upshot of devolution of welfare and related businesses (e.g., housing, workfare programs)—taking place under the rubric of dispersed governance—is state and nonstate management of activities and the governance of subjects. It could be argued that increased public and private agency staff facilitates service and support, as indicated by the help that several people described (e.g., shelter staff's intervention to lift sanctions). Yet, when self-sufficiency is a guiding principle and mission, then regulations, coercion, and disciplinary measures are employed to achieve that end. That being the case, decentralized support creates an environment where people at various levels in the social service system and in disparate agencies use their discretionary powers to investigate, observe, judge, collect information, and direct or mandate the activities of applicants and recipients of welfare and other aid. Their interests, agendas, goals, and timetables so often conflict with those of recipients, thus creating new tensions and exacerbating extant stresses and family insecurity.

The new model of *worker* needing *temporary* aid is the ideal or "deserving" type, similar to the model recipient for unemployment insurance benefits. Yet, the two programs remain hierarchically ranked, with public assistance being far inferior in status, benefit level, and treatment of recipients. This inferior status is manifested in the disregard for recipients' time as evidenced by applicants needing to wait for people and benefit determinations, produce documentation within an unrealistic timeframe, respond to conflicting requests from several different staffpeople, make repeated phone calls that are often ignored, attend numerous mandated meetings, record job searches, take aptitude tests, and even resolve bureaucratic errors. Having inferior status also subjects people to various disciplinary measures.

In the PRWORA era the system has become more complex and inflexible for recipients due to new provisions and measures to decrease the welfare rolls. The accounts of the eligibility processes illustrate that discretionary requests for information create excessive delays. Furthermore, complex administrative processes increase the opportunity for more mandates, tensions, discipline, and traps; this in turn inflates the risk for noncompliance sanctions and case closures. The threat of sanctions and case closures has intensified. Since most parents I met indicated that they have been mandated to workfare, their risk for sanction was increased due to the various tasks that must be completed. Many felt coerced by the threat of a sanction because they had their family well-being to protect. Although the fair hearing process is recourse for the aggrieved, it is yet another administrative procedure that robs poor people of their time and energy in an environment where people have to work *and* work "harder" for their benefits.

Recently, the trend is for welfare agencies to operate in a business-like fashion (Clarke 2004). Traditionally called "clients," welfare recipients are now often referred to as "customers." This linguistic shift is akin to business-model language in the service economy. But unlike company goals in the service sector, customer satisfaction is not a measure of success in a welfare office. Recipients' satisfaction is incompatible with their excessive waiting, the onerous eligibility processes, diversion and delay practices, and countless regulations and disciplining techniques. Waiting and wending one's way through the government assistance bureaucracy subjects poor people to physical discomfort, emotional aggravation, and sometimes despair. When recipients of welfare are required to perform bureaucratic gymnastics that result in the denial of benefits, the "customer" is hardly satisfied. But unlike in a competitive business environment, poor customer service has no downside for welfare bureaucrats. In fact, losing a "customer" has an upside—the welfare count is reduced, and this is a primary criterion of PRWORA's success (cf. Lipsky 1980).

5

Family Needs versus Welfare Limits

Family Pressures and the Need for Government Aid

The earlier snapshots of the suburban families and the experiences of recipients conducting their welfare-related business offer a glimpse of individuals' lives and stresses. Latrice Parker experienced the effects of trauma as a teen when her family and home life became destabilized after her mother's death. Her abandonment, weak family supports, and foreshortened high school education made her ill-prepared for the adult world. When she became homeless and pregnant, she turned to the state for aid. Though Desmond Hughes's need for welfare spanned three decades, it was after his wife's death that he struggled as primary caregiver to maintain a family; he assiduously pursued welfare and other aid. Financial decline beset Roseanne Tate in the aftermath of her husband's incarceration. She attempted to save their suburban house and provide for her children; TANF receipt was integral to her strategy. Anita Ramos turned her life around with the help of private and public aid when she left prison; welfare has been vital to her survival.

Through a life-cycle analysis of forty-two people's narratives, I have identified a variety of similar lifetime pressures that occasioned their need for aid. The foremost pressure was insufficient household income to support a family, stemming mainly from one or more aspects of an inadequate labor market (e.g., low wages, short-term jobs, prolonged unemployment). Other pressures were related to poverty, family issues, caregiving, housing, health, domestic relations, and various bureaucratic systems. People sought welfare cash (AFDC and/or TANF) and other government aid at one or more life stages for a variety of reasons.[1] They include but are not limited to the onset of motherhood; long-standing child rearing;

food inadequacy; unaffordable housing; homelessness; family destabilization such as the breakup, death, or incarceration of a spouse; postincarceration needs; domestic violence; and illness of a child or family member. Some parents experienced the multiple burdens of supporting households alone with little or no support from a partner and the loss of income from a contributing household member. Yet, in many instances it was accumulated stressors that created the need for aid. Many people experienced numerous and often simultaneous or sequential difficulties before they sought assistance. Many exhausted the resources of their personal support systems before doing so. For many poor people the need for welfare arises throughout one's life.

Here I introduce seven more women whose narratives shed light on the myriad pressures and crises that can arise within a family over time. The women include the youngest and oldest of the parents, as well as a mother having one child and another who had the most children among those whom I interviewed. Their stories describe some of the issues that created downward shifts and propelled individuals to seek cash benefits for the first time, for subsequent episodes, or on a continuing basis. While the women's stories are meant to show individual families' need for welfare over time, they also provide an opportunity to consider whether the federal government's lifetime limit on welfare benefits is reasonable over the life span of vulnerable families. Under PRWORA families can only receive federally funded assistance under the TANF program for five years.[2] But because the welfare legislation allows for flexibility, states can impose shorter lifetime limits or provide benefits beyond the federal limit using state funds. New York is an example of the latter; eligible families who exceed the sixty-month TANF limit may receive continued assistance through the state's Safety Net Assistance program.[3] Nevertheless, I use the federal government's timeframe of *sixty* months to show that time limits ignore the reality of the possible protracted need for welfare in a life span.

Shayleen Vaughn

It was a crisp autumn day when I first met Shayleen, a black woman in her very early twenties. By then, Shayleen had already experienced a life on the streets, several noncontiguous periods of TANF totaling "probably a whole twelve months," three episodes of incarceration, and three incidents of homelessness. She recalled the circumstances that led to her receiving welfare. A couple of years earlier, when she was still a teen, Shayleen had been selling marijuana. The police thought she sold narcotics and raided her mother's house where she and her younger siblings had been living. Her mother was not home; she was in "a detox" program at the time. During the drug bust police found her mother's drug paraphernalia and Shayleen was charged with possession. Shayleen asserted, "Me personally, I don't do crack, you know what I'm saying? But I would take that charge a thousand times so my mother don't lose her kids." In other words, she protected her mother to prevent the possible removal of her mother's children by a child welfare agency. Shayleen was charged and incarcerated. Her selfless act proved to be a sad irony. Upon release from a jail term of several months, an order of protection prevented her from living in the same house as her siblings, the very ones she was protecting in the first place. Furthermore, Shayleen could not live with her boyfriend who was residing in what she called a "bullshit shelter." Hence, Shayleen moved to a women's shelter where she received public assistance. Life after incarceration is difficult enough, but she was separated from her family and her boyfriend. At some point she became pregnant. To ameliorate stress her boyfriend sneaked into her shelter room nightly. Both that arrangement and her pregnancy were short lived. Her stress intensified. She recalled her situation:

> And then they're making me run back and forth from DSS to the [shelter]. And it was winter, and I lost the baby. I had a miscarriage. And that was another thing that just made me go crazy. . . . And then when they found out about my man staying there, they kicked me out. I really didn't give a shit. So I said, I'd just be on the street. 'Cause I just didn't understand why I had to lose my baby. I went through a lot of mental changes from when I first started fucking with welfare. They put you through a lot of changes.

After Shayleen was kicked out of the shelter, she did not return to DSS for another placement. She said, "After we got caught I'm like, 'Fuck it. It's summer now. I can go stay anywhere.' So I just went AWOL." By going AWOL from DSS she relinquished her public assistance benefits. It was "illegal" for her to return home. So how did Shayleen survive?

> I slept in cars. I slept in my uncle's car. I used to stay up all night. I used to just do drugs just to stay up all night and just chill. Hustle money up. Everyday I'm trying to hustle up $65, $70 to go stay in [a hotel]. You know

what I'm saying? I used to put myself up for the night and the next day get back on my hustle just to do it again the next night.

I asked Shayleen what "hustle" meant and she explained, "Sell drugs, you know what I'm saying? Sell drugs. Everyday." Shayleen lived on the streets until that was interrupted by a jail term for probation violation. Some time after her release, Shayleen and her boyfriend were living together and she became pregnant again. This and their substandard housing drove her to obtain TANF and placement into a family shelter. Afterward, she gave birth to a baby boy, James. But a warrant for a drug sale during a prior year resulted in a third incarceration. After her jail term, she returned to her mother's house where her son was staying. Shortly afterward she and her son moved back into a family shelter.

The experience of motherhood and the desire to assure James's wellbeing instilled in Shayleen an aspiration for a successful life working in corporate America. Seemingly undefeated by some of the incidents that had led to her homelessness, Shayleen took advantage of opportunities that came her way. While living in the shelter, she enrolled in a certificate program targeted to welfare recipients at an academic institution. At our second meeting, eight months after our initial interview, Shayleen was in her fourth semester and proudly told me that she had written a paper on the poetry of Robert Frost and one on capital punishment and was in good academic standing. Nevertheless, the passing of time meant that Shayleen's TANF tally increased by the same number of months. As a result, Shayleen was approaching the two-year mark of TANF receipt. Mothers who receive TANF at a young age risk losing it while they are still young. Shayleen's intellect, determination, enthusiasm, feistiness, and educational goals are likely to facilitate her pursuit of a successful career, one in which she does not need welfare. But, she has at least sixteen more years of child rearing. If she has more children, the time will increase. Unless the federal law changes, during those years Shayleen can only receive three more years of TANF. In the future, she will not have TANF to ameliorate life's financial crises. If she needs assistance and resides in New York State after reaching the TANF time limit, she may have the protection of the state's Safety Net Assistance program. But if she moves to a state that has no such program, she will join the ranks of women nationwide who have exhausted federal aid and will have to draw on her talents and other resources to stave off economic hardship.

Carole Marlow

For an overwhelming number of women who were surviving marginally, either unemployed or working in low-tier jobs, the onset of motherhood spurred them to seek government assistance to help with maternity and child-rearing expenses. This assistance could have included TANF (or previously AFDC), food stamps, WIC (supplements from the government food and nutrition program for woman, infants, and young children), and Medicaid.[4] Many of the women seeking such assistance lacked the financial support of a male partner, either because partners were absent or their employment could not sustain their families. Many poor women required aid early in their reproductive years. Approximately 60 percent of the women I interviewed, including Carole, had their first child before age twenty-one.

Carole is an African American woman in her thirties who has two young children. She initially obtained a welfare grant due to the onset of motherhood. But her narrative tells much more. Carole told me that she was on social services her "whole life." I asked her why.

> *CM:* Because my mother was. She was mentally disabled. . . . Until she received SSI, she was on public assistance. So I inherited the damage.
> *TL:* And what do you mean by "inherited the damage"?
> *CM:* She went to a mental institution and I went to a foster home. . . .
> *TL:* So from the time you were five to eleven you were in foster care and then from eleven you were reunited with your mom?
> *CM:* Yes, eleven to when she died when I was fifteen.
> *TL:* . . . Where did you go when you were fifteen?
> *CM:* I went back into the [foster care] system. Nobody wanted me.

A few years later Carole went away to school, attending a state college. She said her tuition was "free" because she was a foster child. It was during her college days that she became pregnant. When Carole became a mother at age twenty, Medicaid was a factor in her decision to obtain public assistance. I asked Carole what was going on in her life that led to her decision to "go to DSS": "Literally peer pressure. People telling me, you need to go, you need to go, you need to go. I needed Medicaid, I needed health insurance for my child. I was pregnant. . . . That's how I got it, a month after I had my daughter."

For many women the need for welfare often continues. Carole soon found out that her father had cancer. She left school and moved in with him, but residential doubling-up became untenable. She recalled, "My daughter had colic. My father had cancer. And somebody was screaming at all times. He couldn't deal with the noise in a one-bedroom apartment and I couldn't deal with him yelling about my daughter crying. So there was nowhere else for me to go." Carole entered the shelter system and was eventually placed into temporary housing. After five years she obtained Section 8 housing and subsequently moved into her own apartment where she lived for eight years. During this time she worked at sundry jobs making minimum wage; welfare augmented her paltry pay. She had a son when she was twenty-eight years old. Her daughter's father died; before his death he was not part of her daughter's life. Her son's father is around but "he does nothing" save for when he "babysits" their son sometimes.

At some point, Carole's son got lead poisoning from the apartment paint. Landlord neglect, harassment, and a neighborhood in flux prompted her to move into another Section 8 apartment a few months before we first met. Six months after our initial interview, Carole invited me to her home for a follow-up interview. Her Section 8 apartment was located on a tree-lined street in a middle-class neighborhood. I arrived with a large pizza and Sunkist orange soda and we conversed in the room that functioned as living room and bedroom for her and her son. The exterior bucolic setting belied the scarcity of interior household amenities.

For many recipients, welfare work requirements can create stress. During the visit Carole told me that she had been sanctioned for noncompliance of a workfare mandate. One day she ignored a mandate to attend a job recruitment event for a major retailer opening in the neighborhood because she took her son to the doctor to treat his ringworm. Furthermore, she thought the mandate was redundant since she had already attended a job fair two weeks earlier for the same retailer, where she was interviewed and took a skills and drug test. Although Carole left a message for her caseworker advising him of the redundancy, her monthly $292 welfare grant, $314 in food stamps, and Medicaid for the family had been terminated. This would have been devastating, but fortunately it coincided with the approval of SSI benefits for her son who had been recently diagnosed with a hearing disability. His SSI check was $587 a month. Carole did not intend to appeal the benefit termination but planned to apply for Medicaid and food stamps. She figured that she would relinquish welfare aid, thereby eliminating future workfare mandates. Thus, she could devote time to her son's disability and go to his therapy three times a week instead of working at a low-wage retail job. These are the compromises a poor mother has to make.

Carole said that she began receiving welfare a decade ago although she did not indicate whether it was continuous. She thinks that she was "switched" to New York's Safety Net Assistance program. Although Carole's son is currently receiving SSI benefits for his disability, if his condition improves, that may not always be the case. If Carole has no more children, she will have fifteen years of child rearing before her son reaches eighteen. It is obvious that sixty months of TANF aid is not enough for women like Carole.

Alice Finnegan

Alice, a white woman in her late thirties, is a mother of two teens and a preteen. When she was twenty-one years old and living in a Southern state, she gave birth to her first child. Afterward, she did not work. Her husband was employed "kind of, sort of, in the beginning," but they could not pay the bills. Fourteen months later she had a second child. Raising two babies was a struggle for the young couple. The struggle was exacerbated by her husband's serious drinking problem. Life in the South was not working out and the family moved to New York and lived with Alice's husband's kin. Shortly afterward, the couple broke up. Alice had a weak family support system; her father died when she was young and she had no property, assets, or bank account to fall back on. Consequently, this newly single mother with two youngsters applied for and received AFDC cash, food stamps, and Medicaid.

In the early 1990s Alice took advantage of an opportunity to attend a postsecondary degree program designed for welfare recipients. During her school years, when she was almost thirty, she had her third child. Soon after her baby was born, she split up with her baby's father. About this relationship she said,

> I don't have any financial support. Like the baby's father, he'll throw in five bucks or whatever and give the kid money. That's fine. I mean whatever. But he unfortunately . . . he's not well. . . . He was a heavily drug-addicted

person, way before I knew him. When I met him, he was totally straight and sober. He's just gotten worse. I just try to stay away from him. We broke up when the baby was a baby, when he was born. I mean our relationship was over when the baby came, practically. It was nothing but fighting.

Alice had worked at sporadic jobs when her two younger children were growing up, but her newborn precluded employment despite the fact that she would soon graduate from college with an associate's degree. She said, "I was getting a degree and I got pregnant. . . . It was a bit of a back fall. . . . Breastfeeding for six months, stuck in the house, . . . I didn't go anywhere. It was one of the worst [winters]; we had a snowstorm, five feet of snow every Wednesday. Needless to say, that's all I did was take care of the baby."

Ultimately PRWORA caught up with her and Alice was mandated to work an unpaid workfare "internship" for about six months in a municipal office. Some time after that she stopped receiving TANF and food stamps. Throughout the years Alice always received Medicaid. Years ago she obtained and has retained Section 8 housing. Commenting on the necessity of a rent subsidy to help defray the cost of Westchester's exorbitant housing, Alice said, "I wouldn't have been able to survive without that." She lamented, "I don't know how to pay these rents around here. If I didn't have [Section 8], I would have rags on."

When I met Alice, she had not received TANF for four years, but at some point it became imperative for her to apply for food stamps.

> Like I said, it had been quite a number of years since I've been there [DSS] and I tried not to apply for food stamps. But it just got to the point where I had to because I can't pay the bills and get food. I can't do both. . . . I had a house with no food in it for years now. And I said, "It's time for me to get some food in this house," really struggling, whatever. I mean, I don't feel so bad about that.

Alice estimated that she had received cash assistance for ten years. Her associate's degree is an advantage that she has over others who have more limited education. Thus, she sees herself as having an advantage in the marketplace. However, for over a decade she has been plagued with back pain that often precludes steady employment. She applied for disability but was rejected. Alice has about nine more years of child rearing before her youngest turns eighteen; then she will be just short of fifty years old. Here again we see some of the difficulties of raising a family alone and see that women's child-rearing years go well beyond the TANF lifetime limit of sixty months.

Laney Heath

Laney is a black woman in her mid-forties who raised three children in the 1970s and 1980s. Like many other women working in low-paid work, her income was a combination of welfare and wages. For several years she worked for the post office at night and had a seasonal job during the day. She also worked in retail and ran a child-care business for a few years. When she was about forty years old, Laney had a difficult pregnancy, left a telemarketing job, and began receiving welfare benefits for the third time in her life. After her daughter was born in the late 1990s she went back to the telemarketing firm, making about $15 per hour. The firm was affiliated with a major corporation that was in the throes of a scandal. The effects of the debacle rippled throughout the corporation and its affiliates. In the early 2000s Laney was one of the last employees to be terminated by the sinking firm because she worked in the collections department. She was able to receive twenty-six weeks of unemployment benefits; afterward she resorted to welfare and other government aid. But unemployment was merely one of Laney's crises. She launched into her narration of another life crisis this way: "I was going through a domestic violence issue with my daughter's father. . . . We were separated. . . . He used to call me on the telephone telling me what he was gonna do to me. 'Cause you know, but I had already had an order of protection on him and the whole nine [yards]." Laney shared with me her sentiments for her daughter's father and details pertaining to his violence.

> I loved this man with all my heart and soul. I spent a good deal of my
> life with him and the domestic violence only came as soon as I had her
> [daughter]. It seemed like it was a jealousy issue. And control. And I had
> [thirty-six stitches in my face and] eight hours of plastic surgery. I only have
> just a minimum little scar here [at the side of my mouth]. . . . He split my
> face completely open. And that was the end of that relationship. I went to
> . . . [a domestic violence shelter]. Then he went to jail. I pressed charges.

When he got out of jail of course he couldn't come back with us. I didn't want him back with us.

Laney's daughter's father returned to her apartment some time later "banging and banging and kicking on the door." He "came in swinging." With her voice slightly shaking Laney whispered to me, "I ended up killing him." Because the district attorney had familiarity with Laney's domestic violence history with her daughter's father, she was released on her own recognizance after spending one night in jail. She appeared before a grand jury and was exonerated a month later.

Laney told me about her anguish and how she and her daughter were coping. Therapy for herself and her daughter was imperative. Adding to her posttraumatic stress, Laney became enmeshed in a welfare system snare that resulted in the temporary discontinuance of TANF, food stamps, rental assistance, and Medicaid. This precluded therapy for two months until Medicaid was reinstated. When Laney went back to therapy it was a "welcomed sight." She said, "I'm in my own cell because I carry this around with me every day. . . . I find strength and solace in other things. Instead of falling apart everyday, [my daughter] gives me strength every day. You know what I mean. I have to keep going for her because now I'm the only parent."

Laney stays to herself. Her family support network is frail. Especially after the "incident" she does not "trust too many people" and does not have friends from whom she can borrow. For those women who experienced domestic violence, securing independent economic stability is challenging to say the least. Any mechanism that cuts off services exacerbates that challenge.

Kimberly Fraser

Kimberly is an African American woman in her mid-thirties. When Kimberly left home fifteen years ago, she worked two jobs to maintain the middle-class lifestyle to which she was accustomed. After giving birth to her daughter, Nakeisha, she opted not to work so she could care for her infant. Having exhausted her employer-provided maternity benefits, Kimberly was prompted by the expense of child rearing to seek government aid for the first time. Kimberly recalled receiving cash, food stamps,

Medicaid, and $340 rental assistance toward her $700 per month apartment. Her mother, father, and grandparents also helped. When Kimberly's daughter was a year old, she began receiving child support.

Kimberly's father was in the medical field and, following in his footsteps, she began working as a nurse's aide. As a result, her public assistance was terminated. Her total first-time welfare experience was for eighteen months. Kimberly describes herself as resourceful, and she hustled to get work. She registered with two agencies and worked 7:00 p.m. to 7:00 a.m. shifts making about $8 or $9 an hour back then. Her mother provided child care for Nakeisha while Kimberly worked. She explained, "I only worked night. I didn't miss anything. And that was key for me. And that was my choice to work nights. So that way I could not miss her first step and so on and so forth. And I really didn't want anyone else with my daughter during the day. I didn't want to put her into any type of child care or anything like that. That was my job."

A few years later Kimberly enrolled in college and took the core requirements for a nursing program; she completed a year and a half of coursework. Over the years she had worked in several health care jobs that paid decent wages with very good benefits. When her daughter was a teenager, a series of events led to a household financial catastrophe. Nakeisha was diagnosed with a tumor and shortly thereafter she had surgery. About three months later Kimberly obtained full-time employment. Subsequently her daughter required chemotherapy treatments that lasted several months. Within weeks of starting her new job, Kimberly reduced her hours to care for her daughter. She calculated that she could get by on her part-time salary and savings for a few months, but all the "extras," such as medical co-pays, took a toll. Within a few months her savings were critically low. She applied for public assistance but was deemed ineligible. Two months later, just before Nakeisha finished her treatments, Kimberly's firm downsized and she was terminated; the firm lost a number of large contracts and she was included in the layoffs. She reapplied for public assistance and received TANF for seven months until she found employment.

Kimberly's downward slide was buffered by some middle-class protections such as a family network, education, and work experience. These middle-class safeguards positioned her more favorably in comparison to many others. Nonetheless, thus far, this mother of one child has had to rely on welfare twice for a total of two years.

Patricia Lambert

Patricia, a black woman in her fifties, raised nine children whose ages range from ten to twenty-nine. I asked her how many times or years she relied on welfare. "Wow. A lot. A lot," she replied. She remembered the first time she applied for her own welfare grant when her first child was born in the mid-1970s. She recalled receiving a "little assistance" for about two years before returning to work. When I asked if she could support herself, she replied, "Barely, barely supporting myself. 'Cause I had to get Pampers, food, and plus pay rent out of my pay and I was making like $169 a week at that time." Her son's father augmented her paycheck by giving her $25 a week or whatever he could afford. Patricia's steady work did not forestall the need for welfare. She recalled:

> And then after Mark [her second child] was born and my mother got sick I went back to DSS for assistance because I let them know that my mother was sick and I couldn't work and we couldn't afford a nursing home for her. So I had to stay home and take care of the kids plus my mother, so it was a lot on me. But I always managed. I tried to find a job babysitting in the building, doing something so I could make some extra money for the kids' Pampers and stuff. But it was very hard. Very hard. Unbelievably hard.

Patricia's insecure financial state weakened after her mother died; her mother's SSI disability check had covered the rent. And the burdens of motherhood and factory work were taking a toll. She left the workforce after her eighth child; it became "too much" for her.

> *TL:* And when you stopped [working], did you go back on social services?
> *PL:* I had to because I wasn't getting any money. After unemployment ran out, I wasn't getting nothing. And I had got eviction notices on my door. I was going to food pantries, but that wasn't enough with all those kids. So I had to go back on DSS [welfare].
> *TL:* So by that time you had eight kids.
> *PL:* That's right. And they were like stair steps. And I tried to work. Every time I'd get a job, something happened where I need a babysitter; I couldn't stay on the job long. I would try to get a job babysitting in the building and it became too much for me, too many kids. . . . Ever since I've been on DSS. I've been volunteering here [at an emergency food kitchen]. . . . So this is the best place for me right now because I can

feed my kids. I get food here. The only thing is, I don't get that much
pay. But it's OK for now.

TL: So from 1990 to 2004, that's fourteen years.

PL: I have not worked.

Patricia's last statement was not exactly true. Although it was fourteen
years since she worked in the formal economy and earned a paycheck, for
over five years she volunteered at the emergency food kitchen helping with
daily breakfasts. She worked in exchange for food, clothing, and about $6
or $7 per week for cigarette money.

Until Patricia had her eighth child at age thirty-eight, she worked, and
she claims to have done so during her pregnancies up to about the ninth
month. Then she wanted to devote exclusive time to child rearing. In the
ensuing years, finding employment has been futile and her husband's
salary has been unsteady. Therefore, continuous welfare aid was imperative. Ever hopeful of reentering the workforce, Patricia said,

> [My husband is] a painter. He works with a company. They go out on paint
> projects, houses, stuff like that. But it's not a steady job. He could work this
> week for three weeks. Then the fourth week he won't have to work. And
> then two weeks lapse. And then here comes another job. So he doesn't have
> a steady job, but he will work. And he does not like welfare. . . . By the time
> they talk about this TANF stuff, I'm gonna have me a job. I don't want to be
> on more programs. I've programmed enough [*laugh*]. No more programs.

Patricia's chances for securing a living-wage job to adequately cover the
expenses of the five children who are still living at home (ranging in age
from preteen to mid-teens) are dubious. Patricia is no slouch; her volunteer job required her to rise early and report to work by 6:45 a.m. But, as
a long-time factory worker, Patricia's opportunities are seemingly limited
in the postindustrial service economy. And employers might be reticent
about hiring an exoffender with a prison record for bank robbery, despite
the fact that she has not gotten "in trouble" since a parole violation decades ago. And although she has not "used" heroin for fourteen years,
when we met Patricia had been attending a daily methadone maintenance
program for more than three years where she received a low milligram
dosage. When she finds steady work, she will be able to switch to home
medication.

For Patricia, motherhood began in the mid-1970s. Her children's births were spaced apart over eighteen years from the time she was twenty until she was thirty-eight years old. When her youngest reaches eighteen years old, she will have raised children for thirty-six years. Multiple pregnancies disrupt labor force participation and increase household expenses. Mothers who have large families and even those with smaller families who have children spaced far apart in age are more vulnerable in the PRWORA era because the TANF time limit will expire long before they are finished with child rearing.

Lena Powell

Lena, a black woman, was in her early sixties when we first met in the building where she worked. I asked her about the possibility of posting my study recruitment flyer in the lobby. We chatted and she eagerly volunteered to be interviewed. She explained that her income makes her ineligible for welfare and food stamps, and she was not currently on welfare but had been at various times during her life. Lena began her family of two children in the 1960s. She worked as long as she could remember, saying she wanted to be "independent and take care of myself" and not be "dependent" on social services. In spite of this she maintained, "Sometimes you have to; you have no choice." Her forty-year work history was punctuated by the necessity for government assistance.

Even when employed, she sometimes received welfare to supplement her low income. During periods of unemployment, she received unemployment benefits when eligible and sought welfare when those benefits expired. Lena figured she had been on welfare between six to ten years. As she aged, government aid was vital because her child-rearing responsibilities were protracted by the raising of her two grandchildren. Her teenaged grandson is still living with her. Lena recalled the amount of time that she relied on welfare. "The longest I was on it was when my children were younger. I'd say maybe six years. And I am real rough guessing. . . . And, I've been on [welfare] part-time, sometimes. It has never been a long stretch of time. I can't say it was fifteen years straight. But, it has been a few years here, a few months there."

For a long time Lena had steady government employment. A year after she began working for the State of New York, state office workers were relocated to the World Trade Center after the twin towers were opened because "nobody wanted to rent it." Over the course of ten years she worked in several divisions. Though she was not certain because it was so long ago, she said, "I think I might have been getting help from social services." At some point Lena's daughter, Caroline, wanted to be on her own and wasn't coming home at night. Because of this and other events, Lena assumed much of the parental responsibility for Caroline's daughter, Cindy. She often would have to take time off from work to care for her granddaughter. Lena subsequently lost her apartment "because of all the confusion." Around this time her division was scheduled to relocate to Queens because World Trade Center rents became too expensive; this would have resulted in an immensely inconvenient commute. Thinking about the travel involved, Lena said, "I just couldn't take it." Also, Caroline was having a "problem" with alcohol so Lena had to spend a lot of time with her. Lena resigned from her job. At some point Lena, her daughter, and her granddaughter had been living with Lena's mother who lived in senior citizens' housing. But it became difficult for them to continue to live there because of housing regulations. Lena recalled, "Then, actually we became homeless for a short period of time. . . . We did have social services so they were the ones that put us in a motel." The family initially "stayed in a couple of rough spots."

As a result of issues stemming from Caroline's alcoholism, Lena gained custody of her granddaughter, Cindy. During the eight-month shelter stay Lena still tried to work, securing a few jobs. Eventually Lena and Cindy were placed in several emergency housing units before Lena received a Section 8 voucher, which allowed them to move into permanent housing. Some time later Caroline had son, Will, whom Lena has raised since he was a baby. Lena's granddaughter moved out to be on her own when she was older.

Lena and I were sitting in a coffee shop over lunch one day and she imagined a circumstance that would compel her to apply for welfare: "God forbid, if I lost my job and my unemployment insurance ran out and I had no job or anything." The idea was unsettling, she said, "Not this late in life. I could not stand the pressure." In fact, a year and a half later Lena became unemployed during a month-long work shutdown caused by hazardous workplace conditions and repairs. Fortunately, she received unemployment benefits.

Over the years Lena shared with me her good news and bad. In one phone conversation she spoke angrily about her stalled residential move and the frustrating ordeals with her landlord and the Section 8 housing department. Finally, after six months of bureaucratic delays, Lena and her grandson moved. A kind and gentle woman, Lena graciously invited me to her new home and gave me the grand tour of her "dream apartment" that summer. But a year later she complained about the structural defects, shoddy renovations, and persistent heat problems that not only shattered her illusions but weakened her health and sparked a struggle with the landlord to heat her frigid bedroom in the winter. On the family front, Lena's daughter Caroline was doing very well and had been employed in a retail management position. Granddaughter Cindy lived comfortably with her family. Lena looked forward to retirement and had been making postretirement relocation plans.

On a summer's day four years after we met, Lena called me with some news. She had retired a month earlier and would soon be moving out of state to be closer to her daughter, granddaughter, and great-grandchildren. Her coworkers honored her at a retirement party for her nineteen years of service at that job. Lena had been receiving Social Security benefits and would soon cash in on her employee retirement fund. Her grandson Will had graduated from high school that June. He had turned nineteen in the spring, and while still in school he had been receiving welfare aid on his child-only grant. A month after his birthday his grant was reviewed and his case was closed because it was determined that he was not working. Lena thought that the caseworker knew that Will was exempt from employment because he was still in school. Probably due to an internal communication breakdown, his benefits were terminated. After years of attempting to resolve problems within various bureaucracies, this was the last straw for Lena. Although she surmised that Will's case would have been legitimately closed when he graduated from high school, she was way "too tired" to go through the rigmarole to have the case reinstated. Instead she chose to assume "the burden" and did not attempt to fight for the three months of lost welfare income. With this gesture, Lena ended her dealings with the U.S. welfare system.

Lena raised two generations of children and will be spending her retirement years with a third. She began working when she was in her early twenties and has always valued work. But even so, she at times had to rely on some form of government aid. Recognizing the value of welfare she said, "I always tried to work but there was some point in my lifetime for one reason or another I didn't have a job. So if it wasn't for them [social services], I couldn't have gotten to where I am today." Today, women across the United States do not have the federal welfare safety net that Lena had. If welfare had been cut completely after five years, Lena's life course certainly would have been altered.

The Need for TANF over a Lifetime and TANF Time Limits

The stories of all the parents I interviewed plainly revealed their myriad pressures, tragedies, and crises. Contrary to explanations asserting that welfare program "incentives" cause people to seek and continue to receive welfare (Murray 1984), people are forced to rely on government assistance when crises arise due to structural factors as well as family circumstances. In addition to people who have long been poor, even some people who had a middle-class lifestyle have experienced economic hardship that compelled them to seek aid. Furthermore, many families suffered temporary setbacks throughout their lives, creating the need for the periodic resumption or continuation of AFDC or TANF and other government benefits. For some, the need continues over a lifetime. People's needs are not on a fixed time schedule, and welfare and other government benefits are crucial for survival. Lena said, "Everybody is different. Every circumstance is different. You can't lump people together in a clump and say that's good for everyone." Lena's sage words sum up an important point of the stories—people's family situations are unique. And they speak to the absurd assumption that five years of welfare over a lifetime is sufficient.

The stories demonstrate that women's primary caregiving responsibilities can indeed be lengthy. Children's births spread out over decades, multiple children, and grandchildren can extend a woman's child-rearing years. Though large families were atypical among those I met, Patricia Lambert was one of eight parents who had four or more children. It is apparent from her story that larger families increase the possibility of stresses, burdensome household expenses, and welfare need. However, Patricia could count on AFDC for two decades to help rear her nine children, whose births were spread throughout that time. Many women nationwide are in the same situation as Patricia—their child rearing and need for welfare extends far beyond five years. Many families experienced serious episodic and chronic health crises. Parents' health problems ranged from cancer, HIV-AIDS, diabetes, and at-risk pregnancies to a host of stress disorders. Many of their children were in ill health as a result of some of the same diseases as well as asthma and problems associated with premature births.

Women such as Carole Marlow and Kimberly Fraser who have children in poor health are particularly vulnerable to financial decline because of added stress and expense associated with their children's special needs. Elder care also extends women's caregiving responsibilities. Many women find themselves in situations like Carole and Patricia, taking on the responsibility to care for aging, ill, and dying parents. Family caregiving often results in a person resigning from or being terminated from employment, which can further exacerbate the family's poor fiscal health.

Moreover, women are especially at risk of becoming the sole custodians of their children, bearing the lion's share of the child-rearing responsibilities and expenses. The dissolution of a relationship due to a breakup or divorce can cause tremendous emotional and financial trauma. The death of a partner can destabilize a family, placing enormous strain on the surviving partner. Longitudinal studies show that divorce and widowhood have a negative and prolonged financial impact on women, whereas marital dissolution often improves the economic well-being of men (Holden and Smock 1991). Nearly all of the people I interviewed supported households alone at some time during their lives, which was burdensome in terms of financial provisioning and physical caretaking. The absence of a contributing partner for whatever reason—breakup, death, institutional confinement, hospitalization, denial of paternity, or noninvolvement—has the potential to increase a family's emotional and financial pressures. Yet, even when men are present, some cannot contribute enough to support the family because of their employment in a low-wage, flexible labor force.

Many of the people I interviewed entered adulthood disadvantaged in some way. Some are hampered by loss of a parent, aging out of foster care, growing up in an impoverished environment, homelessness, educational deficiencies, early pregnancies with little financial support, or substance use. People who enter adulthood disadvantaged and whose life circumstances necessitate government assistance experience a paradox. Aid eases dire need or an emergency situation, but often people become subject to regulations and surveillance at an early age. Today this is even more problematic because of workfare and its strict requirements that encumber welfare recipients with additional responsibilities and rules that they must obey or risk losing aid. People seek government assistance to assuage their predicament, but disadvantaged beginnings often handicap them so that they will continue to need welfare over time.

Young mothers fare worse because of the TANF time limit. Recall that

Shayleen Vaughn, who is in her early twenties, has already had experience in the criminal justice, legal, shelter, and welfare systems. For women who are in similar situations in the United States, this is a prospect with unfavorable odds; they will undoubtedly require aid beyond five years. It is unreasonable to think that young women like Shayleen—who entered adulthood disadvantaged, experienced a number of crises, and became mired in various systems—will only need a preset amount of welfare aid in a lifetime. Nowadays, when a woman exhausts TANF early in life, she will not have any reserve later in life. As she proceeds through life, her financial position and life circumstance will mitigate or intensify the threat of time limits. If she experiences hardships that require the continuance of welfare, she edges closer to the point of TANF termination. Reaching a time limit adds to the stress associated with other pressures of poverty and jeopardizes family well-being.

Domestic violence is yet another pressure in the lives of many families. Laney Heath's story tells of the emotional anguish, violence, and gender inequality in abusive relationships. Several women told me that their controlling male partners prevented them from seeking personal fulfillment or continuing education and employment, thus limiting their options to provide family income. Four women fled their homes and sought shelter and domestic violence support (see Davis 2006). The combination of homeless services, TANF, and other supportive aid is vital to women who abandon their homes to escape an abuser. Victims of domestic violence who flee their homes are often traumatized by the stress of abuse, fear, family disruption, and the loss of a relationship, residence, and possessions. Additional pressures stem from starting a new life phase and from solely providing for the well-being of their children. Research shows that having ample economic resources to live outside the abusive relationship is a major factor in whether a battered woman will permanently leave an abuser (Kurz 1999). Such women are further disempowered when a government system cannot accommodate their basic survival needs.

One positive aspect of PWRORA is the Family Violence Option. It grants states flexibility to waive certain requirements for welfare recipients who are victims of family violence.[5] Several women who experienced domestic violence told of their experiences with the waiver program. While procedures are in place to protect welfare recipients, they appear to be inconsistent. Poor domestic violence victims like Laney who suffer severe posttraumatic stress brought on by extreme violence sorely need financial support and a myriad of other support services. Any mechanism—a time limit or sanction—that halts those services leaves them completely adrift.

Of the six people who reported that they were incarcerated, a few indicated that postincarceration services under the auspices of private agencies linked with welfare and other government assistance was crucial to their return to the community. Anita Ramos is one such person (see Chapter 2). Anita has about fifteen more years of child rearing. Given her low level of education and low income potential as a home health care worker, she will undoubtedly require welfare and other government aid over time. Anita figured she was on welfare for about five years. If she has not already done so, she will encounter the TANF time limit soon. Women like Anita across United States who make gallant efforts to change their lives upon their release and who struggle to maintain a family are eventually abandoned by the federal government when a time limit is imposed.

Roseanne Tate, Kimberly Fraser, and others are among those who had middle-class lifestyles but experienced a severe financial decline. This has become a trend.[6] Disparate crises, often combined with other family pressures, can destabilize families regardless of their financial and social position. However, people who have marketable skills, education, and middle-class safeguards and who have tallied negligible or comparatively little TANF usage are better protected than most. But others who enter adulthood with many disadvantages and those who have had chronic stresses and setbacks will need aid beyond the federal limits. The TANF time limit is a mechanism for the federal government to opt out of welfare provisioning for those who have a protracted need. The stories suggest that over the life span TANF might be more accommodative to downwardly mobile middle-income working parents, who, having exhausted unemployment insurance benefits, have had to rely temporarily on TANF for income maintenance until reemployment. The program seems more suited for those who have some safeguards than for the impoverished who need aid throughout their lives. To be sure, TANF is a vital resource for many poverty-stricken people. But over a life course, five years is far from adequate and is socially inequitable given poor people's circumstances.

What is worse, some states are even more unsympathetic to the needs of poor families and have imposed even more severe time limits, for example, twenty-four months. Because the federal government stops TANF funding after five years, because states may choose to impose limits shorter than the federal limit, and because states are under no obligation to extend benefits using state funding, welfare provisioning is uneven and unequal for families nationwide as well as for states. In New York, for example, after people reach the TANF time limit and receive Safety Net Assistance, the state takes on the extra burden of care, assumes added operational and budget pressures, and shoulders exorbitant costs. In states that have made the choice to provide no such state program after five years, families are terminated from the federal welfare rolls and the ultimate responsibility devolves to the individual. No matter what, a time limit for welfare benefits of *any* length is unconscionable and also contributes to inequality in the United States.

6

Insecurity and Inflexibility of "Flexible" Labor

"It's a Struggle"

Harriett Robinson was a homemaker for five years after her first child was born. She started working in the telemarketing industry in the late 1980s and recalled that her first check was $511 for her first two weeks of employment. She worked in telemarketing for about ten years. From the time of her first pregnancy, she relied on some form of public assistance. For the past four years, Harriett has been working as a bus monitor. Harriett begins work between six thirty and quarter to seven in the morning, when she meets the bus driver. They "ride around" and "pick up" kids. Many children board the bus at homeless family shelters. The bus is small, holding about ten kids altogether. It wends its way through morning traffic across the county making drop-off stops at grammar schools and high schools. Afterward, the driver takes Harriett back home, and she will rest for a couple of hours. Then, she said, "at twelve thirty or one o'clock, he's picking me up; now we're going back to pick the kids up from school." Does Harriett get any benefits or sick days? "No, this is one flat pay, $150 a week, that's it." In terms of an hourly wage Harriett said, "It's hard to pinpoint" because she does not get paid by the hour. Inclement weather and other variables can prolong her workday. Harriett explained, "On a winter day, maybe four o'clock, four thirty. But you still get one flat pay a week." And what if the bus is stuck in traffic? She said, "There's no overtime, none of that."

All of the parents I interviewed told me about their employment and welfare history; most had a work history. Some held professional or middle-income jobs, many others had industrial and postindustrial working-class jobs, and a few had worked in union jobs. A minority had negligible work experience; their employment was primarily in the informal economy. A couple of women volunteered for service agencies in exchange for food and goods, or interned for work experience and college credit. Some were mandated to perform unpaid workfare. Many people had been unemployed for protracted periods. Some of the individuals are part of America's low-income working families. According to a national report, in 2002 more than 25 percent of U.S. working families were classified as "low income," that is, their earnings were so low they struggled to survive financially. Of the 9.2 million low-income working families, 2.5 million lived below the poverty line, earning less than $18,392 for a family of four (Waldron et al. 2004).[1]

Those who had low- to middle-income jobs were educated formally or on the job. They held positions as flight attendant, substitute teacher, respiratory therapist, agency program director, military supply specialist, secretary, social work intern, bookkeeper, and postal worker. But they experienced a crisis that set them on a downward financial slide, suffered economic hardship, and consequently sought government assistance. Well-paying union jobs are few and far between, especially for the younger generation. Only Lena Powell, who was in her early sixties when we met, held a union job; a year later the union intervened when she and coworkers were temporarily laid off when their worksite was shut down for repairs. As Mercedes Montgomery's story will soon show, employers move workers into nonunion jobs where they have no protection.

Far more people were employed in working-class jobs, either in factories or, more recently, in the low-wage service sector. Higher-paying working-class jobs in the industrial era have been replaced by lower-waged jobs in the service sector (Ehrenreich 2001; Mollenkopf and Castells 1991; Munger 2002; Nash 1989; Newman 2006; Pappas 1989). A number of people worked in these new working-class jobs as customer service representatives, data-entry clerks, telemarketers, retail clerks, and cashiers. Some received vocational training for potential employment as a home health aide, child-care provider, or security guard; they did this training either through workfare programs or on their own. Several worked in the food-service industry, including fast-food restaurants (see Newman 1999) and supermarket chains. One woman prepared food for school breakfasts and lunches for elementary and high schools. Another worked for a food production company preparing mass volumes of food for various state institutions. Others, including several of the women in their early twenties who had accumulated very little work experience, worked as bus monitors, babysitters, and receptionists. Many of these occupations are primarily held by women in the U.S. segregated labor market.[2] Moreover, wages earned in occupations dominated by women are lower than in those held predominately by men. This is one of many factors that accounts for U.S. women's median wages being 76.2 percent of men's wages.[3] Educational deficits, family caregiving demands, underemployment, and unemployment compelled many people to work in the low-paid service sector, the informal economy, and the illegal labor market.

Carole Marlow worked in low-paid jobs in the formal economy but said, "I made more money hair braiding and babysitting." When braiding hair, she can make from $25 to $40 for a child and $60 to $80 for an adult, depending on the design. Carole explained, "I was doing it before I had any children. In the projects everybody does it. Some of the guys sell drugs, women braid hair; it's lucrative." Carole also chemically colors and straightens hair. She can buy supplies for about $5, and she charges $10 to $20 for her services. Carole said,

> I would starve many a day or month if I couldn't do it. And it's funny 'cause the instructions are right on the box. People could do it themselves but a lot of women want, you know, a female companion, somebody to talk to, tell their problems to. And poor women can't afford the $65 salon that middle-class black women can afford. So they call it the kitchen community. You go in somebody's kitchen, you relax it, you cord it, you curl it, you braid it [*laugh*]. So it's more of how I get my extra money.

Only a small number of women said they had no work experience or negligible work experience. Christina Torres, a mother of three in her late thirties, said she "never" supported her family by working; as a teenager she did, however, work in her family's store. Jodi Mancini, a woman in her forties who did not complete high school, said that as she was illiterate, she could only work sporadically in domestic jobs and still never made enough to support her family. Carissa Simone, a mother of six children who is in her mid-thirties, worked "like once" to support her family and claimed not to have "much skills." Yet, during the course of a narrative she told of buying novelty items wholesale to resell at a local flea market, as well as to a select group of customers. Women's understanding of themselves as not working appears to be based on a cultural perception that their work is not valued or does not contribute to the economy; thus, they cognitively exclude themselves from the labor force. Many did not mention child rearing, per se, as part of their work experience.[4]

At the time of interviews, twenty-eight of the forty-two people said they were not currently working; they received various combinations of government benefits. Two other women worked but did not get paid— one was an intern at a service agency and the other was a long-time volunteer at a soup kitchen. Many who were not currently working had low-wage work histories but had experienced crises that rendered them unemployed. Structural factors and personal reasons accounted for individuals' unsteady employment.

Many parents had positive opinions about the ideology of work and strongly desired lucrative, meaningful, steady employment. Sandee Staton remarked, "I love to work because I hate being in the house, just sitting there. I like to move, I love to be motivated. That's why I've been in school so much. Different jobs. I just try to be out there. But nothing lasts." And very few earned enough income to support a family without some form of government aid. Their jobs in the formal and informal economies did not pay enough or provide enough hours. Moreover, the erosion of wages affected them all. And because welfare income was insufficient, working on and off the books while on welfare is common and evidently essential.

Lorna Webster aptly sums up the realities of working life at the bottom. She said, "It's a struggle. I mean I didn't have extravagant jobs making $12 and $13 an hour; I had low jobs making $8 an hour." Low and eroded wages, inherent in the flexible labor market, contribute to the widening income gap of the past several decades. Harvey (2005) posits that neoliberal policies from the 1970s and forward restored the economic wealth to the upper-class elite and contributed to the expanding socioeconomic inequality. An analysis of New York State income trends by the Fiscal Policy Institute (2006a) provides quantitative proof of the widening wealth gap. Some factors causing this inequality include postindustrial restructuring of work from higher-wage manufacturing to lower-wage service sector jobs, a decline of the union workforce, the diminishing value of the minimum wage, a scant 1.5 percent growth of the median wage from 1990 to 2005, and the erosion of income in real terms for low-wage workers.[5] Conversely, higher income earners experienced an escalation of wages and an expansion of investment income, such as positive capital gains (Fiscal Policy Institute 2006a:16–17).

The average income of the richest fifth of New York families, even after adjusting for inflation, *increased* $51,205 (or 65%) to $130,431 from the early 1980s to the early 2000s. This was five times faster than the growth of average income of the poorest fifth of New York families that increased by only $1,901 (or 13.4%) to $16,076.

. . . the average income of families in the middle quintile grew by 29%, less than half the rate of families at the top.

Average incomes for the super-rich, the families in the top five percent of the income distribution, grew by 94% over this period. This was more than three times the growth rate for families in the middle. (2006a:7, 10)

Inflexibility in the Flexible Labor Market

Income disparity is but one trend in the labor market. The aftermath of the economic crisis of the early 1970s was an era of corporate financial restructuring and labor market transformations. Employers implemented flexible organizational strategies into their production processes and personnel strategies. One type of flexibility strategy is to readjust staff size according to demand fluctuations. Another approach is to hire workers apart from regular, full-time personnel. This approach might include hiring part-time staff or using on-call day and short-term temporary workers, temporary help and contract agencies, people who are self-employed, and independent contractors. Part-time staff and those outside the organization receive few or no benefits, thus lowering organizational costs (Kalleberg 2003).

Part-time employment, less than thirty-five hours per week, is on the rise in the United States. Before 1970 most of the increase in part-time work was "voluntary" part-time workers, mainly women and young people who wanted part-time work. Since the late 1970s the increase is due to "involuntary" part-time workers, those who want but are unable to find full-time work. The trend has moved away from employment that satisfies workers' desire for shorter hours to employers' preference for cost containment and flexible staffing. The growth in part-time work has accompanied the expansion of the service sector that is typically staffed with part-time workers (Kalleberg 2000). It has also been found that women who work part-time involuntarily earn less in wages and benefits than women employed in traditional jobs or who work part-time voluntarily

(Ferber and Waldfogel 1998:5). Hence, nontraditional arrangements and employer flexibility disadvantages workers who would prefer to work full-time and who require ample hours to maintain a family and maximize income.

In contrast to traditional employment, that is, full-time and of an indefinite duration, flexible employment is labeled as nonstandard or nontraditional. Within traditional employment, some employers have adopted flexible work arrangements. These include "flextime," whereby employees have some autonomy in controlling their schedule, and flexible work locations, such as telecommuting or taking work home on occasion. These arrangements purportedly facilitate the employees' conflicting demands of work and home. However, they are generally available in knowledge- and information-based, white-collar, and professional occupations in which the work requires minimal employer supervision and coworker collaboration (Weeden 2005).

The majority of the workers I met had nontraditional employment arrangements in occupations where these types of flexible work arrangements were not an option. Kathy Young, Lorna Webster, Mercedes Montgomery, and Amber Hamilton are four such workers. These four women told me about their experiences on the job, and their stories are representative of the types of situations experienced by women workers and illustrative of the effects of labor practices in the U.S. flexible labor force. Many of their jobs were low wage and did not provide health and other employee benefits. Their narratives demonstrate how flexible labor practices are malleable and generally benefit the employer. Their work schedules are not flexible enough for them to adequately tend to their own and their children's needs, illnesses, or emergencies. Some of the women exhibited flexibility by rearranging their work schedules to accommodate their employers' workforce demands, yet their employers did not reciprocate when they needed it. Flexibility also suited employers, who hired ample staff to accommodate their workloads, but resulted in inadequate hours for an individual employee.

These women I interviewed are typical of other female workers in marginal employment who needed welfare and other government aid to supplement their income or lost wages due to termination. Once they are in the welfare system, they must deal with the machinations of the bureaucracy that include eligibility requirements, delay tactics, workfare, and myriad regulations. And catch-22 situations can intensify their impoverished position. A glimpse of their household economies and the deficit between income and expenses reveals their marginal financial states.

Kathy Young

Kathy is a black woman in her early forties raising her preteen son. She is one of the twelve women who were working for wages at the time I spoke with them. She worked part-time as a library aide. She receives food stamps, Medicaid, and child support and has a Section 8 voucher. Kathy has a long work history in the low-wage labor force. When she was fourteen years old, Kathy worked in a laundry and continued her employment there after she graduated from high school; her highest salary was $7.00 per hour. After ten years at the laundry, she was fired. She was granted unemployment insurance compensation after she won her case for benefits in an appeal process. Some time later she received welfare for about six months. During this time she attended a six-month secretarial training program funded by the state. In the ensuing years she had some low-wage jobs. When she was almost twenty-nine years old, Kathy gave birth to her son. She was unemployed and obtained AFDC cash, rental assistance, and supplements from the government food and nutrition program for woman, infants, and young children. When her son was about six months old, Kathy moved into Section 8 housing with her infant. She raised her son with the help of these government benefits.

At some point Kathy was mandated to TANF workfare activities and was required to seek employment. Four years before we met she found her current library aide job. Kathy's goal had been to enhance her skills, and through her own initiative she obtained security guard training at a local community job-training center. At some point she worked as a part-time security guard making $8.50 per hour to supplement her library aide salary of $8.00 per hour. Neither job had benefits. The combination of wages from these two jobs made her ineligible for the continuance of TANF because she made "too much." The security job was short-lived. She left because her boss hired another person, causing her hours to be reduced, and he miscalculated her time and shortchanged her.

When we met, Kathy complained that she was not even clocking the nineteen hours she was "supposed" to work weekly as a library aide. Her income fluctuated when she took off time without pay. She missed work recently when her father passed away, when she was ill "for a week or so" with the flu, and when she fell in her apartment building and tore a leg ligament. She also does not get paid for snow days.

Working at a job with inconsistent hours is problematic not only because the pay is unpredictable but also because a shifting work schedule can preclude accepting other part-time work and partaking in other activities. And fluctuating hours create administrative work for recipients of welfare who must report any changes that would affect their welfare budget. Frequent reporting can result in bureaucratic mistakes that can take more time and energy to rectify. When Kathy's monthly food stamps had been reduced by approximately $75 a month on the incorrect assumption that she was working more hours, Kathy was upset. She said, "I'm trying to figure out what I'm supposed to do about that. I just asked my boss if she could give me a letter stating that the hours are less now. And give it to Social Services. For food stamps. Because I'm not making that much here, and then they cut my food stamps to $147."

By all accounts Kathy is not making much. Her income not only declined in her current job, but over the years her wages have eroded. Since the time that she worked in the laundry when she was in her early twenties until now, she only realized a wage gain of $1.00 hourly. Based on her wage of $8.00 per hour, a weekly work schedule of eighteen hours would yield a *gross* monthly wage of $576. In addition she received $83 in child support and food stamps of $147. Thus, her total monthly gross income is $806. From this, she pays $117 for her portion of the Section 8 monthly $850 rent, food, clothing, transportation, nonfood sundries, and other household and personal expenses. Kathy and her son take advantage of the dinners served by the churches in her community. I witnessed this at a holiday community church dinner where I volunteered as a server and we chatted in the dessert line. Kathy sometimes volunteers at another church, packing bags at their food pantry. She said, "So I get me a little bag too. So it helps me too." Twice a month she unloads trucks in exchange for a bag of canned goods.

I occasionally saw Kathy in her neighborhood. She once complained about the way the lack of a car limited her job search, employment, and earnings potential. I subsequently gave her information on a work support program administered by a private, not-for-profit social service agency. It provided an interest-free loan for up to $1,500 to eligible parents to purchase an automobile to facilitate employment. When I talked to Kathy two years after we initially met, she had been working at the same job, but her weekly hours were reduced to sixteen. She told me that she inquired about the auto loan but was deemed ineligible because she did not make enough money. This is an example of a catch-22 situation that low-income workers encounter.

Kathy consistently wanted to learn new marketable skills but education was costly; thus, she limited her schooling to the free vocation training offered by the state or community organizations. This training is for low-wage jobs, so Kathy cannot gain a toehold on employment that pays a living wage. Like many others in her situation, she lives in an impoverished state, garnering resources from disparate sources—the labor force, the state, private organizations, and a personal support network.

Lorna Webster

Lorna is a black woman in her early thirties. She lived with her two young children in an emergency housing apartment. She had recently moved there after spending five months in a shelter for homeless families. Lorna holds a GED diploma (high school equivalency). Her first job was at age twenty-one when her father became ill and stopped working in the construction industry. She was employed at a regional department store for about eight months. Shortly before the store went out of business, Lorna found a job at a New York–area fast-food chain. Lorna enjoyed the work world—she was still living at home, she had no responsibilities, and her paycheck was hers to spend.

When Lorna became pregnant, she applied for AFDC cash and medical insurance to cover the maternity expenses. Her low-paid job did not offer benefits. She could not rely on her baby's father for support. She said he "ran off" and "left us stranded" when he found out she was pregnant. She worked just shy of her ninth month and gave birth two weeks later at the age of twenty-three. Lorna had a younger girlfriend with strong maternal instincts who babysat Lorna's newborn. This facilitated Lorna's return to work after two and a half months.

Three months after Lorna started working, she met a man who three years later would become the father of her second child. When she became pregnant again, Lorna required government assistance because she was in dire need of aid. Her part-time job at a retail chain store lacked benefits, and she needed TANF to augment her meager income and the inadequate rations from the government food and nutrition program for woman, infants, and young children. By the time her baby was born, she and the baby's father had broken up. He helped her to some extent, but his job also lacked benefits. In the past Lorna relied on her father's financial support when she needed help, but that was not an option this time—he was now dying.

Lorna's employment had been steady even through two pregnancies. But her low-income wages were consistently inadequate, obliging her to occasionally work at two jobs simultaneously to provide for her children. One time she was ineligible for TANF when she worked part-time as a sales associate at a restaurant chain and full-time as a dietary aide at a hospital. At about this time the hospital found it necessary to lay off many workers. Anticipating her fate, Lorna found employment at a large regional supermarket.

Lorna worked in the deli department and her job entailed cooking prepared foods in a room where the floor drain would stop up. She long suspected a faulty floor drain because it "used to clog and overflow." One day Lorna and her coworkers were unloading supplies. She slipped and fell on the wet floor and a box fell on her. She suffered a shoulder bone splinter and tore her rotator cuff. The injury required surgery and subsequent physical therapy. She did not pursue a lawsuit; she liked her job. During her seven months on disability and convalescence, Lorna received workers' compensation.

When Lorna returned to work, she found an entire personnel change—a new supervisor and team of coworkers. She believed that the new supervisor did not want her back; she was a leftover from the former crew and not part of his hand-picked team. To her dismay her hours were cut dramatically from forty or fifty hours a week to about twenty-two, "which sucked."

Lorna's employment situation worsened—her hours dwindled and she experienced harassment that increasingly intensified. Finally she took her grievance to the store manager whom she knew and thought really cared. Lorna defended her work ethic and past performance, which she believed warranted a promotion. She reminded the store manager that in the past she gave "300 percent" of her time—she came in early and worked longer hours when asked, and she was readily available when coworkers called in sick. Lorna pleaded for more hours. He listened but presented her supervisor's account of the situation—the schedule was tight and they needed to accommodate a "lot of people."

One day Lorna telephoned her new supervisor to report that she would be two hours late due to her child's hospitalization for an asthma condition. When she arrived at work earlier than she anticipated, he had already arranged for a day replacement and sent her home. The next day she discovered that her schedule had been changed without her knowledge. Agitated, Lorna promptly addressed the matter, not with the store manager, who was out of town, but with another manager, who was also new and with whom she had no relationship. Seeing the manager on the phone, she poured herself a cup of coffee to calm down while waiting. On her way to the cash register she noticed the manager was now free and proceeded into his office, forgetting to pay for her drink.

After her meeting with the manager, still in a state of heightened anxiety, Lorna returned to her work station with her coffee in hand. A few minutes later she was instructed to report to security when she had finished with her customer. As a result, she was fired for "stealing" a $1.19 cup of coffee. Thinking she had no recourse, under pressure, anxious, and lacking the protection of the store manager who was out that day, Lorna signed a statement detailing the events. In a subsequent conversation with the store manager, Lorna explained her absentmindedness, assuring him it was an "honest mistake." Although he regretted that the event occurred during his absence, he stated there was nothing he could do because she signed the statement. Adding insult to injury, Lorna was denied unemployment insurance benefits.

After her termination, Lorna's thrifty ways, confidence in finding employment, and "a little nest" of a bank account were her justification for taking time off to spend with her children. After a monthlong hiatus, Lorna sought employment armed with her professionally prepared résumé. But she could not find a job. And within five months her savings had diminished to $173 just before Christmas. Although she made regular partial rental payments, her rent was $183 in arrears and the landlord began eviction proceedings. She applied to DSS for rental assistance but was denied the benefit due to a determination that she had sufficient funds.

Lorna was determined to find employment and save her housing. She sought legal counsel to fight the eviction. (It is unknown whether she pursued free legal aid.) In the process she incurred court fees of $100 for each appearance plus legal costs. This added over $500 to her deficit. As the expenses mounted, she earned some money braiding hair. When she would "do a couple of heads, make like $150," she paid down her debt. But after attempting to resolve the housing issues in the court, she simply incurred more legal fees and was ultimately evicted.

On the afternoon of the eviction Lorna went to the DSS office to seek shelter. Lorna stayed with a friend during her eligibility determination. Her application was denied. This triggered frustrating meetings with DSS, which in turn prompted her to contact a lawyer. After two weeks, Lorna and her two children were finally placed in a family shelter where she received $65 in food stamp assistance during the first month, but no cash. A month later she began receiving $315 TANF cash biweekly and $137 in monthly food stamps. She received a back payment check for $1,500; that money was earmarked for numerous bills and repayment of borrowed money. Lorna reflected on her emotional state during her early days at the shelter: "Oh my God [*laugh*]. I went through everything. Oh God, I isolated myself from my kids. Like, I didn't want to be bothered. I was going hysterical every day over everything, like where we live. Everything changed in my life. . . . Everything. One day you have a life and everything is cool and then you go to sleep and wake up and everything's taken from you."

From the start of motherhood, Lorna supported her family on her own by working low-wage jobs; at times her employment was threatened by a weakened economy or an employer's dire financial condition. Her ambition and work history counteract two stereotypes—that women have babies to secure welfare and that recipients of welfare are lazy and do not work. More recently, the downward trajectory of Lorna's financial state and emotional health and the disruption of her family's residential life are severe consequences for her absentmindedness about a cup of coffee stemming from her frustration associated with a work schedule change. By comparison, the consequences for the employer were minor; Lorna could merely be replaced by another flexible worker.

Mercedes Montgomery

Mercedes is a white woman in her forties who lives with her young daughter, Sophie. She is now estranged from Sophie's father, her partner for over ten years. She worked her whole life and in the mid-1990s began working as a flight attendant. Mercedes said that Sophie's birth was medically complicated and correlates her premature birth to a "low" immune system, which was the basis for her chronic infections. Sophie's recurring illness precluded preschool and demanded the at-home care of her working parents. Because they could not afford child care, Mercedes and her partner alternated missing work to care for their ill daughter. This was particularly difficult for her because of preset flight schedules. She often swapped days with other flight attendants to accommodate her daughter's needs. At some point Mercedes' partner did not want to miss work; conflicts arose as they negotiated who would stay home to care for their daughter.

Ultimately Mercedes' absenteeism culminated in her termination. She explained:

> So basically, they gave me a warning. They said, "Ok, well, instead of being a flight attendant, go on the ground since you're having all this instability." And that was a big mistake. Because when I went to the ground to do like ticketing, whatever, I lost my union. So I wasn't protected anymore. So after five years of working for [the airline], they asked me to resign because I missed six days in one year. And I was like, "I can't really resign. I mean, I have to work." They said, "You missed too many days, you are already on probation, we already put you on the ground, you're still missing [work]. Your husband [partner] doesn't want to help." . . . They were giving me a really hard time. I mean, I understand their point of view. But at the same time, it was only six days in one year, but that was too much for them. So I ended up not resigning. I resisted resigning and I collected unemployment. When I collected unemployment, I became blacklisted throughout the airlines, which is what I was told. You can't be rehired. No one will rehire [you]. . . . Because if you collect unemployment with the airlines, they blacklist you.

Mercedes came to believe that there was nothing she could have done, rationalizing that her employer had the prerogative to hire and fire and she had no union for support. At some point Mercedes filed for and began receiving unemployment insurance benefits. Mercedes continued the job search during an inopportune time when the airline industry continued to lay off tens of thousands of employees in the aftermath of the September 11 terrorist attacks in the United States. Mercedes perceived this as a "double whammy," having come to suspect that she was blacklisted from the industry. Mercedes decided to go back to college and was accepted at a private university. She was able to transfer credits she had earned in the late 1980s.

Not only was Mercedes devastated by her termination, but her daughter's poor health exacerbated her stress. Sophie continued to have medical problems, and Mercedes was on a quest to discover what was wrong through a myriad of medical tests. Mercedes grew angry with her partner, for she felt alone in this endeavor. Eventually they separated.

When Mercedes' unemployment insurance benefit expired, she was strapped for cash. Without unemployment benefits or her partner's financial support, Mercedes applied for rental assistance when her rent was in arrears. But because of a series of bureaucratic errors, Mercedes withdrew her application in frustration (see Chapter 4). A year after her termination Mercedes worked a summer job as an art teacher at a municipal park. After six months of employment she was able to collect unemployment benefits that sustained her through the winter. Mercedes applied for government assistance; at some point her daughter began receiving about $500 per month in SSI disability benefits because of a slight speech disability associated with her premature birth. Mercedes also received food stamps.

A year later Mercedes secured employment in retail sales. She recalled making "probably $400 a week—$300 after taxes, $250 or something." Her salary made her ineligible for continued food stamps, yet eligible for an after-school child-care subsidy of about $60 a week. Her work hours often exceeded forty hours per week, and occasionally she was required to work late nights.

Four months into her employment Mercedes became involved in a DSS bureaucratic fiasco over subsidized child-care payment. Mercedes found a reputable, conveniently located child-care provider that offered enriching activities for children. She repeatedly submitted the requisite documentation to DSS, but the department "kept messing up the paperwork so many times" and did not pay the provider. The provider urged Mercedes to resolve the payment situation and subsequently began to pester her more; Mercedes felt harassed. After four months the provider told Mercedes to remove her daughter from her child care; Mercedes complied. Then she quit her job. She explained, "[In] November I was like, I have to quit, this is just too stressful with this woman breathing down my back about child care and me trying to deal with them [DSS]. It was too much. So I just quit. I left on good terms. But unfortunately I left on good terms, so I didn't get unemployment either. And that's why I ended up back at the [DSS] office."

Mercedes had been living on the cash from her daughter's $500 SSI monthly payment. A $2,000 student loan got her through several months. She described her deteriorating financial situation: "So after January I was really getting tight on money. I didn't get my student loan for the next semester because I am ready to graduate and I'm like, 'Oh my God, I can't survive. I have no food in my refrigerator.'" Mercedes could not rely on financial support from her estranged partner; he was unemployed. When Mercedes was out of food, she would fast but would not let her daughter go hungry. She would call her ex-partner and demand that he pick up their daughter and get her something to eat or take her to his mother's for a meal. Mercedes had not relied on food pantries. She does not have a kin support system and is uncomfortable phoning friends to ask if she could borrow money.

In January Mercedes applied for TANF and food stamps and was denied TANF benefits because it was deemed that she had sufficient funds. When we met in the spring, she had recently begun working part-time making $50 per week teaching art; she also did freelance photography. She was still awaiting food stamp approval after months of administrative snags associated with her caseworker's demand for submission of requisite paperwork (see Chapter 4). A few weeks after our interview Mercedes left me a phone message saying that her food stamp application had been denied.

Mercedes' story is typical of several of the women who experienced downward mobility from professional jobs. In the aftermath of her termination, she was unable to maintain steady, full-time employment. A combination of structural factors and personal issues exacerbated her predicament—an unfavorable post–September 11 employment environment and bureaucratic errors resulting in a child-care fiasco. Like many women who break up with a husband or partner, Mercedes became financially distressed and unduly burdened with child rearing. Without adequate child-care support, women are penalized in the workplace and in the household. And the erosion of wages exacerbates the financial hardship of families.

Amber Hamilton

Amber is a black woman in her late twenties and a mother of two pre-school boys. Her home life during high school years was disruptive, but she graduated at age nineteen. Subsequently she attended a youth educational program for nine months where she earned some college credits and a nursing assistant certificate. She initially worked as a home health aide for a year before securing a job as a certified nursing assistant at a health-care facility where she had "continuous reemployment" for five years. Amber recalled an event that resulted in her first termination from the facility.

> When I was pregnant with my first son, I had placenta previa. I was at work and I was working nights then, and I used to work all the time because I had no kids and 'cause I was young, so I used to just work all the time. I was like a workaholic. I'd work seven days a week 'cause I was able to do it. But when I got pregnant, I told them they had to change the schedule. They made the schedule for a month in advance. I told them, "I cannot stay up like this no more. . . . I need to get some sleep."

Although Amber was five months pregnant, her employer would not change her schedule until she produced a doctor's note verifying that her hours not exceed three consecutive days. Even after that, she was asked for consecutive work when her employer was short-staffed. One night Amber agreed to work a fourth consecutive night, but in the morning she began bleeding due to a detached placenta and was hospitalized for a couple of weeks. Consequently, she was terminated from her job. Amber recalled:

> Yeah, they terminated me. Yep. They didn't call me to the nursing home, they sent me a letter, something about I'm terminated because my doctor put limitations on my work or something like that they said. So they terminated me. But after I had my baby, I went right back there and I said I want my job back or I'm gonna see a lawyer. So by the time I got home, the director of nursing was like, "Amber, when can you start?" So that's how I got back in there.

Amber was reinstated and resumed working there until a crisis happened several years later that led to her second termination in the early 2000s. By this time Amber had another child and they were living in a $1,000-a-month, two-bedroom apartment. She had been working full-time making $14.63 an hour, five days a week. She earned extra money by working double shifts and earned time and a half on holidays. She said during those years she was able to maintain her family. Recalling those times, prior to her termination that led to her becoming homeless, Amber assessed the financial quality of life this way: "I didn't want for nothing. I was happy. I didn't know about nothing [welfare benefits]. I never even seen this in my future for this to happen to me. I had everything I wanted. I had a car. I had everything." Then Amber told the story that led to her financial decline.

In late summer Amber and her two sons went on vacation. Her sons' paternal family lived in a Southern state, and Amber scheduled time for them to visit while she planned to "hang out" with her best friends, who lived in an adjacent state. When the children's aunt came to get them, she assured Amber that she would bring them back to where Amber was staying. On the following Sunday, the day before the aunt was to return the children, Amber called their paternal grandmother to confirm the arrangements. The grandmother told Amber the aunt had to work and was unable to make the trip to return the youngsters. Amber panicked; she felt the family was trying to keep her boys. Even though Amber had to be back to work that Wednesday, she decided to retrieve her sons. But first she needed to wait for the issuance of her paycheck and have the money wired to her, coordinate rental car transportation, drive to pick up her sons, and then continue driving back to New York.

Although she was in contact with her employer, the director of nursing kept calling, telling her they needed her back to work and that she was on "borrowed time now." Amber was conflicted. If she continued to stay to resolve her issue, she risked being fired since she had exhausted her vacation and personal time. But if she returned to work immediately, she feared the family would keep her sons. Moreover, the latter plan would necessitate a return trip to the South plus additional expenses. And she would have to wait to accrue vacation time before she could even make a second trip. Amber felt she had no choice but to stay and work out the logistical arrangements to retrieve her children. By the time she returned to work, she had been terminated for failure to return when she was due back.

Shortly after Amber returned home, she learned that her children's father was "smoking crack and doing all kinds of stuff." In a court proceeding she was granted full custody of her sons. While Amber's previous reflection on her quality of financial life sounds rosy, in reality she did not have "everything," for she lacked sufficient savings to sustain a month and a half of unemployment. She could no longer afford her $1,000-a-month rent. Amber could have accumulated rent arrears until she was evicted, but her conscience would not allow this. She had known her landlord for many years and wanted to be fair to him. Therefore, Amber went to DSS and for the first time in her life she sought welfare and homeless services. She said, "Everything was piling up on me so I just came to the shelter."

Several months after moving into the shelter with her two children, Amber was hired by a staffing agency for home health aide work at $7.00 per hour. Three months later Amber left after finding work with another agency for more money. At this new job Amber was hired as a nurse's aide making $14 per hour and she initially worked twelve-hour shifts. However, soon thereafter, the agency lacked a sufficient number of patients to assign Amber any cases. She said, "I don't want to just sit there 'cause they don't have no work for nurse's aide." So, Amber took the test for a home health aide, a lower-level job, and began to pick up work for $8.00 per hour. Ruminating on her decision to work for lower pay in light of her homeless predicament, Amber said she felt that she had no choice because she needed to earn money. She said,

> I already gotta pay $291 a month to live here [at the shelter]. And they want their money by the first, no later than the tenth. . . . Right now I get $75 food stamps a month. And every fourth and nineteenth of the month I get $37 [TANF cash aid]. And that's it. And I get paid $208 a week. $208! After I cash my check and they take all the money and everything [tax deductions], I put $208 in my pocket.

By the time I met Amber, she and her four- and five-year-old sons had been living in the family shelter for a year. When she first moved into the shelter, her TANF and food stamps totaled approximately $500. When she was employed, her grant was rebudgeted periodically and ultimately reduced to this current amount; she was also required to pay monthly shelter rent. Amber lamented the futility of wage work while living at the shelter and bemoaned her situation when I asked her what it was like working as a home health aide. She said, "I don't like it at all. I don't like it at all. I'm sick of going to this lady's house [patient's private house]. But I have to. I'd rather be at a nursing home somewhere." She surmised that if she makes a higher wage at another job, her shelter rent will increase and she feared that the payment would skyrocket. Amber continued, "They're gonna want like $1,000 for me to live in that room [at the shelter]. 'Cause I know people in here that's paying that to live in that room. And I can't see myself giving them that money. . . . The more you make, they take it. You don't keep that. They take everything." I responded, "So there's no incentive for you to go get a better job? "No," she said, "it's like whatever you do, you can't get out." This thought unnerved Amber and she started to cry.

> AH: And I'm tired of this place. It's like no matter how hard you work, you're stuck. It's like no matter how much I do, I'm not gonna get out of here. That's how I feel. My kids are rebellious now, you know. My son, he tells me this morning, "Get off me, I'm gonna hit you." He pees on himself every day at school. You know. I'm sick of it. They never wet the bed before they came here. My kids wet the bed every night. I gotta buy pull-ups. I can't afford pull-ups. But I gotta buy 'em.
>
> TL: And how much are pull-ups?
>
> AH: Every week I spend $11 on pull-ups.
>
> TL: They're like diapers, right, for big kids?
>
> AH: Yeah. Yep. I mean I'm tired of it. It's like tearing my kids up.

It is astonishing how Amber can hold things together. By the time she pays shelter rent, she has approximately $173 per week left over. Basic survival expenses are costly. She complained about the price of incidentals and washing her family's clothes. And, with winter approaching, she needed coats for herself and her boys.

> AH: [I've] been saving every week, every week so I can get him [her son] a coat. . . . Like my other one [son], I bought him a coat. And I saved, saved, saved. And I go to Burlington Coat Factory and bought him a coat. Now tomorrow I'm able to go get my other son a coat. And then I got to save and save and save so I can get me a coat. 'Cause I don't have a coat.
>
> TL: No winter coat?
>
> AH: No. And it's already cold. I mean I just can't go out there and buy a coat. I gotta keep saving, saving, saving. It's gonna take me about a month for me to get a coat.

Furthermore, working incurs expenses—transportation, food, clothing. It costs Amber $17.50 each week for public transportation round trip; when she does not have the money, she walks. She cuts costs by forgoing lunch. In the morning she spends a dollar daily on a buttered roll and tea to hold her all day. Although wearing street clothes would be slightly cheaper, Amber chooses to wear a $20 uniform (scrubs) to work. She said, "I feel like, more like, you know, I'm really doing something. Like, my job is important when I have a uniform on."

Amber's résumé summarizes her seven years of work experience in the health-care profession. She has "solid experience" as a certified nursing assistant, specializing in "rehabilitative, hospice, skilled, and dementia care." Her summary of qualifications states that she is a "fast learner, dependable, flexible."

Undoubtedly, Amber views her flexibility as an asset without realizing its implications in the twenty-first-century workforce. Indeed, she demonstrated flexibility on the job when no staff were available to cover patients, to the point where she jeopardized her pregnancy. Yet, her employer was inflexible and did not accommodate her high-risk pregnancy and hospitalization and terminated her employment. Years later, her decision to tend to a family emergency rather than immediately report to work was cause for a subsequent termination. Amber's employer demonstrated inflexibility in both situations.

Amber's experiences reveal the tremendous workplace power imbalance and insecurity in today's flexible workplace. After her first termination Amber threatened legal intervention; she was rehired. Her second termination led to her family becoming homeless. She and her children suffered from the stress of shelter living. Her new employment pays less. She is trapped in a labor system and a public and private assistance system where she cannot get ahead. The more she makes, the more she must pay for inadequate shelter living arrangements. Amber's work history also dispels the myth that recipients of welfare are irresponsible and lazy. Amber described herself as a "workaholic" before she had children. After becoming a mother she strove to work steadily, often working double shifts and holidays, and has made great sacrifices to provide for her two children.

Issues for Working Families in the Flexible Labor Force

These and other parents' narratives bring to light issues that are common in the flexible labor force—insufficient wages, labor insecurity and exploitation in the health-care industry, health issues that impede workers' labor force participation, the impact of family caregiving, as well as the ramifications of incarceration on employment and TANF benefits. These issues warrant further exploration.

Insufficient Wages

The U.S. labor system creates such an inequitable divide that it cannot sustain and protect those in lower-tier employment. One factor is the minimum wage. When I began my fieldwork in late 2003, New York's minimum wage of $5.15 per hour had been set at the federal rate since 2000, despite increases in the cost of living. After a political struggle, which included a veto by Republican Governor George E. Pataki, in December 2004 the New York minimum hourly wage was set to incrementally increase each January 1: to $6.00 in 2005, $6.75 in 2006, and $7.15 in 2007.[6] While the increase was seen as a victory by its champions, it is still far from adequate.

Several quantitative measures show just how inadequate these wages are. As illustrated earlier, the minimum wage is at variance with the "housing wage" required to pay for housing costs (National Low Income Housing Coalition 2004). Similarly, workers earning the minimum wage cannot meet the self-sufficiency standard for New York (Pearce with Brooks 2000; Pearce 2004).[7] The standard varies by location statewide. For example, in affluent Westchester County, the self-sufficiency wage in 2000 for a single adult with one preschooler and a school-aged child was $25.50 per hour. Two wage-earning adults ease the burden, but each adult must earn $14.03 per hour (Pearce with Brooks 2000:12). In 2004 for the single adult household this was close to five times the New York minimum wage; it was approximately twice the New York median hourly wage for blacks and Hispanics.[8]

As the narratives demonstrate, workers' ability to provide for their families is further hampered by jobs with insufficient hours, temporary and seasonal work, prolonged unemployment, and wage disparities based on gender, class, and race/ethnicity.[9] Moreover, work is often economically futile. Added to the stress of insufficient wages are work-related and transportation expenses, as well as time management and child-care issues (see below). New or increased wages trigger a recalculation of a welfare budget. This in turn can cause a subsidized housing rental payment increase and the reduction or termination of welfare. Based on insufficient wages and other issues commonly experienced in the workforce, it is understandable that workers cannot gain a toehold.

Flexible Health-Care Workers

A number of the women in this study had been employed in the health industry. Among them, the majority worked in lower-wage employment such as home health aides. Women with little formal education often choose this occupation. Training takes place on the job or through short-term training classes. Because this training is often approved for workfare, some women took classes to fulfill a welfare work activity. Others paid for the class and attended on their own.

According to the New York State Department of Labor, the occupation of home health aide had "very favorable" employment prospects for several years into the future in New York's Hudson Valley region, of which Westchester is a part. The median wage for a home health aide was $22,780 annually in 2006. (Recall that in 2004 the annual income needed to afford a two-bedroom apartment in Westchester with a fair market rent of $1,259 was $50,360; this median wage for a home health aide is not even close.) The job description of the home health aide is to "provide routine, personal healthcare, such as bathing, dressing, or grooming, to elderly, convalescent, or disabled persons in the home of patients or in a residential care facility" (New York State Department of Labor 2006). Because much of the work is assigned through an agency, it is an occupation suited for the flexible labor force.

Some of the narratives of women who worked as home health aides are a testament to the vagaries of home health aide work, the physical labor, inconsistent pay, and scrutiny under which they work. The women who perform work as home health aides, and even as higher-skilled certified nursing assistants, struggle to maintain their families due to the inconsistency of employment. The inability to obtain steady assignments was not uncommon. It becomes apparent why many augment their wages with welfare while employed or when they become unemployed. The following dialogue with Anita Ramos clarifies the irregularity and insecurity of her flexible labor.

> *TL:* So how many years have you worked for [home care agency]?
> *AR:* On and off, five years.

TL: . . . In a month's time or a year's time, how much steady work do you think you had?

AR: Five months, six months steady.

TL: Out of a whole year?

AR: Yeah.

TL: . . . How did you support yourself the other six months?

AR: DSS. I was always on DSS [welfare]. Yeah. The only thing was, I would have to give them my pay stub every week and they would change my income on what they was gonna give me every month [benefits]. So it was very complicated.

TL: That must have been an administrative nightmare for you to figure out that you were being compensated properly?

AR: Yeah, or is my rent going to be paid this month, or do I have to contribute to my rent. Which they do that now.

TL: OK. Can you tell me how that works?

AR: Right now I'm unemployed. My job [agency] hasn't found me a case. If they was to find me a case right now, and if I was to get, let's say $12 an hour, they probably would only find me a case morning shift, which is nine [a.m.] to one [p.m.]; might be five days a week. So it's just $12 an hour from nine to one. Not unless they find me a case that could be $7, four days a week. It was never consistent. You could be on a case for like two months, and then they'll pull you off the case and put somebody else on because they might need you on another place.

TL: Why do they need you somewhere else?

AR: Because of your experience. Because different aides have different experience. And a lot of times, patients they usually ask for what aide they want.

TL: When was the last time you had a case?

AR: Three months ago [*laugh*].

TL: And how long did that last?

AR: I was on that case three months.

TL: OK, so during that period of time, you were employed. How much were you making?

AR: $9.00 an hour. Only in the morning, 9:00 to 1:00.

TL: How much was DSS supplementing?

AR: I wasn't getting ongoing needs [welfare cash]. But they were sending me food stamps which I think was $319. And they was paying [a portion of] my rent, $587.

When income is insufficient, some health-care workers receive public assistance, if eligible, to augment their salary when employed or in between assignments. Others (e.g., Amber Hamilton, who was on staff at a residential care facility) sometimes worked double shifts, enabling them to make a living wage. Melba Jackson, a forty-eight-year-old woman who raised two children and two grandchildren, was a certified nursing assistant. She not only worked double shifts and weekends, but on rare occasions could get more lucrative, private work outside of agency staffing. But for both Melba and Amber their employment was exploitative.

Melba recalled with indignation a job that she was assigned by a health-care agency.

> So I went over there and I filled out the application. They give you a little test and I passed the score with a ninety-five. And then they send you to the Bronx to do the training and everything. And I went down there, riding two buses. . . . And then they tell me all they were paying is $6.50 an hour. I wanted to scream. I said, "Shit, I ain't never made $6.50 an hour." . . . Even at [the Head Start Program in the early 1990s] we made $7.50, $8.00. And you talk about $6.50! I stayed there three months; that was it [*laugh*]. 'Cause they want to give you four hours here, three hours there. Then they want to send you upstate. Uuh-uuh. Then I went one place and the lady wanted me to do her floor. And I asked her, "Where's the mop?" She said, "I don't have a mop." She said, "You know, you can just scrub it, get on your knees and wipe it up with a rag." I said, "I'm [from] down South; I ain't getting on my knees and scrubbing floors down South. You think I'm coming all the way to New York to scrub a damn floor." She said, "Oh, I'm gonna make sure I tell." I said, "I don't give a damn." As a matter of fact, I went outside and I called the agency. I said, "This lady don't have a mop. She want me to get on the floor and scrub her floor with a rag." She lost her mind, please. I ain't getting down there. So I told them, "I told you before, I ain't with housework." I clean shit all day long.

Also, recall that when Amber worked for an agency, it could not provide her with assignments as a nurse's aide, but could assign her to jobs for which she was paid $6 less per hour. Undoubtedly, Amber had higher-level skills that could have been utilized if necessary on these lower-level jobs. Thus, her labor also was exploited.

Furthermore, health-care workers are often subjected to intensive scrutiny during the hiring process and during their employment (e.g., disclosure of criminal records on applications, urine testing for drugs). Prior to the job that Melba just described, she resigned from another agency when she knew she would test positive on an unscheduled drug test. This occurred on a Monday morning after she "had got high that weekend" at a birthday party.

Moreover, employees working in low-tier jobs must *prove* that they cannot accommodate employers' staffing demands. In Amber's case, she was required to submit a doctor's note indicating that she could not work a specific number of consecutive days during her pregnancy.

The balance of power always rests with the employer but never more so than in low-tier jobs. In low-wage occupations the employer has tremendous control over employees, as evidenced by these workplace regulations. In contingent employment the employer exercises additional control by flexibly assigning work, tasks, and hours to employees; employees are at the mercy of those who devise malleable workers' schedules and assignments.

Health Issues That Impeded Steady Wage Work

In the course of their narratives, some people revealed data about their medical conditions. The extent of their ill health was remarkable. Three people are infected with HIV/AIDS. One woman is a diabetic, has a liver disease and posttraumatic stress disorder, had recent umbilical hernia surgery, and was being diagnosed for cancer. Another is a cancer patient. One woman was mending a torn leg cartilage from a fall in her poorly maintained apartment building. Another suffered from panic and anxiety attacks all her life. One woman has a thyroid condition; her weight fluctuates drastically in times of stress. Another woman also experiences weight fluctuation from stress and currently suffers from migraine headaches. A young mother suffered from postpartum anxiety attacks and attention deficit disorder. A mother in her thirties was recently diagnosed with mild depression for which she was prescribed antidepressants. One woman had a dilation and curettage procedure and was being watched for breast cancer due to a persistent cyst. Some women had miscarriages. One mother complained of a leg cramp that she had for two months. One woman became very ill with bronchial asthma and was forced to quit college in her first semester. At least four people had missing teeth. During my interviews, people's stress was apparent. A couple of women broke down in tears when they described the burdens, anxieties, and combined pressures of motherhood, caregiving, employment, finding affordable housing, shelter living, and getting through everyday life.

While it is unclear to me what impact PRWORA specifically had on the health of these individuals, it is evident that some health conditions impeded an individual's ability to work certain jobs or to work at all. Mandated work and workfare activities had the potential to create more stress for some individuals.

Many women lost work and wages because of their pregnancies. Abby Armstrong is a diabetic and quit her $7.50 per hour home health job during the third trimester of a high-risk pregnancy. Carole Marlow was forced to quit a job when she was "miserably" sick from gestational diabetes throughout her entire pregnancy. When Anna Moreno was pregnant with her third child, she worked as a bookkeeper making $10 per hour. She became depressed and stopped going to work. When she could not give her employer an answer as to when she would return to work, she was fired. We saw that Amber Hamilton worked as a certified nursing assistant when her doctor prescribed limited hours after which she was hospitalized for placenta previa; this led to her termination.

Alice Finnegan has had severe back problems that restrict her employment options. Charlotte Thompson also has back problems and cannot sit or stand for prolonged periods. She believes she could be exempt from workfare requirements but said, "I have a hard time seeing disability next to my name." She decided to opt for pain management instead of back surgery. Vanessa Geller once worked as a postal worker and sustained a few injuries on the job. Unrelated to work, she was stuck by a car crossing a street and at some point was unable to work. She received welfare until she became eligible for Social Security Disability. Lena Powell was diagnosed with diabetes; she was hospitalized at least twice, once when she was first diagnosed and another time when she had complications due to medication. Fortunately, Lena had medical benefits and sick days in her union job.

People spoke about their children's health problems, which include cancer, asthma, HIV/AIDS, muscular dystrophy, spinal meningitis, and problems associated with premature births—water on the brain, delayed speech and walking, mental retardation, and emotional disorders. Asthma was prevalent in many families. Children's ill health posed special burdens on families. Complications arose on the job when working women had to miss work to care for their children when they suffered from common childhood illnesses as well as chronic diseases. The issues associated with children's health are particularly stressful when they occur simultaneously or serially with other family pressures.

Caregiving

Women's caregiving responsibilities throughout their lives are at odds not only with the TANF time limits, as elucidated in the previous chapter, but with their position in the labor market. Many women chose not to work while their children were young. Some quit or were terminated from jobs when their employment conflicted with their caregiving responsibilities, which may or may not have stemmed from health issues. For many, their decision to leave the workforce either voluntarily or through a termination led them to seek government aid. The tensions among paid work, home work, and motherhood have been well documented and experienced by women of all classes in different ways (Hochschild 1997). An outcome of mandated welfare work requirements is that poor women are unable to forgo wage labor or take a hiatus from the workforce and stay at home to rear their children. Regulations control their labor, often resulting in jobs caring for children other than their own. The labor of poor women in domestic and child-care employment facilitates others to work in higher-paying jobs (Susser 1991; Colen 1995). Prior to TANF, workfare mandates were not as rigorous and the timeframe exempting postpartum employment was greater; therefore, some poor mothers were able to raise children with no labor force participation, or varying degrees of participation, when they received welfare. Today work requirements are stricter. Among the women I interviewed, I found that many had returned to work several months after giving birth, due to workfare mandates, as well as personal choice or economic necessity (e.g., Lorna Webster and Amber Hamilton). Regardless, the workplace is not accommodating to working mothers whose employment and caregiving responsibilities are at variance with work expectations. Employment and child-rearing demands often collided, resulting in a crisis.

Caregiving extends to other family members. At least three women quit their jobs during a parent's illness. Patricia Lambert noted that she could not afford a nursing home and had to stay home to take care of her sick mother. Abby Armstrong quit her $12.25-per-hour job at a nursing home to attend to her ill mother who moved in with her and whose disability money helped pay for household expenses. Sandee Staton quit her data-entry job and moved upstate to care for her mother who was suffering from AIDS.

Child Care

While child care is a concern for all working families, poor and single parents are confronted with added pressures in terms of support and costs. Mercedes Montgomery's story elucidates the woefully inadequate child-care supports in the workplace. As a national agenda item, child care for working families receives inadequate attention and monetary support. Therefore, parents must devise strategies to accommodate children and work. Partners often worked split shifts enabling one of them to stay home with the children. When a couple separates, the noncustodial partner is often solicited to perform this obligation. Several women relied on members of their personal kin and other support networks for child care. Others relied on private child care, some of whom received child-care subsidies.

Some factors that parents consider when selecting a child-care facility are subsidies, affordability, availability, safety, cleanliness, the provider-child ratio, stimulating environment, and schedule flexibility.

State-subsidized child care is an option for some families. It has an application process requiring the completion of forms by the applicant and others (e.g., child-care provider, school, and landlord). To receive subsidized child care an applicant must be deemed eligible and must use an approved provider. As with other programs, eligibility requirements for child-care services can dissuade applicants from seeking aid. For example, a draconian eligibility requirement for subsidized child care was instituted in mid-2004 in New York State. A custodial parent or caregiver must actively pursue child support from a noncustodial parent through the court. The person must demonstrate that she or he already has a court order for child support or is in the process of obtaining one. This necessitates establishing paternity if it has not already been established. At the very least the regulation is time-consuming and has precarious implications. A mother might not know, and thus be unable to prove, the whereabouts of a child's father or know his social security number. The regulation propels a family into the legal system. A court proceeding could be risky and emotionally upsetting for a woman who must confront the child's father, especially if he had been abusive. Although a person has the right to claim "good cause" not to actively pursue child support, the process is onerous and the burden is on the individual to establish that good cause exists. Applicants and recipients can be penalized and denied child care if they do not comply. Many do not know what recourse is available. This regulation has been a significant deterrent to obtaining a subsidy for child care.[10]

Joyce Scott, a facility director, told me about the circumstances under which she had reinstated three children to her child-care center. The mother of the children was denied a subsidy for three months because she could not provide information on the father in order for the state to pursue child support collection. The mother was required to sign an affidavit and swear under oath that she did not know how to locate the man. When she did so, this enabled her to resume the child-care arrangements. The director's anecdote illustrates the difficulties and penalties poor mothers must endure, and the disruption of a child's routine. One can imagine how this three-month disruption also affected the mother's life as she scrambled for other resources or faced employment termination. The latter is not far fetched; Mercedes Montgomery's bureaucratic morass vis-à-vis the delayed child-care payment by the state was the basis for her decision to quit her job (see Mercedes' story).

Affordability is a major consideration. The monthly fees for one reputable child-care provider was $890 for full-day care from 7:00 a.m. to 7:00 p.m. and $300 for after-school care from 3:00 p.m. to 7:00 p.m. Joyce Scott placed child-care fees into perspective. She said that a child in full-day care can potentially spend 240 hours per month at the center (12 hours x 20 days).

> So we're looking at what, maybe $3 an hour. Which isn't a lot when you're talking about the care and safety of your child. But when you make $8 an hour, or even if you're someone who makes $10 to $15 an hour, that becomes a lot. Because taxes are taken out. You have other expenses that you have to take care of. So if you can't get a subsidy, it's almost hard to pay for child care privately. Especially in a market that is saturated with so many subsidies. Most of your centers, they ask the rate that the Department of Social Services will pay. . . . Because they know that that's what social services will pay. Landlords know what Section 8 will pay. And so the market is artificially

inflated. And so the parent who makes $20,000 working in a municipal office or as an entry-level person in a professional setting, they have a hard time affording child care.

A day-care subsidy may be granted to New York TANF recipients who work or who are in engaged in mandated workfare activities. For non-TANF recipients, state subsidized day-care subsidies cover part of the costs; parents must pay the balance. Costs vary throughout the county and subsidies are time limited. Initially when Roseanne Tate started receiving TANF, the full cost of her prekindergarten son's full-day child care was approximately $1,200 per month; as a TANF recipient she paid nothing. Later on when Roseanne's son entered kindergarten, the monthly fee was $600 for after-school care from about noon to roughly 6:00 p.m. The child-care provider was able to reduce the fee to about $400 through private scholarship funds. Of that, Roseanne received a subsidy but was required to pay about $260 per month for her five-year-old son. Her two preteens went to a recreational facility or to a friend's house after school during the school year. When school was closed, she arranged for the children to attend holiday and summer camps for which she paid $45 per day. Among the women I met, Roseanne appears to have the highest annual income (approximately $35,000 annually) and her job offers her some schedule flexibility. Even for her, it is a strain to support her three children and manage her household on her own.

Availability of safe, affordable child care is yet another issue. Several women said that providers are reluctant to accept children who receive subsidies because of the bureaucratic procedures and payment delays by DSS. One woman's perception is that a lot of the providers who *do* accept subsidized child care provide "ghetto care." Conversely, I visited quality day-care centers that accepted state-subsidized child care.

Ginger Anderson, a black single working mother of a three-year-old daughter, recalled her search for child care. Ginger first checked out a center that she attended as a child; it had a three-year waiting list. Assessing one facility near her house, she said that "the maintenance was disgusting." She thought it was because the facility was in close proximity to housing projects. She finally settled on a quality day-care center in her neighborhood. But Ginger subsequently transferred her daughter to a church-affiliated day-care center across the county from where she lived and worked. Although this required her to drive her daughter approximately twenty miles round trip twice daily, Ginger made the switch because the new day-care center provided breakfast and lunch and required a uniform, all of which reduced expenses.

The availability of child care is problematic for evening and night-shift workers, especially single parents without a partner to share child-care responsibilities. During the course of my fieldwork, Target, Best Buy, Stop & Shop, T. J. Maxx, and other retailers opened along a stretch of establishments in Mount Vernon. These and other such stores employ low-income, flexible workers for day and evening work. Some supermarkets around the county are open until midnight. A day-care director told me of a young boy who leaves the day-care facility at 7:00 p.m. and walks to where his mother works at the local supermarket to give her a kiss before going to his grandmother's house where he stays. If he is up, he might see his mother when she comes home from work after midnight.

A *safe* environment is a prime selection criterion. Some women were apprehensive about leaving their children in others' care. Some feared child abuse. Mothers of children in poor health have added concerns when they entrust their sickly children to others. Latrice Parker has a desire to work and was considering day care since her toddlers can now talk. She explained:

> *LP:* 'Cause I'm very paranoid for my kids. If something happened to them, I want to be able to get there. I'm willing to work. I'm willing to do whatever. But I need my kids to be safe while I'm doing what I do, while I'm working and stuff. I need them to be safe.
>
> *TL:* And you don't think they'd be safe in a day care?
>
> *LP:* Yeah, now they would because they're older and they can tell me what's going on. It's too much stuff going on in this world. All this molestation and all this touching. And I have a daughter, and I don't play that. I mean, my son, they do it to little boys too.

Some fears were not unfounded. Lorna Webster recalled a time when she was in a workfare program and had subsidized child care for her three-year-old and infant sons. She discovered that the provider was a drug addict when one day she went to pick up her sons and the police were raiding the child-care provider's house. Lorna said. "So if I didn't get there on time, my kids would have been gone." In the aftermath of that scare Lorna did not want to use child care. Sometime later she decided not to attend a mandated workfare program regularly. But after she was referred to a child-care umbrella organization in the county she felt reassured by their recommendation and then complied with workfare requirements.

Even when parents are satisfied with the day-care facility, the time constraints and logistical arrangements are often stressful for working parents and their children. A parent who has a long commute to work must arrange to drop off a child before work. Working overtime, traffic jams, and mass transit delays can result in being late in retrieving a child before the facility closing time. Some providers charge a late fee based on time increments. Some children start their day at the day care as early as 7:00 a.m. and leave at 7:00 p.m. Facility director Joyce Scott said to me, "Imagine being two or three years old and having to spend almost twelve hours with a day-care provider. That's a long day for anyone and especially a small child."

Like other government assistance programs, subsidized child care is fraught with traps and conundrums. One mother made a tactical decision to reject a $2,500 raise six months after the commencement of her employment. Her rationale was that had she accepted the increase, she would have exceeded day-care eligibility standards and would have lost her subsidy for her child.

Subsidized child care can cause complications for flexible workers who were approved for a set number of child-care days per week. Many people work temporary jobs, are on call, have schedules that change weekly, or work inconsistent hours. For example, if a home health aide has an opportunity to work extra days during the week or on a holiday, she must scramble to arrange child care. Joyce Scott said that often a person in that situation will inquire whether the child-care center can take the child for the day. Parents are not even sure if they can afford to pay for the day out of pocket, but working gives them the opportunity to make extra money.

In New York a parent receiving cash assistance has the right to be excused from a work activity if she or he is unable to find an appropriate, accessible, affordable, and suitable child-care provider for a child under thirteen years old. There are DSS procedures in place to help a parent secure such a provider (New York State Office of Temporary and Disability Assistance 2005b). Nonetheless Joyce observed, "And I've seen parents lose their benefits because they couldn't secure steady child care. So it's a catch-22. If you don't have child care, you can't work. If you don't work, and they [DSS staff] feel you're eligible to work, then you are sanctioned and you don't receive the benefits. So it's difficult. It's difficult."

When working parents cannot secure child care (e.g., they are ineligible for subsidized child care or the cost for private payment is prohibitive), they must devise alternate strategies—quit working or enlist the help of (ex)partners, adult kin, or friends. Some after-school care options include children staying at home unsupervised or in the care of an older sibling, visiting friends' houses, or joining neighborhood clubs. Latch-key and unsupervised arrangements can be risky.

In summary, for working parents the criteria for child-care selection are affordability, availability, security, and nurturing environment. For low- and marginal-income workers, subsidized child care might be possible, if they are deemed eligible. Joyce Scott said, "If you're lucky to get a subsidy, then you're really fortunate." But even so, the combination of employment and child care in the flexible labor market is difficult. Employment in the low-wage labor market is often hard and unsatisfying. And considering the extra expenses associated with work, the travel involved, and the cost and stress of child-care arrangements, employment is often viewed as futile.

Incarceration

Since 1970 the U.S. prison population has increased seven times over, caused in part by the mandatory sentencing laws stemming from the Reagan administration's "war on drugs," the proprison lobby (Niman 2000), and the growth of the prison industrial system in rural deindustrialized areas (Street 2001). While blacks are approximately 12 percent of the U.S. population, they are 50 percent of the two million incarcerated Americans (Street 2001). African Americans comprise 51 percent of the New York State and 91 percent of the New York City prison populations (Niman 2000). These statistics indicate that black families are disproportionately represented in the prison system. Among the people I interviewed, six had been incarcerated at some point in their distant or recent pasts. It is unclear to me the extent to which a criminal record was a factor in their subsequent (in)ability to obtain employment and support families throughout their lives.

Shayleen Vaughn and Margarita Carlos are in their early twenties; both were incarcerated. If their criminal records hinder their employment prospects and they continue to receive TANF, this does not bode well for them in light of the impending TANF five-year time limit. Three decades ago Patricia Lambert was incarcerated, but since then she has not been involved with the criminal justice system. When we met, she had been out of the formal workforce for fourteen years, although she volunteered at a soup kitchen. When I saw Patricia about a year later, she still was not employed. In fact, due to some changes at the kitchen, she was no longer volunteering for "cigarette money."

Desmond Hughes was incarcerated for approximately a year when he was twenty-seven and has been incarcerated five times since. Desmond earned a bachelor's degree; some of the classes were completed during his first incarceration when he was selected to enroll in a college program. This was in the 1980s when funding and ideology supported education in the prisons. When I first met Desmond, I asked him if he had an extensive work history.

> Not really. No. The majority of years that I've been on my own, either I was in the streets, I hustled, or I worked from time to time. But it is not the best work history. It's not the most regular. But I supported myself and my son and my son's mother for at least ten years prior to her death. It has been just my son since. And I got temporary work off and on and I was on social services.

Out of the mainstream workforce for long periods, Desmond sold marijuana and cocaine. But this resulted in repeated incarcerations. Throughout my fieldwork Desmond was constantly looking for work. He found temporary, odd jobs, like working with a contractor doing masonry work. About a year after our first interview I unexpectedly saw him at a Department of Labor office at a recruitment day held by a national retailer that planned to open a store in the area. Desmond applied for work even though he did not have a car and the store would be located across the county from where he lived. Desmond was smartly dressed in a dark suit and crisp shirt. He made quite an impression on me and I told him so, remarking that he looked very professional. Desmond was not hired.

Anita Ramos completed the sixth grade and is in her mid-thirties. Ruth Jenkes, who earned a bachelor's degree, is in her mid-forties. Both were incarcerated years ago. Their early years were fraught with substance abuse, homelessness, separation from their children, and other hardships. As the postincarceration travails of Anita show, ex-offenders face numerous issues when they leave prison—securing housing and public assistance benefits, obtaining custody and reuniting with children, and finding sustainable employment (see Chapter 2).

Parents face many of these legal and civil barriers, as well as problems obtaining student loans and immigration issues. Issues continue to plague people with prison records long after they have served their formal sentences. In fact, the federal government continues to punish ex-offenders. A provision of PRWORA imposed a lifetime ban on TANF and food stamps for individuals convicted under federal or state law of a felony involving the use or sale of drugs after August 22, 1996. The ban remains enforced irrespective of circumstances or subsequent rehabilitation efforts. States have the flexibility to pass legislation so that the ban is not imposed (Hirsch et al. 2002). Although New York does not impose this ban, it is instructive to briefly discuss this rule here in the context of devolution. Furthermore, it is yet another example of how PRWORA can be implicated in creating more stress and poverty in poor people's lives.

Allard's research analyzing the effects of the lifetime ban on women and children reveals that as of December 2001, forty-two states were enforcing the ban in full or in part (since then a few more states opted out of the ban). Her 2002 report indicates that in the twenty-three states investigated, an estimated 92,000 women were affected by the ban at the time. The U.S. "war on drugs" and this TANF ban disproportionately affect minorities—48 percent of the women affected by the ban were African American or Latina. Although the ban does not extend to the children, an estimated 135,000 children risked a reduction of family benefits. The lifetime ban has serious implications for parents, especially minority and recovering mothers, for it endangers their chances to obtain cash, food, drug treatment, and other supports to raise a family (Allard 2002).

This federal ban is in blatant contradiction to the ideology of PRWORA that emphasizes personal responsibility and self-sufficiency. Prior to the 1996 welfare law both Anita Ramos and Ruth Jenkes benefited from an array of postincarceration services, which they highly commended, enabling them to make a transition from prison to the community, gain custody of some of their children, and create a family life. In the PRWORA era, large numbers of parents are at risk nationwide. If parents cannot provide the basic needs for themselves and their children when they leave prison, it is possible that their situation might draw the attention of a child welfare agency. Historically, children, particularly black children, have been removed due to issues related to poverty (see Roberts

2002). Legislation that permits states to impose a lifetime ban on welfare benefits is an extremely punitive measure in light of the fact that many incarcerations stem from the illegal drug trade used as an employment option for those locked out of the mainstream workforce for a host of reasons ranging from lack of education to racism.

Some important insights can be drawn from the narratives of the suburban parents I interviewed. Most had an employment history (cf. Edin and Lein 1997), they are hardworking, and they experienced insecurity in the flexible labor force. Their nonstandard employment was part-time, temporary, and seasonal; they lacked union protections and workplace supports; their hours were irregular and wanting; and their wages were insufficient and eroded over time. The insecurity of the workplace extended to women in middle-income jobs who, for a variety of reasons, experienced such a financial decline that they resorted to TANF and other aid.

The working parents are integral to the so-called flexible labor force, yet for them it is quite inflexible. Their stories convincingly illustrate that flexibility suits the employer, whereas it is often detrimental to the employee. Employers' flexible labor practices significantly contributed to employees' labor market insecurity, often resulting in unemployment. Employees often took pride in their ability to exhibit flexibility on the job. Yet employers often did not reciprocate when employees needed schedule flexibility in order to handle emergencies or personal issues. Inflexible labor is quite incompatible with the child-care and elder caregiving responsibilities of working-class parents. When this incompatibility cannot be reconciled, unemployment is often the upshot. For many low-wage workers, temporary or agency work has become an option because of the recent labor market trend of outsourced and temporary staffing. While agency work is a source for employment, it is an unsteady one.

Some of the low-paid jobs that had "very favorable" employment prospects are those that are integral to the workfare strategy (New York State Department of Labor 2006). The training is short term for some of these occupations, and, more significantly, poor people's labor is often mandated to fill local labor demands through workfare programs. Home health aide is one such occupation. This and other caregiving occupations, integral to the gender-segregated labor market, are generally dominated by women and typically performed in the domestic sphere; wages are low and work is demanding, often physical. As illustrated, many of the jobs do not pay wages that meet the self-sufficiency standards for New York (Pearce with Brooks 2000; Pearce 2004). Furthermore, even when workers are able to support their families from month to month and perhaps even accumulate savings, their reserves are generally inadequate in the face of financial emergencies. Responsible working parents who cannot earn enough to make a living, let alone accrue a sufficient personal economic safety net, experience the failure of the labor market. For many people nationwide who need continuous TANF aid, the U.S. government eventually also fails them when they are cast from the federal welfare system. The ideology of personal responsibility and self-sufficiency through work and the "success" rhetoric of policy makers and others who support neoliberal workfare strategies obscure the reality of the labor market.

7

Work First, Workfare, and Education

Work: A First Priority

Personal responsibility, self-sufficiency, and work-first ideologies are manifested in federal and state welfare legislation, policies, language, bureaucrats' attitudes, workfare requirements, and even welfare office decor. In a New York DSS Service Center, framed posters on the waiting room walls inscribe an ideology of personal responsibility in English and Spanish. One read: "Self-sufficiency. Temporary Assistance for Permanent Change. Believe that you can do it." New York State's Temporary Assistance program embraces a work-first principle and expects that recipients "will consider work their first priority and will view work as the goal of the program, regardless of the number of barriers the individual and family may have to overcome to attain that goal" (New York State Office of Temporary and Disability Assistance 2000:5). Employment is considered the best way to achieve self-sufficiency.

Nationwide, the work-first principle is backed by federal mandatory work requirements. Recall that states are obligated to meet federal work participation rates and must ensure that recipients of TANF work or participate in work activities. Fifty percent of all families are required to engage in work-related activities; single parents must participate at least thirty hours per week, twenty hours if a child is under six. Ninety percent of two-parent families must engage in work activities for a combined average of at least thirty-five hours per week; fifty-five if they receive federally funded child care. Some of the activities that count toward work participation are employment, work experience, and job search and job readiness assistance. Some others include on-the-job training, vocational educational training, and job skills training directly related to employment.[1] Since the 1996 welfare law, access to education and educational options have diminished and restrictions have worsened. Essentially, employment, even if unsustainable, has taken precedence over education. Recipients are expected to seek employment and accept a job when offered. TANF recipients' access to education is severely hampered by work-first pressures, the limited options that count toward fulfilling mandated work requirements, welfare program approval, and funding earmarked for specific education (cf. Polakow et al. 2004). The number of TANF recipients participating in allowable education and training that would lead to employment advancement is low in most states. For example, in fiscal year 2004 in New York State, of the recipients who were counted as working, only 13 percent were enrolled in vocational training (lower than the 15 percent national average) and fewer than 1 percent were enrolled in job skills training. Yet the state is permitted to place 30 percent of all families (that count toward its 50 percent participation rate) in vocational educational activities (Renwick 2006). But even that is not enough.

Although some people I interviewed were offered different types of job training, others approached their DSS caseworkers about educational options and had been dissuaded, flatly denied, or threatened with a sanction if they attended a nonapproved program. When Roseanne Tate received TANF in the aftermath of her financial decline, she was refused the training that she requested. After a decade-long hiatus from the labor force while she raised her children, she began a job search but lacked the confidence she had years earlier while working as a secretary. She knew computer basics but did not know if her skills were up to par. She felt that the free, basic computer classes offered to her were inadequate for her needs and requested more advanced training. Her caseworker felt otherwise and did not approve the training, claiming that she would acquire the skills on the job.

Mercedes Montgomery went back to college after she lost her airline industry job. When she subsequently slid into financial decline, she applied for public assistance. She recalled that during that time she was "offered no kind of vocational or educational training whatsoever." Mercedes thought that a person could not be in school while receiving welfare benefits and she feared repercussions.

> A lot of women I was with, including myself, had to hide the fact they were going to school at night. Or pursuing an education. Because that would be used against them. You can't do that, you can't be in school. . . . No, I never

told anyone. I kept it a total secret. So here I was, this woman learning about gender oppression and cultural oppression in school and, at the same time, experiencing it in the day. It was very interesting.

Anita Ramos, who earlier described her insecure labor as a home health aide, had some thoughts about the lack of education alternatives and the work-first principle in the PRWORA era:

> I think welfare has changed because they no longer give you the help that you need for [people] like me. Dropping out in the sixth grade, I don't have a high school diploma. They never push you to get your education to like stay off of DSS. Sometimes I feel like they always want to keep you on. Which is bad. They never gave me the opportunity to go into a training program. They always wanted me to go back to work. And every time I went back to work, it was always a job that I really didn't want to do.

Carissa Simone, a longtime welfare recipient who lacked a work history in the formal economy, said, "I always expected for welfare to send me to go get a trade or send me to school for anything. And they never did that." It is not clear whether Carissa asked about educational options. But having completed the tenth grade, Carissa could have benefited from high school equivalency education, as could many of the others who had limited education.

Some people did not know about allowable training activities that could count toward a work requirement because they were misinformed, misdirected, or not told by welfare caseworkers (cf. Kahn and Polakow 2002). It was Nellie Blake's therapist who told her about the ten-week child-care training that she attended. Shayleen Vaughn received literature from an academic institution about its free certificate program targeted to people on public assistance. She figured the institution received her name from DSS but recalled that no caseworkers counseled her. She said, "Nobody sat down and talked to me and told me, 'Well, we'll help you with this, we'll help you with that.' I had to go on hearsay, you know." At first she was not interested in the program but changed her mind after "seeing a lot of girls that I grew up with . . . saying, 'Oh, it works.' And then you get funding from here; you get funding from there. . . . There's a lot of things out there but they're [DSS] not gonna tell you. You got to really get into it and find it out yourself." Shayleen elaborated:

They [DSS] tell you whether you're eligible for that [welfare grant] or whatever shelter they're gonna send you to. They don't tell you about none of the programs that you can use to better yourself. All they tell you is that you have sixty months. You know what I'm saying? So you better get on with whatever you're gonna do. Me, personally, I don't want to work in a fucking [drug store]. I don't want to work in a dead-end job. I'm not gonna be bagging anybody's groceries because I know I'm smarter than that. So I'm going for the gusto. You know, forget the shelter. So that's why I enrolled in it. Basically I'm trying to move forward.

When we met for a second time, Shayleen's studies in the ADVANCE program were well under way.

Many of the people I interviewed were also kept in the dark about rule changes pertaining to education. One was a New York State law favorable to students receiving public assistance that had been in effect since 2000. The law required "that certain work study and internships shall be counted toward a client's work activity requirements and that districts shall make reasonable efforts to ensure other work activity assignments do not conflict with the student's academic schedule" (New York State Senate 2004; see also New York State Assembly 2004). The legislation resulted from a grassroots initiative spearheaded by the Welfare Rights Initiative within Hunter College of the City University of New York in response to the dramatic drop in university enrollment following the strict workfare initiative under welfare reform legislation (see Loffredo 2001). However, based on my queries, information about the Work-Study and Internship Law seems not to have been well disseminated. In fact, I gave the particulars to a few women who were enrolled in college or eager to learn about their educational options. None recalled being informed. Anna Moreno assertively said her caseworker "never" told her about it when she was a student and was mandated to work. That was unfortunate because it would have been applicable in her situation when she worked at an internship in college.

Anna is a Puerto Rican woman in her late twenties. When she was fifteen, she dropped out of high school. She had two children while in her teens. After she had her second child, she was still living at home in a two-bedroom apartment with many others. To alleviate the overcrowding, she moved into a shelter and then into Section 8 housing. In her late teens she began working; this became imperative when her husband was incarcerated. Initially she worked as a cashier making $4.25 per hour; she relied on welfare and other public assistance to supplement that wage. At a subsequent job where she worked on an assembly line, she learned accounting skills and rose to head bookkeeper after telling management, "I can do more than this; come on, give me a break, give me a try. . . . I'm a fast learner." Anna changed jobs a few times. While she was working as an accounting clerk making $13.50 per hour, she enrolled in a bachelor's degree program majoring in social work. When she lost that job, she relied on unemployment insurance until the benefits expired. Then she applied for TANF and food stamps because she ran out of money. During her first meeting at the welfare office, she recollected that her caseworker said, "Well, if you get accepted and you get approved, you're gonna have to go to work." Anna continued,

> I tried to explain to him that I was working on my bachelor's. And at
> the time I was doing an internship. . . . I told him, there's no way I can
> participate in the work program if I'm doing an internship. He said, "Well,
> go to school at night." And I said, "The internship is three days a week, nine
> to five, and I have classes two days a week so that's the whole week." And
> I told him the internship placement has to be during the day. He was nice
> enough in that he told me that he understood and he commended me for
> going to school and trying to pursue my education, but it wasn't up to him.

The caseworker instructed Anna to return to the welfare office a week or so later and told her that the application processes would cease if she did not make the appointment. In order to comply she missed one of her classes to attend an orientation where she joined a group of people who were directed to a computer and told, "Look on the Internet and just find a job. Apply." Anna recalled that the facilitator told the group, "I expect you guys to be here four days a week, Monday through Thursday from nine to four." She remembered her confrontation.

> I raised my hand, I said, "Well, I'm in school and I intern" and so and so
> and so. I gave her a rundown on my situation. And she was like, "Basically
> that's not my problem. I have nothing to do with that. I'm just running this
> here workshop." And she said, "If you don't come in, your benefits will be
> discontinued." I just got up and left. I didn't even wait for her to finish up. I
> said, "You know what? I'm in school. . . . I'm not dropping out of school for
> nobody." And I just stormed out of there. I walked out. And that was it. And

> I received a letter saying that because I refused to participate in the program, . . . that my application would be discontinued.

The irony of Anna's situation vis-à-vis the work-first ideology was that she *was* working. It was unpaid labor three days a week during her senior-year internship placement.

Anna's application was ultimately approved. She does not know what swayed the decision—the promise by her caseworker to speak to his supervisor to see what he could do, or, as she said, maybe she "fell through the cracks somehow." For ten months Anna received approximately $320 monthly TANF cash for her and her three children. But she received a subsequent letter saying that if she did not participate in the workfare program, her benefits would be discontinued. Looking back, Anna said she "was really afraid, 'cause I knew I was always in danger. I felt like . . . the following month I was gonna have no benefits. That was pretty scary." If Anna had been told about the New York Work-Study and Internship Law, and her internship hours had been applied to her workfare requirements, she probably could have avoided this angst-ridden ordeal.

When her internship ended, Anna remained on the job for a short period earning $15.00 per hour, but her welfare benefits and food stamps were discontinued. Then, she went on to a master's program in social work. Anna worked hard and struggled to raise her family on little. If she had not received TANF and other public assistance, she might not have graduated, or not graduated when she did, precluding her acceptance into an accelerated graduate school program at a prestigious university. Compared to her other jobs, as a social worker, Anna will have a far greater chance to raise her family with independent means and to help others in need.

Parents' pursuits of and access to education are influenced by career aspirations and their current level of education. They are limited by their assets, debt obligations, financial aid, public policy, time, energy, child care, transportation, and the imperative to work (whether mandated or by choice). Of the forty-two people interviewed, Anna was one of the seven who have a college degree. Ten other women have some college, ranging from a single class to senior status. But many were educationally disadvantaged and thus experienced wage erosion and have dismal future earnings potential in the low-wage labor market. Thirteen women only have a high school diploma or General Educational Development (GED) equivalency. Twelve women did not complete secondary education. Of those, two did not finish grade school. Some completed training in areas such as computer, secretarial, word processing, cashier, home health aide, nurse's aide, electrocardiogram, and phlebotomy. Some paid for training themselves, and others attended the training through a workfare or other state-financed program.

Some women had educational and career aspirations that they were exploring or actually pursuing—obstetrics and gynecology, media studies, physician's assistant, and penning a book. Some strongly desired an education for careers in social work, psychotherapy, and accounting. A few women had ambitions—such as a career as a physical therapist or marine biologist—but figured those were dreams that would go unfulfilled, requiring major investments of time and finances, which they lacked. Others merely desired a high school equivalency diploma or to complete a degree so as to increase their marketability and earnings potential. Some had modest goals that would not yield high incomes—to become a nurse's aide, "get into computers," or work in some caring capacity with children or the elderly. Nonetheless, a common aim was self-improvement, as reflected in the oft-used term to "better myself." People unequivocally recognized the value of education for themselves and their children. A twenty-eight-year-old black mother of five children said, "I want to get my GED. Basically because I try to instill in my kids how important school is." This sentiment was elucidated in Jones's research (1993). He observed a "culture of achievement" among the majority of poor parents in a Head Start program who attempted to instill values and attitudes in their children that would help them to succeed despite myriad obstacles common among impoverished families. Yet, recipients of welfare face many barriers to education, including today's welfare policies that emphasize work first.

Workfare Experiences

During their time on welfare the majority of the parents that I interviewed participated in workfare, some of which spanned the AFDC and TANF periods. Some people presumably escaped workfare because of an exemption, such as having a child under a certain age, domestic violence, or disability. Workfare encompasses a range of mandated work activities. One form is a work assignment in which an individual works without compensation in exchange for welfare benefits. A few parents found this appalling, likening it to "sharecropping" and "free labor," or thought it absurd when it paid the equivalent of a welfare grant (see Boris 1999). Laney Heath gives her assessment of this type of workfare.

> They are sweep-the-street programs. They're clean up my kitchen programs at the nursing homes. They're programs like that. And you don't even wanna go. You know that if you don't go, you won't get your benefits. . . . So it keeps you going. But you get no other incentive. . . . These places, they're short budgeted. If you would want to stay, they really can't pick you up [hire you]. But they need the help too. So you are helping them, but you're not getting any help.

Another type of workfare is a welfare-to-work program. Thirty-two of the forty-two parents were required to attend some variation that included short-term job search and job readiness assistance programs, job skills training, or a program designed for welfare recipients at an academic institution. People had various opinions and experiences, depending on the type of program, tasks required, staff, regulations, hassles, and their education and work history. From people's descriptions it appears that the most common workfare programs that they engaged in were short-term (usually six weeks) job search and job readiness assistance programs. Some liked the program, considered the program to be useful in general, or believed it practical for others but not themselves. Some thought their experience to be futile or an unproductive use of time. A few complained that they were merely given a newspaper section with classified advertisements and a phone book and told to make "cold calls." Several found a job during the time they were in a program, yet some of them thought that they would have found employment regardless.

People described programs administered by state and nonstate agencies contracted by the state or county; they were cognizant of sanctions that would be imposed if they did not attend. The short-term job search program assumes the availability of jobs and that one can find employment during that period; many did not find jobs during their first program and were assigned to another. The insecure labor market was not implicated in people's unemployment. Instead the blame was often directed to the individuals, sometimes in a demeaning fashion. Some of the resounding criticisms were the lack of available jobs and the pressure to find one. People wanted an employment service that matched their skills to occupations and provided leads for suitable jobs. Lorna Webster, Sandee Staton, Chandra Alexander, and Shayleen Vaughn told about their programs.

Lorna remembered the TANF workfare mandates imposed on her. About two months after the birth of her second son, she received a letter from the welfare agency regarding work eligibility. She subsequently met with a caseworker with her résumé in hand and recalled their conversation: "I know I am able to work. But I just had a baby. And I had a cesarean. So I need time to heal. And they're like, 'Well, we can only give you like four weeks and then you have to get back out there and you have to find a job.'" Lorna attended the job search program, but it did not meet her expectations. She thought the program was ill suited for her particular needs and that it was a waste of time. She was also critical of the overall failure of the labor market, caseworkers' condescending attitudes, and their failure to supply her with tangible employment leads.

> I mean it got to the point where I was really pissed off about it. Because just imagine eighteen people in the room. One person in a suit and tie, clean cut, telling you, "You can get a job, you just don't have the skills, you just don't have the tools." I've had jobs all my life. Don't tell me what I don't have. Give me leads. Don't give me lectures. . . . But they don't do that. They want you to sit there and listen to their lectures and play these little interview games. I mean don't get me wrong 'cause [for] somebody who's never had a job, it's a start, it's a jump off. But for me, I've been there, I've done that, I know how to get a job. Tell me where they're hiring, don't tell me I need to go get a job. Give me papers saying, "Well, these six places are hiring, go fill out applications." Out of those six, I guarantee three would be calling me back because I'm a good worker. I have letters of recommendations that you wouldn't believe. . . . Just from reading the letters you would hire me. But they're telling me, "Oh no, why don't you have a job now?" "Because the economy is screwed up, you retard." That's why I don't have a job. But to them, it's like nobody gets a job because nobody's able, or you're not capable of getting one. They make you feel like you are less than what you are.

On a subsequent occasion Lorna was assigned to another work search program. Her search for full-time employment was self-motivated and diligent, and she complied with program requirements in order to avoid a sanction. Lorna took advantage of the bus passes and clothing allowance that were program benefits. She said that the latter "wasn't a lot," but she was able to purchase about "eight outfits." However, her lament was similar to that made about the first program—she wanted solid leads to pursue. She said,

> Because with the program, I was doing my own thing, really; . . . sign the sign-in sheet, snatch up some papers, make a couple of phone calls and leave. I already had my week set though. So basically I just went there so I wouldn't get cut off so it would look like I was really trying to work with their program. But what they have you doing is insane. It's insane. They have you looking through the phone book, calling places out of the phone book. . . . If you're gonna call yourself an employment center, you should have places that are ready to employ. . . . Help me become employed, don't help me do the things that I'm already doing on my own that I don't need you for. That's a waste of time. . . . Doing all this crap that we already know what to do. If we didn't, we wouldn't have a résumé. If we didn't, we wouldn't have a work history. Get us leads. . . . That's all I want.

Some other women had experiences with multiple job search and readiness programs over time. Sandee Staton, a mother of three in her thirties, has a work history extending back to her teen years. During a nine-year gap she raised her children, and she took secretarial courses at a local college. Sandee returned to work in the late 1990s when her youngest was about a year old. For many of her working years she relied on public assistance. Although she tried to get off, something unforeseen happened that required her to lean back on social services.

Over the years Sandee was assigned to four programs. Therefore she was duly qualified to make an informed assessment. She thought that for her, the programs were inappropriate and inadequate. Sandee said, "When they started the reform, it was better because they helped you in the work program, helping you try to get a job. But for some of us, it didn't help us. It just ended us back in another work program, another work program doing the same thing." She remembered telling the job counselors that she had her résumé and had work knowledge and experience. She explained to them, "All I needed was a job. I don't need the program." Sandee did not believe she needed help writing a résumé, training on how to conduct herself on an interview, or advice on where to go to buy clothing for the job search. Yet, she admitted that she picked up some useful tips watching films on mock interviews. And, in the last program she made use of the facility's computers and databases for her job search.

Chandra Alexander, who is in her early twenties, was mandated twice to attend a job search program. She "liked the program a lot, a great deal." Her work history included a five-month stint as a supermarket cashier in her high school years. During the height of a tax season she worked as a receptionist and secretary at a tax service firm. For about six months she was employed as a cashier and usher at a local movie theater. When Chandra attended the first six-week welfare-to-work program in the early 2000s, she had not worked in a year. She had had a baby in the year before. Although she felt confident about writing a résumé, she took a workshop in order to improve upon hers. She found the PowerPoint and Excel classes to be helpful, especially since she was looking for a secretarial or reception position in which it was likely that she would use computers. Throughout the first six-week program Chandra applied for about thirty secretary, receptionist, retail store sales representative, and cashier positions. She said she went "everywhere"—Best Buy, Circuit City, Victoria's Secret, Target, and various stores at the Galleria, an urban mall. No one called her back. Feeling very qualified initially, the search left her discouraged and unemployed. About a year and a half later she was mandated to another job program. Her job search was a repeat of the first; so was the outcome.

Shayleen Vaughn spoke about being in a mandated welfare-to-work program after she was released from prison and living in a shelter for single women.

> And they sent me to [nonstate agency]. That was supposed to be getting you ready for the workplace, learning how to do a résumé. . . . They would give you a long-ass sheet with like twenty dots. Somehow you gotta go and you gotta fill out all these applications. . . . Where though!? There's nowhere that's accepting work. You see some places say they're hiring. Then you go in there, you go fill out the application, and then that's one. Meanwhile you gotta find nineteen other ones for this month.

Shayleen was not given leads. She said, "They were trying to tell me how to do a résumé and all this shit. I already worked, so like man, forget this, unless they send me to a work site then I'm not really gonna do it. And then I went AWOL. So I didn't really care." She further explained:

> And I'm like, I'm trying to tell these motherfuckers that I'm pregnant, like, you know what I'm saying. And they're telling me that unless you are seven months pregnant, that you have to go to [the workfare program]

still. I believe it was like either five or seven months. And I'm like, "No, I don't want to go work, cause I'm like sick, I'm getting sick." I'm throwing up and doing all this shit. And they're making me do all that. . . . I had a miscarriage.

Many people recognized the benefits of the programs for others, but not necessarily for themselves. Some benefited from skills training, the use of a technology-equipped employment center, transportation and clothing allowances, and child-care subsidies. However, the services come with strings attached—governance by the state and private agencies, through surveillance, discipline, and sanctions. Workfare in any form is a type of coercion. While unsatisfied "customers" can exercise choice and leave the program, many parents are coerced into complying. Parents risk forfeiting benefits essential for their families. Moreover, the overriding theme among the four women's stories is that each wanted more from the workfare program—a job. Indeed, each had some work experience and felt they knew how to write a résumé. They were generally frustrated by the push into what they perceived as a lackluster labor market. And their qualifications and searches were aimed toward the low-wage service sector where they would have little opportunity for career and salary advancement. Some women's narratives reveal the contradictions in the messages they received in the workfare programs. Lorna heard, "You just don't have the skills, you just don't have the tools." The focus is on the deficits of the individual. There is a lack of consideration for systemic issues that create significant obstacles to employment in the core sector and sustained economic independence.

Additionally, several people completed job skills training or vocational training. Some of the programs they described as being approved generally fell into the areas of remedial education, high school equivalency training, and job skills training. Some programs include "soft skills" training; soft skills are associated with personal traits and nontechnical skills. Some of the vocational classes that people attended sought to train people as health care aides, office workers, and child-care workers. The approved classes seem to be geared mostly toward the demands of the local, low-paid flexible labor market. Under the workfare model, it is an individual's personal responsibility to be self-sufficient, but the short-term job search and job readiness programs and the job skills programs are not enough to help workers realize that aim. Even if a program led to employment, economic independence was wanting.

Postsecondary Education

For most parents, their lack of higher education credentials is a barrier to those jobs that pay a self-sufficiency wage. Several women whom I interviewed wanted to attend or go back to college to enhance their career and earnings potential. Four of the seven college graduates earned a degree before the 1996 welfare legislation, a time when some states actually encouraged recipients to enroll in college. In the pre-PRWORA era, under the Job Opportunities and Basic Skills Training program created in 1988, states promoted access to higher education for recipients of AFDC; postsecondary education could include two- and four-year college programs as a job training option. Today, postsecondary education can count as a work activity, but recipients of welfare desiring a college education are thwarted by the work-first ideology and severe restrictions. Following PRWORA, states had flexibility within federal guidelines to design the types and duration of allowable educational and training programs that count toward TANF work participation. All but one state allowed some form of postsecondary education, though their strategies allowing TANF recipients access to education ranged from permitting enrollment in short-term vocational programs to support for students in four-year degree programs.[2] Rules varied nationwide. Significantly, most states imposed restrictions and requirements. Some states limited postsecondary education that would count as a work activity to a short duration (e.g., six, twelve, or twenty-four months). Most states required that a degree program lead to employment and that the student combine education with other work activities (e.g., unsubsidized employment), maintain a certain grade point average, make satisfactory progress, and finish the program within a specified time (Center for Women Policy Studies 2002). The latter is a challenge because low-skill and low-income students take longer to complete basic education, skills training, and degree programs (Center for Women Policy Studies 2004; Martinson and Strawn 2002). Assuming approval for a postsecondary educational program, the demands of employment and other workfare requirements, coursework, and homework, on top of household and family caregiving responsibilities and obtaining child care, can be overwhelming for a poor parent receiving welfare. Moreover, absent financial aid, the cost of tuition is prohibitive.

Multiple demands on poor parents are not only a deterrent to enrollment but can also contribute to college dropout rates. In fact, since PRWORA, TANF recipients' college participation rates plunged nationwide (Center for Women Policy Studies 2002). In New York for example, from 1996 to 1999 City University of New York enrollment among students who received public assistance dropped from approximately twenty-seven thousand to about ten thousand (Price et al. 2003:20). The restriction on education under TANF is yet another example of how things are "way stricter and harder" *after* the 1996 legislation.

Students' Experiences

Ruth Jenkes, Vanessa Geller, Desmond Hughes, and Alice Finnegan attended college in a comparatively supportive environment within which they earned a degree *before* PRWORA legislation. They received welfare benefits while attending college and *did not* have to strictly comply with mandated work requirements. Ruth Jenkes voluntarily participated in a workfare program while she was attending college. She recalled that the workfare program was not mandatory and her workfare experience counted toward college credits. And she was able to receive child care for her two-year-old son. To help pay for her education she had grants and also earned income at a part-time job. But she needed AFDC to augment her salary; she also needed Medicaid. Ruth earned a bachelor of arts degree in business in the early 1980s. Vanessa Geller said she obtained student loans for an associate's degree program, which helped because "otherwise I wouldn't really have had money to eat, money to go to school or anything." She also received food stamps and cash, which was "barely enough to get by." She remembered that she had to push for herself and learn from other recipients about entitlements because most of the caseworkers would not volunteer the information. When I asked whether the caseworkers were supportive of her academic efforts, she recalled that they were basically neutral. She said, "The workers I guess they were just leaving me alone 'cause I was in school. They were just like, 'Oh well, she's going, she's trying, just leave her alone.' You know. That's basically what I remember." She also recalled receiving transportation money for school. At some point Vanessa began full-time employment in a government job where she worked for about seven years. When she began working, she quit school because the work hours interfered with school and her courses were not offered at opportune times. Nonetheless, Vanessa eventually finished her AAS and went on to earn a BA and MA.

Desmond Hughes began his college education in the late 1970s, which he financed with the aid of Pell and TAP education grants that he had to "stretch as far as possible." He received public assistance and recalled that the welfare agency "didn't have any problem with a person who was striving or trying to move ahead and on welfare and going to college also." In the early 1980s he was incarcerated for a little more than a year during which time he was selected to enroll in a college program that held classes in a state prison. Nine months into his jail term he was allowed school-release whereby he attended classes on the college campus. After his prison release, he was able to continue college until he graduated about a year later. However, finding it difficult to secure work after his incarceration, Desmond had to rely on public assistance.

Several women attended postsecondary education workfare programs administered by academic institutions in partnership with DSS. These programs changed over the years in response to welfare reform legislation. One such program was the Learn Then Earn program.[3] A program representative told me that when the program began it emphasized academics, but because of welfare reform it has since pulled back on education and now focuses on "training, training, training." She acknowledged that this was a disadvantage to students because they need an education; but they also need jobs, so it is now a training program. Undoubtedly the program is influenced by the "work first" principle; hence, the "training" is focused primarily on preparing for employment. Because the overall program receives funding from a block grant and is contracted through DSS, it is accountable for specific measures such as recruitment, retention, and upgrades. The representative said that the latter is any "positive movement" of students in the workforce. This ranges from employment or additional employment hours to a salary increase.

Another New York academic institution offered the ADVANCE program to recipients of welfare; it spanned the AFDC and TANF years. After welfare reform legislation, the main program offering was downgraded from a two-year associate's degree program to a one-year certificate program. Alice Finnegan and Shayleen Vaughn attended the program more than a decade apart and describe their experiences.

Alice Finnegan recalled that she received a letter from DSS in the early nineties, *before* PRWORA. She said the letter stated, "Either find a job or you can take this assessment test to go to school. There's a program that's available, or something about there's money available for you to go to school." She remembered choosing between at least two colleges and a variety of programs such as nursing, water abatement, and X-ray technician. She chose the ADVANCE program, a two-year associate's degree program designed for welfare recipients. Students continued receiving public assistance benefits while enrolled. The classes were scheduled around children's school hours; during the summer the state paid for child care. Alice majored in office technology and took the required academic subjects, such as English literature, social studies, European history, and myriad computer courses. In addition to the academic and vocational classes, the students were prepared for entering the work world. An entrepreneurial course, geared to women starting their own businesses, covered such topics as bookkeeping, marketing, and securing start-up funds. Representatives from local businesses periodically addressed specific topics. Alice recalled that college was a transforming experience.

[Before entering the program] some of these girls couldn't even spell and they had high school diplomas. They couldn't write a paper. They didn't know how to type. We all learned how to type. I didn't know how to type when I got there. That was our first class, to learn how to type. Once you learned how to type, the doors were wide open. And just like I said, the self-esteem aspect, I'm getting emotional thinking about it because it was such a good experience. And now, it was such a hard experience. Did we cry and have breakdowns! I was home typing papers until 3:30 in the morning and I had two little kids. And it was a hard time. But it was so worth it in the end. I didn't want to leave. . . . You felt like you were smart. You felt like you were doing something for your kids. You were getting an education so you could get a better job. . . .

We used to have a ball, I mean laugh. Definitely we had a lot in common. White or black it didn't matter because we all struggled. And we all were married to jackasses that didn't take care of us. You know, unfortunately, we all made bad choices. And so we all came from the same boat, we all struggled. . . .

I mean that was like the greatest experience in my life. Because being on welfare all those years and not really going anywhere personally and everything and really feeling like I'm doing everything for everybody else. You know, 'cause I had two kids and was taking care of my mother, taking care of everybody. And going to school gave me an opportunity, really my self-esteem really, really raised that time. . . . So there was only a handful of white people, otherwise it was Spanish and black. And I graduated with distinction. You know, a couple people graduated with honors, I didn't. But I did graduate with distinction, so that was really, a really good experience. I love school. I really did. And I did well in it.

Alice graduated, earning an associate of science degree. Cognizant of the benefits of the program, Alice offered a concrete suggestion to policy makers: "have people go to school," that is, offer an academic or vocational degree program for people on welfare.

For Alice, a career after college was halted by the rearing of a third child, and she has been plagued by back problems that limit the type of employment she chooses. Yet, Alice has worked and has not received TANF for a few years, but recently had to apply for food stamps. However, having an associate's degree, rather than merely a high school education, gives Alice an advantage in the labor market. It was also a springboard and incentive to continue her education. When we met, she applied to a local college and felt confident that her forty credits would be transferred.

Shayleen Vaughn attended the ADVANCE program in the PRWORA era slightly more than a decade after Alice. By this time the program had changed in response to welfare reform. When we met for a follow-up interview, Shayleen was in her fourth semester of the one-year certificate program and had earned a high grade point average in the previous three. She described some of the courses.

> *SV:* All right, my first semester I took a technology seminar, which was they teach you how to basically fiddle around with Microsoft Word. You learn how to edit documents, all kinds of stuff. Language Seminar, that's writing. I wrote a persuasive essay; my persuasive was on medicinal marijuana. And I got an A on it. . . . College Prep Seminar. It's basically teaching you procedures of going to school. How to take notes. You know, sometimes you gotta take a recorder to class. You gotta learn how to deal with your professors 'cause they're all different. Like everybody's teaching style is different. I've got Keyboarding. [And a computer course]. That was good too.
>
> *TL:* What's that about?
>
> *SV:* Basically for people who are not computer literate. It teaches you how to save, how to print, real cut and paste, basic shit. You know what I'm saying? But it's really good for people who don't know 'cause you'd be surprised how many people are not into the whole computer revolution.

TL: Were you bored with that, because you knew all that?

SV: Yes.

TL: So how did you deal with that boredom?

SV: How did I deal with that? The first marking period I excelled in everything and I got straight As. But I was bored. I was like, "Man, this is shitty." The only thing that's helping me is Language Seminar because I like to write. So the professor was helping me with my writing and everything. You know, putting things together. But I just said to myself, "maybe it will get harder," and it certainly did. . . . But after that I also did a poetry thing and I did it on Robert Frost. Now, . . . you never know how many things fly over your head until you get the knowledge and it's like, "Whoo, I know that." And I'm so proud to be able to say, "I know that."

After she briefed me on a variety of courses, I asked Shayleen what some of the most useful classes were.

SV: The writing class, the keyboarding class, the employment preparation, and all of the business kind of classes, you know, where you're learning the professional jargon. Those are the concrete ones that I like. Also now I'm learning how to deal with Excel, Microsoft Excel. And I've been knowing about it, but it's good to just get in there and really, really learn how to do it. You know, with the formulas and things like that. 'Cause that's what employers are looking for. So it's definitely, I would recommend it for anyone. But you know, you've gotta have drive. If not, it's gonna drive you up a wall and you're gonna be like, "Forget it."

TL: You seem like you have overdrive.

SV: Yeah, 'cause I'm an overachiever.

Shayleen's comments were less enthusiastic when she described parts of the curriculum that seemingly aimed at modifying an individual's behavior. She described a workshop series:

SV: It's about basically teaching you how to deal with your children. 'Cause you know we all mostly got little babies and stuff. 'Cause my son is unruly. He's, whew [*laugh*]. He fights and everything and he's only thirteen, fourteen months.

TL: Is it like a parenting class?

SV: Yeah. Basically.

TL: So what do they teach you?

SV: They teach you how not to hit your kids. How to deal with the pressures, like how to deal with them when they get fussy. You know, do you get fussy or do you try to help them. They help you with trying to nurture your kids. There's a lot of stuff that we do subconsciously, that we do without really noticing that it can change your kid. Things that you do and that some of them things I didn't know. Like the way that you deal with anger, your kid will learn how to deal with anger because of what they see you do. That I really don't like it because I feel that I could be getting something else. . . . I really want to look into web design so [the parenting workshop] is like pissing me off [*laugh*]. We got Nonviolent Communications. That's a workshop where we're reading a book and it's kinda good 'cause I do need to learn how to disagree without being offensive. You know, that's something that we definitely don't come programmed with already. We come into the world not knowing how to deal with people all the time, how to deal with our anger and to have compassion.

TL: That's a whole class called Nonviolent Communications?

SV: Yep, we gotta book and we gotta read a chapter and do papers. Ahhh [*exasperated*]. I feel we can get rid of that too. . . . Then we had Business Communications. That class was useless. Oh, I think it was just the professor [*laugh*].

TL: So what was Business Communications?

SV: Basically we were learning how to write memos. She'd give us a memo where somebody was clearly out of their mind writing, you know, in all caps with fucking exclamation points, like they're yelling at you. And you gotta exercise your nonviolent communication [*raises her voice*] and put it in a way that's not gonna be offensive, things like that.

Shayleen said that she "learned so much. It fascinates me." I asked how she thought the training would affect her future. She replied, "It's gonna affect my future in a major way, in a major positive way 'cause it's getting me ready to work in the corporate world. You know, you don't wanna be going into nothing blind. Plus you got that paper saying, 'Oh, we're behind you.' [The academic institution] is behind me. They're saying that I'm good; you know? So why wouldn't they want to hire me?" After commenting to Shayleen that it sounded like she had a positive response to the program, she said, "There's nothing bad that I could say about it. It's a good program." Shayleen ends the program with a six-week internship followed by a six-week job search.

Shayleen's school hours fulfilled all but eight hours of her weekly welfare work obligation. She said, "They're [DSS] saying I have eight unaccountable hours," therefore she has to comply with an "employment thing." She was mandated to engage in a work activity in which she took an aptitude test and received multiple packets of "useless information." From those, she said she has to complete assignments "otherwise they'll start fiddling with your fucking benefits. And I just can't afford that." Shayleen viewed this ongoing task as "a major pain" because she does not have the eight hours for that charge. After a full day at school she picks up her son, James, from daycare, comes home and tidies up, makes dinner, has play time with her son and his "daddy," and bathes James before putting him to bed. After that she begins her homework because she wants to get as much out of the program as she can, striving for straight As.

Both Alice and Shayleen seemed hungry for knowledge and were enthusiastic about the ADVANCE program because it afforded them a chance to learn and excel in an academic environment and boost their self-esteem. The differences in the program influenced their experience and outcome. Alice was able to choose a degree program from an array of colleges and degree programs, whereas Shayleen's choices were limited. Both had computer technology courses, but it appears that Alice's curriculum had more of an academic focus since it was longer and was a degree program. Alice's curriculum included entrepreneurial courses geared toward the empowerment of women in the workplace. In the personal responsibility and self-help era, Shayleen described what seems to be a parenting class that focused on behavior modification based on middle-class norms. Importantly, because Shayleen's school hours were not enough to meet her welfare work activity obligation, she was assigned a workfare task by DSS that she felt pressure to comply with to avoid a sanction. It is not yet clear whether the ADVANCE program will help launch Shayleen into a career in corporate America, but she was enthusiastic and felt confident that the academic institution's name will enhance her résumé.

The Value of Academic Credentials

Education alone cannot safeguard against periodic financial decline or persistent poverty spurred or exacerbated by personal crises, physical and emotional hindrances, caregiving priorities, flexible labor practices, insecure labor, wrong turns, and a host of other pressures that prevent people from finding and maintaining employment or keep them trapped in low-wage employment. We have seen that Desmond's work history in the formal economy was irregular. Having had much difficulty finding work, he resorted to the illegal drug trade. Consequently, this resulted in multiple incarcerations. Ruminating about some job prospects, he thought that in some instances employers were reluctant to hire him for entry-level jobs because he was "over qualified." It is not clear to what extent Desmond was passed over because of his criminal justice record and racism. Likewise, Ruth Jenkes's career never fully took off after she graduated from college. She worked as a "Gal Friday" in the media industry, but then became "actively addicted" when crack "hit like a tornado" in the mid- to late 1980s. At some point she was incarcerated. However, with the aid of AFDC and other public assistance benefits, as well as postincarceration services designed to give women a "second chance," Ruth obtained residential, counseling, drug treatment, financial, and transportation services. Ruth recovered but had some prolonged periods of unemployment, especially after her incarceration. Her checkered employment history ranged from "menial things" to work as a case aide and family shelter advocate. Ruth has a large social network and lately views herself as a "freelance consultant." She had been working part-time at assorted nontraditional jobs. Though the lack of benefits is a definite drawback, the arrangement gives her some time to raise her youngest, which is "more important than anything else." For about seven years Vanessa Geller was a government employee and suffered some minor injuries on the job. After two separate accidents unrelated to work, falling down steps and being hit by an automobile, Vanessa became eligible for Social Security Disability benefits. When we met, she was unemployed and raising her toddler.

Eighty-three percent of people I interviewed have less than a college degree and almost a third did not complete secondary education. This has contributed to their weak position in the volatile, low-wage labor force where their wages have eroded, earnings and advancement potential is poor, and they are exposed to (in)flexible labor practices. And as I have shown in this book, countless pressures and crises can trigger financial decline; these can be particularly devastating to poor people. The lack of education might have contributed to their decline. Conversely, educational credentials might have ameliorated a crisis or aided in the recovery. Because of this, it is even more important for poor and educationally disadvantaged people to be given a range of opportunities for further education.

It has been documented that current or former welfare recipients with low skills and educational levels experience little earnings growth over time because of limited opportunities for upward mobility. Moreover, education and skills have become more important determinants of employment opportunities and wages than experience (Martinson and Strawn 2002). Much evidence has linked the acquisition of skills and educational attainment with earnings power. For example, California's TANF program, CalWORKS, allowed TANF recipients to attend a community college for eighteen to twenty-four months as a means to satisfy TANF work requirements. A study tracking employment rates and earnings of recipients who exited California's community colleges in 1999–2000 revealed positive economic outcomes. Among the findings were these: CalWORKS students were twice as likely to be employed year-round after attending college than before. The more education they received, the greater their earnings increase. The CalWORKS students who completed a vocational certificate or associate's degree program had higher earnings and employment than those who completed nonvocational programs. The median annual earnings of associate's degree graduates were five times greater two years out of school than their earnings prior to entry (Mathur et al. 2004).

Similarly, U.S. Census data from 2003 found that earnings increased significantly with each level of educational achievement. People who dropped out of high school experience the lowest lifetime earnings. Compared to women who *did not complete* high school, women who had some exposure to college increased their earnings by 57 percent; women who completed a bachelor's degree increased earnings by 182 percent. Compared to women who *completed* high school, women who had some exposure to college increased their earnings by only 5 percent; those who completed a bachelor's degree increased earnings by at least 59 percent. Comparing women of different races and ethnicities demonstrates that minority women received the largest gains. Furthermore, higher education reduces poverty, especially among minority women. U.S. Census data from 2004 shows that for African American women the poverty rate decreased from 41 percent among those without a high school diploma to 17 percent for women with some postsecondary education and to 5.3 percent for those who completed college. Among Latinas, the poverty rate dropped from 32 percent among women without a high school diploma to 12 percent for those with some college and to 5.9 percent for those who earned at least a bachelor's degree (cited in Jones-DeWeever and Gault 2006:4–5). Additionally, compared to less educated individuals who received welfare, those with higher educational levels are less likely to return to welfare (Center for Women Policy Studies 2002).

What is flatly ignored in the welfare system is the "culture of achievement" (Jones 1993); many women I met yearned for an opportunity to improve their situation through education. A resounding criticism among the parents is that educational options are limited to the DSS-approved programs that count toward mandatory work requirements. And, even if given the chance to attend an approved program, a person might not necessarily prefer it. Limiting options to state-approved programs restricts the freedom of individuals to choose their educational path. Some of the parents who have taken short-term training do not get the opportunity to utilize or maximize the newly learned skills because they fail to find employment or the employment is temporary or short-lived. Technology is sometimes obsolete by the time a person secures a position or masters a skill. Women especially must be afforded education opportunities throughout their lives. Caregiving responsibilities, coupled with poverty-related issues and crises, can often inhibit women's ability to put their newly acquired skills to use. Many parents raise their children with no or little help from men or a support network. Therefore, education and an array of support services (e.g., financial aid, child care) for parents are necessary to help adults achieve economic independence and balance the pressures of home, work, and school.

Most people did not have the money or financial aid to pursue their desired course of education. Those who pursued school obtained government grants and loans. However, research indicates that financial aid only covers a fraction of tuition, and aid has diminished in recent years at the same time that the cost of higher education has skyrocketed. For example, the real value of a Pell grant is half of what it was in the 1970s; the average Pell grant in the 2003–2004 academic year covered only about a third of the cost of an average public two-year college (in Jones-DeWeever and Gault 2006:1). Furthermore, if parents manage to attend school, they must arrange for child care and reorganize their time to accommodate this additional responsibility. Moreover, for TANF recipients whose education is counted as an approved work activity, the work mandates, rules, and limitations and the multiple demands of school, work, and home often impede the completion of their degree.

Advocates for the poor and research policy recommendations have long promoted allowing class time and homework time to be counted toward work activity, and stopping the TANF clock on time limits when recipients are engaged in education and training. The combination of educational preference, financial and TANF aid, suspension of work assignments and welfare time limits, child-care subsidies, and other supports would seem like a more successful national strategy for poor adults to achieve self-sufficiency than programs forced upon them to satisfy work requirements. But such a strategy is the antithesis of neoliberal approaches aimed to shrink the welfare state and of the work-first philosophy to move low-income workers, especially women, into the low-wage economic sector.

After I finished my fieldwork and analysis, the situation became grimmer for recipients nationwide after TANF was reauthorized as part of the Deficit Reduction Act of 2005. Some changes in the TANF program were predicted to result in more recipients having to engage in work activities. New federal regulations also had implications for students and those desiring an education. At first, an interim rule set by the federal government in 2006 no longer permitted states to count participation in a baccalaureate degree program as a work activity under the category of vocational educational training. But this was reversed in the 2008 final rule that implemented changes enacted in the Deficit Reduction Act. States will be permitted to count a variety of postsecondary educational activities as a work activity under the category of vocational training; these include hours spent in associate's and baccalaureate or advanced degree programs. This, and a few new rule changes, such as allowing homework to count as a work activity, will benefit students. Still, the rules are complicated and many are restrictive, such as limiting vocational educational training to *twelve months* in a lifetime. No matter what, the work-first philosophy trumps education.

8

Divergent Interests

Parents Do What They Have to Do

A primary interest of the suburban parents that I met is to provide for the family and, as some have said, "do what I have to do." For most people that meant working, rotating between the employment and the social service systems, and augmenting income with or solely relying on public assistance benefits, as well as deploying emergency and ongoing strategies to get by. For many, one such strategy is reliance on a network of kin support; this has long been recognized as a survival strategy by poor people (Stack 1974; Susser 1982). People's extended kin support network included blood relatives; spouses, partners, and "exes," most notably fathers of children; kin of children's fathers; and fictive kin and friends. Support networks ranged from ones that were extremely frail and tenuous consisting of a few individuals, to ones that were steadfast, reliable, and extensive.

Kin commonly and frequently babysat or provided child care when a parent worked, especially when families doubled-up in households and a household member had an accommodating schedule. Children's grandparents often provided child care and other support. Anna Moreno's stepfather moved in with her for a few years when he had nowhere to go. Although he had no income, his residency allowed Anna to return to work five months after giving birth. He took care of her children and cooked. Anna said, "Even if he had $100 I wouldn't have asked him for anything 'cause he was doing so much more by watching the kids." Women sometimes called on ex-husbands and former partners who are the fathers of their children for child-care duty. This provides a time for children to spend with their father, and, moreover, a father's caregiving is less risky than entrusting child care to another, especially if a child welfare agency posed any threat. Relatives and others gave or loaned people money for continuous expenses and one-time emergency needs. These ranged from a parent subsidizing her adult child's rent to a family member buying food when the cupboard was empty or Pampers when a child wore the last diaper in the house. Many people lacked a car and so borrowed vehicles, carpooled to work, or depended on kin and others for intermittent and regular transportation. Long-term unemployed people often relied on kin and friends to hire them for odd jobs like painting and moving furniture; women braided hair for cash or barter. Throughout a lifetime various kin also gave emotional support in quotidian situations or in periods of crisis.

Support networks are sinuous; over time people move in and out of lives. Because the networks are dynamic, specific individuals' capacity to provide can change over time. Thus, the types and extent of support varies. For example, when Carissa Simone began raising a family close to a decade ago, her mother was using drugs and the two were not in contact. Carissa said that her mother "couldn't really offer me anything" during that period. Yet, a few years later her mother went into recovery. Carissa said that since then, "She is the one that helps me tremendously now. . . . She's the one that pays cable, light, phone . . . ; she's the one that pays everything. . . . My mother is very supportive to me and my children. She's like the father figure at home. The kids respect her. She's the man. You know."

The burdensome cost of housing is a key factor that causes impoverishment and drives families to obtain government housing subsides and other public assistance, as well as to seek help from others. The homes of kin became emergency havens when families lost housing due to a variety of situations that caused a housing crisis. Conversely, some of those I spoke with also extended their homes to others in need. In order to specifically care for an ailing kin, an adult child often moved into a parent's home or vice versa. Some households clearly benefited by the pooling of multiple incomes and support.

Though support networks are crucial, they cannot shield families from impoverishment. Moreover, kin usually cannot shoulder the full burden of another's housing emergency. Doubling-up frequently becomes untenable because of family tensions, overcrowding, and domestic violence, and it is often impractical due to illegal tenancy. For a variety of reasons many poor people do not necessarily have a sustaining support network that can ameliorate a crisis. In fact, some people relied on someone who eventually created a situation that plunged the person seeking help further into poverty. Some people noted that they did not trust friends to keep their state of affairs confidential. Some were reluctant to call on family to help because their kin were in ill health or had their own families to support, or they did not want to burden kin with their problems. In other cases asking for help conflicted with their image of being a responsible adult and parent. Nonetheless, many people declared that their family was vital to their survival at some point. Amber Hamilton enumerated the individuals who helped her as well as her ambivalence about asking for help.

> The only reason I'm making it in here [the shelter] is 'cause I have a boyfriend [he lives in a separate shelter unit]. . . . He has two kids. And we help each other. Like he didn't have no money to wash his clothes the other day. And I had it, so I gave it to him. If it wasn't for him, I'll be struggling. And if it wasn't for me, he'd be struggling. You know. 'Cause we buy food together. We do everything together. . . . My sister. Even my sixteen-year-old brother, he came down here two Fridays ago to give me $40 out of his own little money, you know. He tried to help me. My mother. I do have family and friends. I do have support. But I don't wanna put all that [on them]. Come on, they have their own. And I can't see myself putting all my weight on them like that. You know. But if I need anything, they'll give it to me. Like I have my kids' family, like their grandmother. Like last year she bought them boots for Christmas.

An extended kinship network is integral to a larger support system comprised of supportive individuals and professionals from public and private agencies. As more welfare provisioning has devolved from the government, poor people have gone to community and faith-based organizations. Earlier I have illustrated the paradox; some services entail the governance of recipients by numerous people. But people do rely on nonstate entities for food, clothing, eviction prevention, utility assistance, legal aid, housing, employment training, and other needed services. Laney Heath has very little family and does not have many friends. She sees herself as an independent person and has no support network of people from whom to borrow. But she knows all the food pantries and volunteers at some of them. She and her daughter take meals at the local churches. Laney volunteers her time at a community center. In return she stops by for clothes and sundries and has even relied on the center to help pay to have her electricity turned back on. She said that the agency is her "backbone."

Women also told how they manage household finances. Janetta Prysock moved into emergency housing after she fled her abusive husband. Although she does not pay rent, she manages her household budget for herself and two children on $622 a month from welfare and food stamp benefits. She lamented that after you consider utilities, food, "toilet paper and everything, that money really does not suffice for everything when you really budget it down. . . . I have to budget my money down to the last penny . . . but thank God I had the military to teach me how to budget." When Celeste Woods's three children were all under the age of ten, she was forced to quit her low-paying job because her son, who has "multiple disabilities," was "in and out of the hospital." She had to "stay put" and thus resorted to public assistance because her children's father "wasn't making it" and she did not want to put any financial burden on her mother. Her son received SSI and she received rental assistance and around $600 in welfare cash and food stamps monthly. She said, "I would put some money on this bill and I'd put some money on that bill. . . . I wouldn't put all my money on one bill. I would divide it and try to hold money and buy like little things I needed, or go to the Laundromat or whatever."

Among the parents I met, Roseanne Tate appears to have had the highest annual income. But it is still a struggle to support her three children on her own and manage the household on about $35,000 annually. Working incurs commuting, wardrobe, child care, and other costs. Roseanne received a subsidy but paid about $260 a month for child care for her youngest child during the school year. When school was not in session, she paid $45 per day for her children to attend camp during the summer and holidays. I commented, "That's a big chunk of your salary."

> RT: Yeah, yeah. Aside from household bills [*laugh*].
> TL: So how do you survive?
> RT: I take from Peter to pay Paul. Or I don't pay at all [*laugh*]. Right now I haven't paid my fuel bills [$250 a month in early spring]. But I expect a tax refund, so I'm holding them off.

Income tax refunds undoubtedly provide timely relief for many low-income workers, especially if they qualify for an Earned Income Tax Credit.[1] Mercedes Montgomery used her tax refund to make back rent payments. Recall from her story that she opted to use this money instead of continuing a frustrating ordeal with a welfare office that made numerous errors on a number of rental assistance checks, precluding their use. Another time she used her income tax refund for food while awaiting a decision on her application for food stamps, which was ultimately denied. Alice Finnegan purchased a computer for résumé writing and her job search with her refund.

Some people employ unconventional strategies to provide for their families. Lucy Middleton's included "bin shopping" and "scrapping." She and her husband rummage through the bins for donated clothing located in parking lots. She said, "My husband actually jumps inside the bins and takes clothes out. I can't afford clothes for the baby." Lucy sits in the van and makes her selections and puts back what she does not want. She said, "I stopped getting embarrassed." They have gotten stopped by passersby who told them that the clothes were for poor people. Her retort: "Yeah, I know." Lucy and her husband also go "scrapping" when they want to save for something special. She explained, "So whenever we see cans and bottles . . . we pick them up, cash them in. He has this jar. He's filling it up to take [their child] to the zoo." New York requires a five-cent deposit on certain glass and plastic bottles and cans, such as soda and beer. Refund machines are often located outside supermarkets. Compared to more affluent neighborhoods, poorer areas have a larger number of machines to accommodate scavengers.

Alice Finnegan suffered a lot of back pain for fifteen years and sometimes cannot walk. Though she wants to work and support her family, the pain limits what she can do. She applied for disability benefits but was turned down. Consequently she works "a little bit here and there." Because she will "go the whole week with no money," she brings in small amounts of cash in different ways.

> I'm really not surviving right now. I do everything that I can. . . . I'm meeting with you [for the $20 interview payment], that's one thing. Stuff like that. I'll do those international research things, those marketing things where they say, "Can you test this skin cream for $25?" I do that from time to time. Every little bit helps. . . . Sometimes I'm collecting those cans. I mean not too much. I'm talking like I make $5 for gas or something if I'm really desperate. . . . I mean I don't like to but sometimes it's what I have to do until the paycheck comes in. I'm behind on everything right now. I'm behind on my rent; I'm about $300 behind. My ConEd is $200; they are going to turn me off. I am going to try to keep the cable on. And the car insurance, I'm always late with that. Like I just worked Passover. I did

a Passover job. So I earned a little extra money. But then my back went out two times in the last week. So this is why I don't do a lot of side work anymore. I just physically can't do it.

Before her recent approval for food stamps Alice often had a sparse cupboard. She said, "I would go to the supermarket and I would go straight to the dented can/crushed box bin and that's where I would get most of my stuff. I'd go get all the ten-cent vegetables and the dollar cereal box. Everything generic. Everything that was on sale."

The suburban families I met make heroic efforts to manage a household and raise children as best as they can. Their attempts to get ahead are so often stymied by the vagaries of the low-wage labor market and onerous federal and state welfare policy. Moreover, continual welfare reform has made it even more difficult.

Governments' Agendas: Continued Welfare Restructuring

New York State's Assaults

Parents told me about their lives during a period when President George W. Bush was in office and George E. Pataki governed New York State. During their Republican administrations the state and federal governments proposed and made some changes to welfare policy that did not support the interests of struggling parents. Ongoing welfare restructuring presents new challenges for families and for those who advocate on their behalf.

Commencing his first gubernatorial term in 1995, Governor Pataki initially headed New York during a national economic boom. Beginning in fiscal year 1999–2000 personal income tax receipts grew by double digits for three consecutive years, helping to produce a budget surplus despite the implementation of a multiyear tax reduction plan in the 1990s. But then a number of factors coalesced to create budget problems. These included the Wall Street and dot-com bubble bursts, the fiscal consequence of the attacks on September 11, 2001, a national recession, and the unsustainable multiyear tax reduction. At the start of fiscal year 2002–2003 New York estimated that the state faced a budget deficit of $6.8 billion. Although the state initiated a number of spending and revenue actions to reduce the deficit, by fiscal year 2003–2004 the estimated budget gap rose to $11.5 billion. Governor Pataki proposed spending cuts to close the gap, but the New York Legislature reduced those cuts and adopted measures to increase revenue, one of which was a temporary income-tax rate increase on higher incomes (the top rate was still half of what it had been in the mid-1970s). By fiscal year 2004–2005 the projected budget deficit was $5.1 billion, and by 2005–2006 it was reduced to $4.2 million (Coughlin 2004; Fiscal Policy Institute 2005).

Due to welfare reform and the restructuring of New York State's welfare program, New York State witnessed a dramatic decline of more than one million welfare recipients from January 1995 to November 2004 (Renwick 2005). Despite the decline, assaults on New York's poor continued. In a fiscally weak environment New York State planned or moved ahead with further welfare program changes that would reduce funds to low-income families. The 2004–2005 New York State budget proposed a number of measures that would drive poor families further into poverty while closing less than 1.8 percent of the state budget gap (see Fiscal Policy Institute 2004). Here I will mention two: welfare grant reductions for families with disabled members and full family sanctions.

Effective July 2004 the New York State Office of Temporary and Disability Assistance (OTDA) adopted a regulation that changed the budget calculation methodology for a household receiving Temporary Assistance benefits that included a member who received Supplemental Security Income, a disability benefit. Approximately twenty-seven thousand households with children were initially affected by the change, which resulted in an average monthly grant reduction of $90 per family and a reduction of nearly $200 for some smaller families. The Pataki administrated estimated a savings of $30 million from the change. Soon afterward a lawsuit on behalf of the affected families ensued. A September 2007 final judgment in the *Doe v. Doar* class action suit declared the regulation illegal because it violated the state's Social Services Law; it directed OTDA to proceed with a plan to increase benefits prospectively and retroactively to compensate families affected. Thus, because the reduced budgeting method ceased, new applicants and families currently receiving public assistance began receiving higher monthly welfare grants. Affected recipients who were no longer receiving welfare were to have had the opportunity to have their eligibility assessed but would be unable to receive retroactive awards if deemed ineligible for public assistance. In the end, almost fifty thousand families were affected by the benefit reduction due to additional families applying for public assistance over the course of the multiyear litigation

(Empire Justice Center 2007). Despite the retroactive monetary relief distributed among the affected families, in the interim years impoverished families suffered financial loss because of measures taken by the state to reduce the budget deficit.

In fiscal year 2004–2005 Governor Pataki proposed full family sanctions. In New York a sanction results in benefits being withheld on a pro rata basis, that is, the cash is reduced or cut from the noncompliant adult's portion of the benefit grant. The governor's proposal was not enacted in fiscal year 2004–2005, but it was proposed again in his fiscal year 2005–2006 budget proposal. A rationale behind the full family sanction was that it would alter the behavior of those adults who would rather accept a pro rata benefit reduction than comply with work mandates. Advocates for poor people object to punishing an entire family for a recipient's infraction or a welfare system error. My research supports the common belief among welfare advocates that an inordinate number of sanctions are caused by bureaucratic errors or caseworker demands that are either impossible or illogical for a recipient to meet (e.g., a mandated meeting that conflicts with another agency meeting). Full family sanctions posed a major threat for many families. Approximately 10 percent of families in New York State are in sanction status at a given time (Doar 2005). Fortunately for recipients, the proposal for full family sanctions was not enacted; one view is that advocacy pressure blocked passage. Yet the continuing attempts by the state to reduce or terminate benefit grants, trim the welfare rolls, and push people into the workforce seem relentless. One such attempt by the state to temporarily remove recipients from the welfare rolls prompted me to engage in the following letter-writing campaign organized by an advocacy group.

New York families who reach the Family Assistance (TANF) program sixty-month lifetime limit may be eligible for continuation of assistance through the state's Safety Net Assistance program. In mid-October 2005 the OTDA proposed a rule change that would have had injurious effects on families who had reached the limit. When I analyzed the details of the proposed rule in the *NYS Register*, I learned that individuals reaching the sixty-month limit applied for Safety Net Assistance by using an abbreviated application form (not the long standard form that I described in Chapter 4). Albeit short, the form was used because "the State wanted recipients who were able to work to acknowledge their need to achieve self-sufficiency and affirm their need for continuing assistance" (New York State Office of Temporary and Disability Assistance 2005a:29). The form was also used so as not to overburden local social service districts with the thousands of recipients who would reach the time limit after December 2001. (The Family Assistance TANF-funded program began in December 1996. Families receiving *continuous* aid would have reached the sixty-month limit in December 2001.) If a recipient did not complete the application by the sixtieth month, the welfare case was supposed to be closed. However, the state instituted a process so that cases were automatically converted from the TANF-funded program to Safety Net Assistance to ensure that the state would not incur federal penalties for using TANF money after sixty months, which may have happened if the state had inadvertently left cases active or failed to process applications by the deadline. According to OTDA, the combination of the abbreviated form and the automatic conversion "diluted the self-sufficiency message the State sought to send" by creating a "seamless process" whereby benefits were not interrupted (29). The proposed rule called for the closure of a TANF case at the end of the sixty months, requiring the recipient to apply for Safety Net Assistance via the standard application process. This would necessitate a forty-five-day wait period for consideration of Safety Net benefits. Importantly, estimates indicated that approximately 10 to 20 percent of the recipients would not apply for Safety Net Assistance, thus resulting in program savings.

By the time of the proposed rule change in October 2005, the number of recipients who reached the TANF time limit decreased from forty-four thousand in December 2001 to approximately nine hundred a month, so the time appeared feasible for the state to make an administrative change. The rationale was that the current level of cases reaching time limits "now allows for a process that more effectively conveys to the recipient the expectation that they attain self-sufficiency within a certain timeframe and now makes this proposal administratively viable for local districts to do" (29).

The proposed rule change was reported in an article in *City Limits* that quoted then OTDA Commissioner Robert Doar:

> We have a lot of families who are going past the five-year time limit, and who we think—and the counties think—haven't been forced to do enough to help them go off of cash welfare. . . . We want there to be a sense of urgency, both in these folks and the counties. It's in the best long-term interest of families that they take advantage of supports for working people and move off cash assistance and [find] work. (McMillan 2005)

With background information and a nuanced reading of the rule changes, I wrote a pointed email in December 2005 to the OTDA opposing the rule change. I pointed out that the state's assessment considered the economic impact (there was none) on social service districts but did not consider the adverse economic impact on the nine hundred families per month predicted to have their cases closed. I cited the state's position that the change would enable local districts "to more accurately assess the recipients' needs and engage them in more appropriate self-sufficiency activities" (New York State Office of Temporary and Disability Assistance 2005a:29). I indicated that case closures and loss of cash would likely create a family crisis, so an assessment during a crisis imposed by the state would unlikely be more accurate. Moreover, the state had sixty months to assess the recipients' needs. I noted that the state projected a savings of millions—between $4.79 million and $9.58 million (30)—the first year and urged the state not to reduce state costs at the expense of poor New Yorkers.

A month later I received a letter from a deputy commissioner of the New York State Office of Temporary and Disability Assistance informing me of the withdrawal of the proposed regulation as written due to the "possible negative impact on clients and local operations" that the commentators raised.[2] Advocates considered this a tremendous victory. However, it was apparent from additional language that the state will continue its workfare offensive. The letter stated that "OTDA is considering various options for a new regulation and/or administrative directive" with the goal to help recipients achieve self-sufficiency and to impress upon them the temporary nature of welfare. Additionally, the state anticipated TANF reauthorization changes by the federal government and was bracing for increased work participation rates at the risk of financial penalties to the state.

TANF Reauthorization: Continued Welfare "Reform"

In August 1996 when PRWORA was enacted, TANF was only authorized and funded for five years with September 30, 2002, as the expiration date. In February 2002 President George W. Bush's reauthorization proposal initiated the process of TANF reauthorization. President Bush's proposal did not increase the TANF block grant and child-care funding, yet it considerably stiffened TANF work requirements through a number of measures that would have put increased pressure on recipients and states at a time of rising poverty rates and escalating unemployment rates during a jobless recovery following a recession.[3] The proposal maintained the PRWORA five-year ban on TANF benefits for legal immigrants entering the United States after 1996, and it allocated funding that would strengthen initiatives promoting "healthy marriages" and abstinence education (see Coalition on Human Needs 2002 for details on these and other provisions). Following President Bush's proposal, legislators introduced bills and amendments, held hearings and debates, rewrote bills, and voted on legislation. In the November 2002 elections, Republicans gained control of the Senate and held their majority in the House. Though the reauthorization process began in 2002, because of Congressional contestation and delays, TANF continued to operate through many short-term extensions that allowed states to receive TANF funding. TANF was reauthorized through September 30, 2010, by President Bush on February 8, 2006, as part of the Deficit Reduction Act of 2005.

The Deficit Reduction Act (DRA) did not increase the TANF block grant funding of $16.5 billion annually. The law retained most of the TANF provisions enacted under PRWORA and contained a number of new ones; most notably, it made significant changes related to work. Work participation rates stayed the same, but some changes will make it challenging for states to achieve the rates. States receive credit for reduced caseloads; for years this resulted in a significant reduction of the participation rates for many states because of sizeable caseload declines. The DRA revised the credit calculation method reducing states' credit potential, thus effectively increasing their work participation rates. And families receiving assistance in separate state programs who had been previously excluded from the participation rates are now included. Failure to meet the all families participation rate in the first year could result in a 5 percent reduction in TANF funds available to a state, and the penalty increases in subsequent years. At the time, it was predicted that the changes would require states to take various measures to achieve the rates and avoid federal monetary penalties—these measures ranged from making increased investments in workfare programs and work supports to restricting access to assistance. The legislation also directed the U.S. Department of Health and Human Services (HHS) to issue standard definitions for the twelve TANF categories of work activities (Parrott et al. 2007; U.S. Department of Health and Human Services n.d.).

In June 2006 HHS issued and made effective an interim final rule implementing the changes. Notably, the twelve countable work activities were narrowly defined, thus rescinding the flexibility that states had in determining what counted toward work participation. Many of the provisions were severely restrictive. In February 2008 HHS published its final rule, which had an effective date of October 1, 2008. The final rule clarified and made some changes to the interim final rule, addressing some of the concerns voiced by many during a comment period after the interim rule (see U.S. Department of Health and Human Services 2006a, 2008). The DRA legislation and the two subsequent HHS rules are highly complex. My reading of the rules leads me to believe that, overall, the provisions will put more workfare pressures on recipients. While future ethnographic research can shed light on the effects of the regulations that resulted from the DRA, the point I want to make here is that welfare "reform" has persisted as a government aim. The TANF reauthorization is yet another key event in welfare history, consistent with the tenor of PRWORA welfare debates where reproduction, marriage, and workfare were central to the debate and outcome. Ultimately, DRA provisions resulted in increased work participation, the delineation of extant work activities, more burdensome state reporting and verification procedures, and increased monetary penalties for state's noncompliance. None of this bodes well for recipients of welfare.

Epilogue

A New Era—A Global Economic Crisis and the Obama Administration

If ever there were a moment that illustrates inequality in the United States, we see it in the government's response to the catastrophic economic meltdown during the final months of the Bush administration. The Emergency Economic Stabilization Act of 2008 was signed by President Bush in October 2008. Almost overnight the federal government passed legislation to spend $700 billion to aid the failing economy, much of which was used to infuse capital into the banking system. This bailout stands in stark relief to the paltry monthly cash that destitute people receive in welfare benefits. New York's basic welfare grant (nonshelter portion) had not increased for almost two decades. For years advocates had been pushing to raise the grant through lobbying, call-in and letter-writing campaigns to legislators, and other efforts. In December 2008 New York State's Democratic governor, David A. Paterson, announced his fiscal year 2009–2010 executive budget. In it he proposed an increase to the basic welfare grant of 10 percent per year over three years beginning in January 2010. In early 2009 the enacted budget agreement included the welfare grant increase; it was set to start in July 2009. For a family of three the grant had been $291 a month. In the first year of the increase the family will realize a monthly gain of $30. Three years out a family of three will receive $388 a month. While this is a start, it hardly constitutes beneficence in light of the magnitude of the federal bailout to failing banks and other corporations.

Now consider the names of the acts related to welfare reform and the bailout. "Personal responsibility" is a key concept inscribed in the title of the Personal Responsibility and Work Opportunity Reconciliation Act of

1996. Public support and legislation for welfare reform were influenced by ideologies that blame poor people for their situation and insist that they assume full responsibility for themselves and their family, regardless of the structural forces that create social inequality. Because of devolution, the government abdicates its responsibility to the poor and pushes it onto individuals through mechanisms that ultimately force recipients off the welfare rolls and into low-wage jobs or leaves them completely adrift. The bailout act, the Emergency Economic Stabilization Act of 2008 (and the accompanying rescue fund, the Troubled Asset Relief Program), is devoid of any inference to behavior or even accountability. We do not get a sense of the *irresponsibility* of policy makers, corporate elites, and others who championed deregulation and other neoliberal practices that have spurred and fueled the extant global economic crisis and contributed to U.S. inequality and poverty for decades. In the neoliberal and neoconservative environment, there appears to have been little moral obligation or political will to adequately provide for the American working class, let alone poor families. The playing field worsened for poor people. The minimum wage does not provide a living wage. Welfare benefits became temporary; the policies became stricter and abetted the movement of cheap, mostly poorly educated, female labor into low-wage jobs in the interest of profit. And continued welfare restructuring has resulted in persistent assaults on needy people.

At the start of the Obama administration we have begun to see changes. On February 17, 2009, President Obama signed the American Recovery and Reinvestment Act of 2009, a $787 billion economic recovery package comprised of spending programs and tax measures designed to stimulate economic activity and employment in the sinking economy. The package contains some provisions to aid low- and moderate-income families. Among them, an additional $2 billion will be provided under the Child Care and Development Block Grant that will help states provide childcare subsidies to more low-income working families, such as Roseanne Tate's, and to other families in which parents are engaged in education or training. The new Making Work Pay Credit will provide tax relief of up to $400 per worker. Some of the working mothers I interviewed benefit from the Earned Income Tax Credit; this credit has been expanded. All of the parents that I met received aid from the federal food stamps program at some time in their lives, and many said that it was not enough to get them through the month (as of October 1, 2008, the program was renamed the Supplemental Nutrition Assistance Program). Approximately

$20 billion has been included in the stimulus package, most of which will be used to fund a 13.6 percent increase to maximum food stamp benefits for approximately fourteen million households comprised of thirty-two million individuals. Additionally, the legislation allocates funds to extend unemployment insurance coverage by additional weeks, increases benefits by $25 weekly, and provides incentives for states to reform their programs to make benefits available to more low-wage and part-time workers (Center on Budget and Policy Priorities 2009; see this for a synopsis of these and other spending and tax provisions).

Unemployment insurance is a crucial benefit for displaced workers. Many of the parents that I interviewed were able to receive unemployment benefits when they became unemployed because at the time they met the eligibility requirements. Yet, at times people were not eligible because their earnings were too low or they did not earn wages within the qualifying timeframes. Not having this financial safety net is particularly troublesome during periods of high unemployment when workers have difficulty finding jobs. As of January 2009, nonfarm payroll employment had declined by 3.6 million since the start of the recession in December 2007; half of this decline occurred in the prior three months with job losses across all major industry sectors. The unemployment rate rose to 7.6 percent in January, and the number of unemployed people rose to 11.6 million. The number of people who worked "part time for economic reasons," that is, involuntary part-time workers, rose to 7.8 million. This was an increase of 3.1 million over the prior twelve months and includes people who preferred full-time employment (U.S. Department of Labor 2009). That people are having a hard time is evidenced by the 15.3 percent rise from December 2007 to December 2008 in the number of people across the country participating in the federal food stamps program (U.S. Department of Agriculture 2009). In this economic crisis unprecedented numbers of middle-class families across the United States will be applying for government benefits for the first time, just like Roseanne Tate did when her house was in foreclosure. More people will find themselves in a situation like Amber Hamilton and Lorna Webster, whose inadequate savings could not avert eviction after their job termination; among other benefits, they received welfare. For Amber, it was her first time. Massive layoffs, work reduction, and other ramifications of the financial downturn will send new and returning recipients to the welfare office.

In light of this, one might expect that U.S. welfare rolls had already been escalating. Yet, that had not been the case across the country by the end of 2008. Having amassed the most recent data available for every state, the *New York Times* reported in February 2009 that between 2007 and 2008 the welfare rolls were cut in eighteen states, expanded in twenty, and remained flat in twelve, fluctuating less than 3 percent. U.S. welfare rolls were at or near their lowest in forty years. Some of the reasons noted in the *Times* article for roll reduction were that obstacle-ridden programs resulted in deterrence, the federal fixed block grant allocation might have dissuaded states from increasing rolls and bearing increased costs, recipients' benefits were discontinued due to noncompliance of workfare mandates, and states closed cases to facilitate meeting work requirements and thus to avoid federal penalties (DeParle 2009). It is not difficult to imagine impoverished individuals around the country undergoing strict eligibility processes at the welfare office. Some probably already have or will be made to jump through hoops, just as Desmond Hughes did. For how many will the exercise prove fruitless because of benefit denial? Furthermore, how many across the country will not apply for welfare benefits because they had already exceeded their lifetime limit?

The American Recovery and Reinvestment Act of 2009 provides some relief to states to help fund increased TANF caseloads. Simply put, an emergency contingency fund was created; the funding is capped at $5 billion for two years. Those states that have provided more families with assistance and have increased their expenditures under their TANF program will be able to receive federal funding to cover 80 percent of their increased spending in basic assistance; short-term, nonrecurrent aid; and subsidized employment. Additionally, a provision in the act will ensure that a state's work participation rate will not increase as a result of rising welfare caseloads. However, even though the rate does not change, the number of people mandated to work will increase, as the same percentage will apply to a larger caseload (Parrott 2009; Parrott and Schott 2009).

President Obama called for a "new era of responsibility" in his inaugural speech (2009a). This language is manifest in the title of U.S. budget for fiscal year 2010, *A New Era of Responsibility: Renewing America's Promise.* His "message" therein speaks about "an era of profound irresponsibility" that preceded the fiscal crisis (Obama 2009c). In this new era, *responsibility* purportedly encompasses all Americans. This marks a shift from a focus on poor people exclusively. But will this era be a time when Americans stop blaming poor people for their situation? Or one in which governments stop their assaults on them? In 2010 TANF is scheduled for reauthorization. TANF reauthorization proposals must consider relaxing, suspending, or at best eliminating harsh TANF provisions such as time limits, intense workfare requirements, and punitive sanctions especially in view of the battered economy and soaring unemployment.

President Obama's recovery agenda and the federal budget placed an emphasis on education. In a televised address to Congress the president asked "every American to commit to at least one year or more of higher education or career training. This can be community college or a four-year school; vocational training or an apprenticeship" (Obama 2009b). The president's stress on education needs to be reflected in TANF policy— ideally through a shift from work first to education first by promoting and supporting various levels of education and training over an individual's lifetime. Training will be especially important for those parents who might want to compete for jobs in industries that the stimulus package will create, for example, so-called green jobs. More generally, TANF reauthorization should consider reduction of poverty rather than welfare caseload reduction as a measurement of the success of the welfare system. Myriad national and local antipoverty advocacy organizations have devised poverty reduction strategies that ought to be reviewed and considered by lawmakers and integrated into new legislation that affects our nation's poorest people. Lastly, in this new political era we need to move beyond the rhetoric of personal responsibility and take action toward economic justice.

Notes

Chapter 1

1. The basic welfare grant is the nonshelter component of New York's temporary assistance grant. The shelter allowance (rental assistance) increased in 2003. Each allowance has a maximum depending on family size. The shelter allowance varies by county. The maximum monthly shelter allowance for a family of three in Westchester County is $426.

2. The names of all research participants have been changed to protect their identity; some identifying features might have been changed. In a few instances in participants' and in my own quotations, I omitted a small number of inconsequential words or short phrases to reduce repetition and maximize readability. Westchester County became a domicile of President Clinton; the Clinton's purchased a house there in 1999.

3. The "Section 8" Housing Choice Voucher Program, created in the 1970s, is federally funded housing assistance awarded to low-income families with children (in 2000, 61 percent), elderly (16 percent), people with disabilities (15 percent), and others in need (8 percent). A voucher pays for rent and utilities for housing on the open market. The program is administered by the U.S. Department of Housing and Urban Development (HUD) and is run by state, regional, and local public housing agencies. Families apply locally. Waiting lists are very long; the national average in 2000 was twenty-eight months. Some waiting lists are so long that they are closed to new applicants. The income eligibility limit is a percentage of the local area median income, a calculation set by HUD annually. A payment standard is set by the housing agency based on a percentage of the fair market rent. Typically, the voucher directly pays the landlord the payment standard less 30 percent of the family's income; the family pays the balance. Landlords are not obligated to rent to families with vouchers. Once a family receives a voucher, they have a fixed period (generally sixty days) to secure an apartment. If the family is unsuccessful, they will lose the voucher. This is not uncommon due to affordable housing shortages,

reluctance of landlords to rent to voucher holders, and other complications (Center on Budget and Policy Priorities 2003).

4. *Out of Reach*, a publication and Internet-based tool of the National Low Income Housing Coalition, compares wages and rents in various counties, metropolitan areas, nonmetropolitan areas, and states. A web-based report generates a "Housing Wage." The publication states: "For each jurisdiction, the report calculates the amount of money a household must earn in order to afford a rental unit at a range of sizes (0, 1, 2, 3, and 4 bedrooms) at the area's Fair Market Rent (FMR), based on the generally accepted affordability standard of paying no more than 30% of income for housing costs. From these calculations the hourly wage a worker must earn to afford the FMR for a two-bedroom home is derived. This figure is the Housing Wage" (National Low Income Housing Coalition 2005). For more information on the calculations see the coalition's website.

5. The average length of the initial interview was an hour and a half. Upon completion, I paid $20 for the interview.

6. Follow-up is a much-noted problem for longitudinal research among homeless people and other marginalized populations; see McKenzie et al. 1999.

7. I was influenced by pioneering feminist anthropologists who have reworked various conceptions of the life-cycle framework to include a focus on women. Feminist theories influenced anthropologists to (re)examine cultural groups and analyze women's experiences, often within the context of key life events and rituals such as childbirth, childhood, marriage, divorce, aging, death, and funeral rites (e.g., Abu-Lughod 1986; Goodale 1971; Shostak 1983; Weiner 1976). Silverman (1975) examined life crises in the life cycle of women in northern Italy in the late 1960s. She perceived life crises to be "those periods in the life span at which there is some interruption in continuity—a transition from one culturally defined stage of life to another, and at which there is regularly expected individual stress" (309). Life-cycle crises such as birth, puberty, marriage, menopause, and death have often been found to be disruptive in various ways cross-culturally (Erchak 1992). In addition to and in between transitional life-cycle crises of these types, impoverished families experience economic and family pressures that have varying consequences (see Chapter 5; see also Barrow and Lawinski 2009; Mullings and Wali 2001).

Chapter 2

1. For racial/ethnic identification, I use the term that the person used.

Chapter 3

1. The people whom I interviewed that received welfare rarely used the formal program names or their acronyms but referred to the welfare program simply as "welfare," or being "on welfare." Most people who gave their opinions about

welfare valued the program as a vital financial resource. But their disparate critiques were influenced by their personal experiences, treatment by welfare office staff, program rules, and the negative stereotypes and stigma associated with the program and its recipients.

2. ADC cash aid was for the needs of children. In 1950 aid was extended to mothers.

3. A 1941 Bureau of Public Assistance review of ADC programs in eighteen communities in six states revealed that "these policies were subject to a wide range of interpretation and despite years of agency experience in dealing with families, 'suitability of the home' and 'fitness' of the parent were still indefinable" (cited in Bell 1965:41). Bell posited, "In the absence of objective guidelines hard-pressed local workers had to infuse meaning into the range of phrases: 'suitable for health and care,' 'safe and proper,' 'satisfactory place,' or 'of benefit to the child to continue living therein'" (1965:41).

4. By December 1940, only 360,000 families were enrolled in ADC. Between 1940 and 1945, the rolls dropped by 25 percent. After World War II the rolls increased 132 percent between December 1945 and December 1950. Yet, in 1950 only 635,000 families obtained ADC. Between 1950 and 1960 the rolls rose only 17 percent in spite of the growing urban and agricultural unemployment (Piven and Cloward 1993:116–17).

5. At the beginning of the twentieth century more than 90 percent of blacks lived in the South. By 1960 about 50 percent lived in the North (Piven and Cloward 1979:189).

6. According to the U.S. Women's Bureau, the unemployment rate for women was 3.7 percent in 1947. In 1949 it rose to 6 percent and fluctuated between 4.8 and 7.2 percent during the next fifteen years. Black women's unemployment ranged from 7.3 to 11.8 percent during the period from 1955 to 1968 (in Abramovitz 1996:320–21).

7. In 1900, 87 percent of blacks were engaged in agriculture and domestic services. By 1960, the percentage diminished to less than 10 percent in agriculture and 15 percent in domestic services. "Northern urban ghettos" had depression-level unemployment rates. In a Detroit census tract wholly populated by blacks, 41 percent of the black men were unemployed in 1960. Likewise in census tracts in Chicago, Los Angeles, and Baltimore in which 90 percent or more residents were black, the unemployment rates ranged from 24 to 36 percent (Piven and Cloward 1979:189, 267).

8. Many scholars challenged Moynihan and the cultural explanations of poverty by demonstrating that adverse circumstances, structural conditions, discriminatory practices, and other factors define and make poverty; poverty is not the consequence of a distinct culture (Hannerz 1969; Jones 1993; Leacock 1971; Liebow 1967; Stack 1974; Susser 1982; Valentine 1968). Nevertheless, explanations that link poverty to "culture" have a long history (see Mink 1995), and cultural myths, misinterpretation, and conservative ideology have proved to be tenacious.

9. States were required to set up employment and job training programs. At the start WIN was a voluntary program, but in 1971 the federal government mandated participation of AFDC recipients who had no preschool children or special responsibilities at home. The WIN program was grossly underfunded, lacked sufficient resources, and was ineffectively managed. The program became merely a registration requirement (Blank and Blum 1997; Bane and Ellwood 1994).

10. Since 1962, the Social Security Act authorized the Department of Health and Human Services to grant states a waiver to federal welfare program provisions. During the Reagan administration the waiver policy was liberalized for the purpose of experimenting with AFDC. Before 1992 a few states sought approval to test minor program changes through the AFDC waiver process. Between 1992 and 1996 President Clinton persuaded states to apply for waivers; thus, the requests vastly increased. In the era of welfare "reform," requests were now radical; states requested approval to restructure AFDC through provisions such as work requirements, sanctions, time limits, family caps, and children's school attendance. By 1996 forty states and the District of Columbia had federal approval to waive specific AFDC provisions, although not all were fully implemented (Rogers-Dillon 2004:19; Schram 2000:104; Haskins 2001:108). Rogers-Dillon views the explosion of the waiver program between 1992 and 1996 as a "revolution in welfare" even before the 1996 welfare reform legislation and posits that it was the waiver program that defined welfare reform and ultimately resulted in the demise of AFDC (19).

11. This is a brief sketch of the politics of welfare and content of the welfare bills. For fuller accounts see DeParle 2004 (chapters 6–8) and Rogers-Dillon 2004.

12. Entitlement came about in the late 1960s and early 1970s when some Supreme Court decisions provided the basis for an interpretation that states were required to provide AFDC benefits. Also, AFDC law defined eligible classes of families and required states to provide aid to families in the classes if their income was below the limits set by the state (U.S. House of Representatives, Committee on Ways and Means 1998).

13. See Peck's definition of workfare and analysis of welfare structures and workfare strategies (2001:1–27).

14. All titles refer to an individual's position during the time period discussed.

15. In 1996, the year PRWORA was legislated, 13.7 percent of all people were below the poverty level. In 2000 during a strong economy when the poverty rate dropped to 11.3 percent, the U.S. Census Bureau indicated that the rate was not statistically different from the 1973 record low of 11.1 percent. Following the 2001 recession, it reached 12.7 percent in 2004 and dropped slightly to 12.6 percent in 2005 (U.S. Bureau of the Census 2006, 2000b). See Chapter 8 for an analysis of rising unemployment rates during this time.

Chapter 4

1. When people recalled their welfare and work history, they told me what happened to them in various situations. Their narrations might contain some inconsistencies and contradictions to welfare rules, which I do not attempt to resolve.

2. Susser (1982) and Davis (2006) provide an analysis of some regulatory aspects of New York's welfare program in the pre-PRWORA and PRWORA eras, respectively.

3. For specificity on mothers' pension programs see Bell 1965 and Mink 1995. For the Aid to Dependent Children and the Aid to Families with Dependent Children programs see Piven and Cloward 1993; Susser 1982; Kingfisher 1996.

4. The *Welfare Rules Databook* is updated periodically; see the Urban Institute website (*www.urban.org*) for the most recent version.

5. PRWORA set states' minimum work participation rates and the minimum number of hours per week that a recipient of TANF must participate in allowable work activities. Both increased over time. Since 2002, 50 percent of all families are required to participate. For single parents the requirement is at least thirty hours a week, twenty hours if a child is under six. Ninety percent of two-parent families must engage in work activities for a combined average of at least thirty-five hours per week, fifty-five if they receive federally funded childcare. See Chapter 7 for a list of the twelve allowable work activities.

6. Article XVII of the New York State Constitution reads, "The aid, care and support of the needy are public concerns and shall be provided by the state and by such of its subdivisions, and in such manner and by such means, as the legislature may from time to time determine" (New York State Constitution).

7. Safety Net Assistance is for single adults; childless couples; children living apart from any adult relative; families of persons found to be abusing drugs or alcohol; families of persons refusing drug/alcohol screening, assessment, or treatment; persons who have exceeded the sixty-month limit on TANF assistance; and aliens who are eligible for Temporary Assistance but who are not eligible for federal reimbursement (New York State Office of Temporary and Disability Assistance 2002a:3). The Family Assistance program (TANF) is funded 50 percent by the federal government; state and local dollars equally fund the remaining 50 percent. The Safety Net Assistance program is funded 50 percent each by state and local dollars.

8. The Office of Temporary and Disability Assistance is the principal state agency that oversees New York State's welfare program.

9. The *New York State Plan and Executive Certification* states that a parent or caretaker is to engage in work once the state determines that the person is ready or once the person has received assistance for twenty-four months, whichever is earlier. It lists the exemptions from federally countable work activities: "a. Custodial parents or caretakers of children under one year of age for a total of 12 months (lifetime), with only three months exemption for any one child of the parent or caretaker, unless the district decides to use more than the three

months or all of the maximum 12 month period for any one child; b. A woman who is pregnant, beginning 30 days prior to the medically verified date of delivery of the child; c. Individuals who are ill, incapacitated, sixty years old or older or disabled pursuant to State law; d. An individual whose presence is required in the home as a caretaker of an incapacitated family member; e. A child who is under sixteen years of age or under the age of nineteen and attending full time a secondary, vocational or technical school" (New York State Office of Temporary and Disability Assistance 2002b:1–2).

10. To protect Desmond's identity, citation standards for the letter will not be used here.

Chapter 5

1. TANF (and its predecessor AFDC) is one among many federal, state, and local assistance programs that people obtained. The others included but are not limited to food stamps, housing assistance, unemployment insurance benefits, Medicaid, Supplemental Security Income (SSI), and Social Security Disability Insurance (SSDI). Some also obtained child-care subsidies, school lunch, and food supplements from the nutrition program for Women, Infants and Children (WIC).

2. A TANF fact sheet offers this distillation of the lifetime limit: "Families with an adult who has received federally funded assistance for a total of five years (or less at state option) are not eligible for cash aid under the TANF program." Also, "states may extend assistance beyond 60 months to not more than 20 percent of their caseload. They may also elect to provide assistance to families beyond 60 months using state-only funds or Social Services Block Grants" (U.S. Department of Health and Human Services 2006b).

3. According to the *Temporary Assistance Source Book*, "Safety Net Assistance [SNA] is comprised of a cash and non-cash component. An individual or family may only receive cash SNA assistance for a lifetime limit of 24 months. After an individual has received cash SNA for 24 months they may be categorized as non-cash SNA, if otherwise eligible. There is no time limit on how long an individual may receive non-cash SNA. Persons who are exempt from work requirements or are HIV positive, and are not determined unable to work due to the abuse of drugs/alcohol, are exempt from the twenty-four month lifetime limit on cash Safety Net Assistance. Under the non-cash Safety Net Assistance component, the shelter allowance and utilities (including heat) must be restricted. The recipient may receive the remaining grant as cash" (New York State Office of Temporary and Disability Assistance 2005b:9). The benefit provided as noncash could be in a form such as a two-party check or voucher.

4. For many, Medicaid was an impetus for enrollment in AFDC because it paid for the medical expenses associated with the birth of a child. Prior to PRWORA, eligibility of Medicaid was tied to enrollment in AFDC or SSI. Recipients of AFDC were automatically eligible for Medicaid. PRWORA severed the link

between Medicaid and TANF so that Medicaid eligibility is not tied to TANF eligibility (see Cornelius 2003; Ku and Garrett 2000).

5. In 2004 New York was one of the forty-one states, along with the District of Columbia, that adopted the Family Violence Option (FVO). Six other states had equivalent policies regarding waivers and three had no FVO-equivalent policies. In 1998 New York implemented regulations whereby public assistance applicants and recipients are screened using a standardized form. A voluntary response that affirms the presence of domestic violence triggers referral to a domestic violence liaison. Along with other tasks, the liaison assesses the credibility of the assertion, informs victims of options for protection and support, makes service referrals, and determines the need for a program requirement waiver. A waiver temporarily suspends a public assistance program requirement, for example, time limit, work activity, or child support enforcement cooperation, if it is deemed that a requirement would put the individual or children in jeopardy. Waivers are for an initial period and subject to periodic review (Legal Momentum 2004; New York State Office of Temporary and Disability Assistance n.d.a.).

6. The Fiscal Policy Institute (2006a:19) cited U.S. Census data reporting a decline between 2000 and 2004 of seventy thousand families in New York State with middle incomes between $35,000 and $150,000, two-thirds of which fell below the lower bracket of under $35,000.

Chapter 6

1. In 2002 a family of four was considered living in poverty when the annual income was less than the poverty threshold of $18,392. A family of four was considered low-income when annual income was less than $36,784, that is, 200 percent of the poverty threshold (in Waldron et al. 2004).

2. The following occupations are predominantly held by women as indicated by the percentage of women in those occupations: secretaries and administrative assistants (96.6 percent); child-care workers (95 percent); nursing, psychiatric, and home health aides (87.8 percent); personal appearance workers (83.4 percent); cashiers (75.7 percent); waiters and waitresses (74.3 percent); and customer service representatives (70.0 percent) (compiled by the Institute for Women's Policy Research in Caiazza et al. n.d.:15, from SF4 files of the 2000 census, U.S. Department of Commerce, Bureau of Census, February 2004).

3. The median annual earnings in 2002 for women working full-time, year-round was $30,100; this was 76.2 percent of men's earnings. The earnings vary by geography and race/ethnicity (Caiazza et al. n.d.).

4. Although raising children is work, it is categorically unrecognized, uncompensated, and undervalued in a capitalist system (see Eisenstein 1979).

5. According to data reported in 2006, since 2000, the 21 percent decline in New York manufacturing jobs was steeper than the U.S. decline. Those industries in New York with the most job gains since 2000 were in the areas of health

care, social assistance, government, educational services, and food/drinking places. Jobs in these sectors typically pay less than middle-income jobs in those industries that lost a lot of jobs since 2000. These include manufacturing; information, professional scientific and technical services; and wholesale trade. The Fiscal Policy Institute reports: "The average wage for sectors that lost job share over the 2000 to 2004 period is $64,382; more than two-thirds higher than the average wage of $38,074 for the sectors that gained job share" (Fiscal Policy Institute 2006b:3–4).

6. In 2003 the federal minimum wage was $5.15. In 2007 the federal minimum wage increased in increments; in July 2007 the new wage of $5.85 took effect. It increased to $6.55 in July 2008 and to $7.25 in July 2009. In July 2009 the New York minimum wage increased to $7.25 per hour as a result of the increase in the federal wage rate. Some industries (e.g., restaurant) have a lower rate, making allowances for tips.

7. The self-sufficiency standard was developed by Diana Pearce, who was then a director of the Women and Poverty Project at Wider Opportunities for Woman, as part of a state project for family economic self-sufficiency (Pearce with Brooks 2000). The self-sufficiency standard is a measure of income adequacy. It "defines the amount of income required to meet basic needs (including paying taxes) in the regular 'marketplace' without public or private/informal subsidies" (3).

8. In New York the median hourly wage in 2004 for white workers was more than $16 an hour, for blacks it was slightly more than $13 an hour, and for Hispanics was just less than $12 an hour (Fiscal Policy Institute 2006b:27).

9. In New York in 2004 the median female hourly pay was 84 percent of the median male hourly wage. Wage disparities for workers in the twentieth percentile (low wage) were as follows: Non-Hispanic white workers earned $9.63 an hour. This was $1.50 more than black workers and nearly $2.00 more than Hispanic workers (Fiscal Policy Institute, 2006b:27–28).

10. In mid-2009 a law was passed in New York eliminating the requirement that a custodial parent actively pursue a court order for child support as a condition for receiving subsidized child-care assistance.

Chapter 7

1. TANF recipients must participate in the twelve allowable work activities. The core activities that count toward work participation are unsubsidized employment, subsidized private-sector employment, subsidized public-sector employment, work experience, on-the-job training, job search and job readiness assistance, community service programs, vocational educational training, and providing child-care services to someone participating in a community service program. The noncore activities are job skills training directly related to employment, education directly related to employment, and satisfactory attendance at secondary school or in a course of study leading to a certificate of general equivalence. Most hours of participation must come from core activities,

for example, the first twenty hours of a thirty-hour weekly requirement (see U.S. Department of Health and Human Services 2006a, 2008.)

2. New York State does not permit participation in a four-year college program as a countable work activity, but it allows participation in a two-year college.

3. The names of the workfare programs, Learn Then Earn and ADVANCE, are pseudonyms. They mimic the names of typical programs that herald the work ethic and imply a positive outcome of the program and employment.

Chapter 8

1. The earned income tax credit (EITC) is a refundable federal income-tax credit for low-income working individuals and families who claim the credit when they file a tax return. It reduces their tax burden and may result in a tax refund when the EITC exceeds taxes owed. There are eligibility rules pertaining to factors such as marital status, family size, and income. To receive the EITC in the tax year 2003 a taxpayer having two or more children had to have earned less than $33,692, or $34,692 if married filing jointly (Internal Revenue Service 2004). In that tax year about 22.1 million working families and individuals received the EITC; $2,100 was the average EITC among families with children (Greenstein 2005).

2. To protect the sender's identity, citation standards for this letter will not be used here.

3. PRWORA was implemented during a strong economy and a period of job growth through 2000. In August 1996 the U.S. unemployment rate for those sixteen years and older was 5.1 percent, the rate declined to 3.9 percent by December 2000. When President George W. Bush announced his proposal for the reauthorization of TANF in February 2002, it was in the wake of the 2001 recession. The unemployment rate was 5.7 percent, and during a jobless recovery it rose to 6.3 percent in June 2003 (it had not reached that level since early 1994); it remained fairly steady in the 5 percent range until TANF was reauthorized in early February 2006 (U.S. Department of Labor 2007). See Chapter 3 for information about rising poverty rates during that time.

Bibliography

Abramovitz, Mimi. 1996. *Regulating the Lives of Women: Social Welfare Policy from Colonial Times to the Present.* Rev. ed. Boston: South End Press.
———. 2000. *Under Attack, Fighting Back: Women and Welfare in the United States.* Updated ed. New York: Monthly Review Press.
Abu-Lughod, Lila. 1986. *Veiled Sentiments: Honor and Poetry in a Bedouin Society.* Berkeley: University of California Press.
Allard, Patricia. 2002. Life Sentences: Denying Welfare Benefits To Women Convicted of Drug Offenses. February. Washington, DC: Sentencing Project. *www.sentencingproject.org.*
Bane, Mary Jo, and David T. Ellwood. 1994. *Welfare Realities: From Rhetoric to Reform.* Cambridge, MA: Harvard University Press.
Barrow, Susan M., and Terese Lawinski. 2009. Contexts of Mother-Child Separations in Homeless Families. *Analyses of Social Issues and Public Policy* 9(1):157–76.
Bell, Winifred. 1965. *Aid to Dependent Children.* New York: Columbia University Press.
Blank, Susan W., and Barbara B. Blum. 1997. A Brief History of Work Expectations for Welfare Mothers. *The Future of Children* 7(1):28–38.
Boris, Ellen. 1999. When Work Is Slavery. In *Whose Welfare?* ed. Gwendolyn Mink, 36–55. Ithaca, NY: Cornell University Press.
Brenner, Elsa. 2005. Housing Market Is Still Going Strong. *New York Times,* February 6. *www.nytimes.com.*
Caiazza, Amy, April Shaw, and Misha Werschkul. n.d. *The Status of Women in the States. Women's Economic Status in the States: Wide Disparities by Race, Ethnicity, and Region.* Washington, DC: Institute for Women's Policy Research. *www.iwpr.org.*
Center for Women Policy Studies. 2002. *From Poverty to Self-Sufficiency: The Role of Postsecondary Education in Welfare Reform.* Washington, DC: Center for Women Policy Studies. *www.centerwomenpolicy.org.*
———. 2004. *A Profile of Low Income Women Students in Postsecondary Educational*

Institutions. Washington, DC: Center for Women Policy Studies. *www. centerwomenpolicy.org.*

Center on Budget and Policy Priorities. 2003. *Introduction to the Housing Voucher Program.* May 15. Washington, DC: Center on Budget and Policy Priorities. *www.cbpp.org.*

————. 2009. *American Recovery and Reinvestment Act of 2009: State-by-State Estimates of Key Provisions Affecting Low- and Moderate-Income Individuals.* Updated March 3. Washington, DC: Center on Budget and Policy Priorities. *www.cbpp.org.*

Clarke, John. 2004. *Changing Welfare, Changing States: New Directions in Social Policy.* London. Sage Publications.

Clinton, Bill. 1992. Acceptance Speech to the Democratic National Convention by Governor Bill Clinton From Arkansas. July 16. *www.4president.org.*

————. 2006. How We Ended Welfare, Together. Op-ed. *New York Times,* August 22. *www.nytimes.com.*

Coalition on Human Needs. 2002. President Bush Unveils TANF Reauthorization Agenda (2/28/02). Plan Undermines Support for Low-Income Families. *Human Needs Report Article.* February 28. Washington, DC: Coalition on Human Needs. *www.chn.org.*

Colen, Shellee. 1995. "Like a Mother to Them": Stratified Reproduction and West Indian Childcare Workers and Employers in New York. In *Conceiving the New World Order: The Global Politics of Reproduction,* ed. Faye D. Ginsburg and Rayna Rapp, 78–102. Berkeley: University of California Press.

Cornelius, Llewellyn J. 2003. Fixing that Great Hodgepodge: Health Care for the Poor in the U.S. In *Rediscovering the Other America: The Continuing Crisis of Poverty and Inequality in the United States,* ed. Keith M. Kilty and Elizabeth A. Segal. New York: Haworth Press.

Coughlin, Teresa A. 2004. *State Responses to Budget Crises in 2004: New York.* February. Washington, DC: Urban Institute. *www.urban.org.*

Davis, Dána-Ain. 2006. *Battered Black Women and Welfare Reform: Between a Rock and a Hard Place.* Albany: State University of New York Press.

DeParle, Jason. 2004. *American Dream: Three Women, Ten Kids, and a Nation's Drive to End Welfare.* New York: Viking.

————. 2009. Welfare Aid Isn't Growing as Economy Drops Off. *New York Times,* February 2. *www.nytimes.com.*

Doar, Robert. Commissioner, New York State Office of Temporary and Disability Assistance. 2005. Testimony. *Assembly Standing Committee on Social Services. Public Hearing #2. The Effect of Welfare Reform Policy in New York State.* September 21 (transcript).

Edin, Kathryn, and Laura Lein. 1997. *Making Ends Meet: How Single Mothers Survive Welfare and Low-Wage Work.* New York: Russell Sage Foundation.

Ehrenreich, Barbara. 2001. *Nickel and Dimed: On (Not) Getting By in America.* New York: Metropolitan Books.

Eisenstein, Zillah R., ed. 1979. *Capitalist Patriarchy and the Case for Socialist Feminism*. New York: Monthly Review Press.

Empire Justice Center. 2007. *Low Income Disabled Families Claim Victory as State Actions Found Illegal*. October 16. Albany, NY (on file with author).

Erchak, Gerald M. 1992. *The Anthropology of Self and Behavior*. New Brunswick: Rutgers University Press.

Ferber, Marianne, and Jane Waldfogel. 1998. The Long-Term Consequences of Nontraditional Employment. *Monthly Labor Review*. May. 3–12. *www.bls.gov*.

Fiscal Policy Institute. 2004. *Balancing New York State's 2004–2005 Budget in an Economically Sensible Manner*. January. Latham, NY: Fiscal Policy Institute. *www.fiscalpolicy.org*.

———. 2005. *Balancing New York State's 2005–2006 Budget in an Economically Sensible Manner*. January. Latham, NY: Fiscal Policy Institute. *www.fiscalpolicy.org*.

———. 2006a. *Pulling Apart in New York: An Analysis of Income Trends in New York State*. January 26. Latham, NY: Fiscal Policy Institute. *www.fiscalpolicy.org*.

———. 2006b. *The State of Working New York 2005: Treading Water in a Tenuous Recovery*. January. Latham: NY: Fiscal Policy Institute. *www.fiscalpolicy.org*.

Foucault, Michel. 1984. The Body of the Condemned. Panopticism. Complete and Austere Institutions. In *The Foucault Reader*, ed. Paul Rabinow. New York: Pantheon Books.

Fraser, Nancy, and Linda Gordon. 1996. The Genealogy of Dependency: Tracing a Keyword of the U.S. Welfare State. In *For Crying Out Loud: Women's Poverty in the United States*, ed. Diane Dujon and Ann Withorn, 235–67. Boston: South End Press.

Friedman, Donna Haig, with Rosa Clark [et al]. 2000. *Parenting in Public: Family Shelter and Public Assistance*. New York: Columbia University Press.

Goodale, Jane C. 1971. *Tiwi Wives: A Study of the Women of Melville Island, North Australia*. Seattle: University of Washington Press.

Goode, Judith, and Jeff Maskovsky. 2001. Introduction. In *The New Poverty Studies: The Ethnography of Power, Politics, and Impoverished People in the United States*, ed. Judith Goode and Jeff Maskovsky, 1–34. New York: New York University Press.

Gordon, Linda. 1994. *Pitied but Not Entitled: Single Mothers and the History of Welfare 1890–1935*. New York: Free Press.

———. 2002. Who Deserves Help? Who Must Provide? In *Lost Ground: Welfare Reform, Poverty, and Beyond*, ed. Randy Albelda and Ann Withorn, 9–25. Cambridge, MA: South End Press.

Greenstein, Robert. 2005. *The Earned Income Tax Credit: Boosting Employment, Aiding the Working Poor*. Revised August 17. Washington, DC: Center on Budget and Policy Priorities. *www.cbpp.org*.

Gueron, Judith M., and Edward Pauly, with Cameran M. Lougy. 1991. *From Welfare to Work*. New York: Russell Sage Foundation.

Hannerz, Ulf. 1969. *Soulside: Inquiries into Ghetto Culture and Community.* New York: Columbia University Press.

Harvey, David. 1990. *The Condition of Postmodernity: An Enquiry into the Origins of Cultural Change.* Cambridge, MA: Blackwell.

———. 2005. *A Brief History of Neoliberalism.* New York: Oxford University Press.

Haskins, Ron. 2001. Effects of Welfare Reform on Family Income and Poverty. In *The New World of Welfare*, ed. Rebecca M. Blank and Ron Haskins, 103–36. Washington, DC: Brookings Institution Press.

Hirsch, Amy E., Sharon M. Dietrich, Rue Landau, Peter D. Schneider, Irv Ackelsberg, Judith Bernstein-Baker, and Joseph Hohenstein. 2002. *Every Door Closed: Barriers Facing Parents with Criminal Records.* Washington, DC: Center for Law and Social Policy; Philadelphia, PA: Community Legal Services. *www.clasp.org.*

Hochschild, Arlie Russell. 1997. *The Time Bind: When Work Becomes Home and Home Becomes Work.* New York: Metropolitan Books.

Holden, Karen C., and Pamela J. Smock. 1991. The Economic Costs of Marital Dissolution: Why Do Women Bear a Disproportionate Cost? *Annual Review of Sociology* 17:51–78.

Internal Revenue Service, United States Department of the Treasury. 2004. *IRS Outlines EITC Eligibility for 2003 Tax Year.* January. Page last reviewed or updated October 31, 2007. *www.irs.gov.*

Jones, Delmos J. 1993. The Culture of Achievement among the Poor: The Case of Mothers and Children in a Head Start Program. *Critique of Anthropology* 13(3):247–66.

Jones-DeWeever, Avis A., and Barbara Gault. 2006. *Resilient and Reaching for More: Challenges and Benefits of Higher Education for Welfare Participants and Their Children.* Washington, DC: Institute for Women's Policy Research. *www.iwpr.org.*

Kahn, Peggy, and Valerie Polakow. 2002. Struggling to Live and to Learn: Single Mothers, Welfare Policy and Post-Secondary Education in Michigan. In *Work, Welfare and Politics: Confronting Poverty in the Wake of Welfare Reform*, ed. Frances Fox Piven, Joan Acker, Margaret Hallock, and Sandra Morgen, 157–71. Eugene: University of Oregon Press.

Kalleberg, Arne L. 2000. Nonstandard Employment Relations: Part-time, Temporary and Contract Work. *Annual Review of Sociology* 26:341–65.

———. 2003. Flexible Firms and Labor Market Segmentation: Effects of Workplace Restructuring on Jobs and Workers. *Work and Occupations* 30(2):154–75.

Katz, Michael B. 1986. *In the Shadow of the Poorhouse: A Social History of Welfare in America.* New York: Basic Books.

Kessler-Harris, Alice. 1982. *Out to Work: A History of Wage-Earning Women in the United States.* Oxford: Oxford University Press.

Kingfisher, Catherine Pélissier. 1996. *Women in the American Welfare Trap.* Philadelphia: University of Pennsylvania Press.

Kingfisher, Catherine, ed. 2002. *Western Welfare in Decline: Globalization and Women's Poverty.* Philadelphia: University of Pennsylvania Press.

Ku, Leighton, and Bowen Garrett. 2000. *How Welfare Reform and Economic Factors Affected Medicaid Participation: 1984–96.* February. Washington, DC: Urban Institute. *www.urban.org.*

Kurz, Demie. 1999. Women, Welfare and Domestic Violence. In *Whose Welfare?* ed. Gwendolyn Mink, 132–51. Ithaca, NY: Cornell University Press.

Leacock, Eleanor Burke. 1971. Introduction. In *The Culture of Poverty: A Critique*, ed. Eleanor Burke Leacock, 9–37. New York: Simon and Schuster.

Legal Momentum. 2004. *Family Violence Option: State by State Summary.* Created December 2001, updated July 2004. New York: Legal Momentum. *www.legalmomentum.org.*

Lewis, Oscar. 1966. The Culture of Poverty. *Scientific American.* 215(4):19–25.

Liebow, Elliot. 1967. *Tally's Corner: A Study of Negro Streetcorner Men.* Boston: Little, Brown.

Lipsky, Michael. 1980. *Street-Level Bureaucracy: Dilemmas of the Individual in Public Services.* New York: Russell Sage Foundation.

Loffredo, Stephen. 2001. Poverty Law and Community Activism: Notes from a Law School Clinic. *University of Pennsylvania Law Review* 150:173–204.

Martinson, Karin, and Julie Strawn. 2002. *Built to Last: Why Skills Matter for Long-Run Success in Welfare Reform.* May. Washington, DC: Center for Law and Social Policy and the National Council of State Directors of Adult Education. *www.clasp.org.*

Mathur, Anita, with Judy Reichle, Julie Strawn, and Chuck Wiseley. 2004. *From Jobs to Careers: How California Community College Credentials Pay Off for Welfare Recipients.* May. Washington, DC: Center for Law and Social Policy and the California Community Colleges Chancellor's Office. *www.clasp.org.*

McKenzie, Michelle, Jacqueline Peterson Tulsky, Heather L. Long, Margaret Chesney, and Andrew Moss. 1999. Tracking and Follow-up of Marginalized Populations: A Review. *Journal of Health Care for the Poor and Underserved* 10(4):409–29.

McMillan, Tracie. 2005. Welfare Withheld: New State Reg Would Delay Benefits. *City Limits WEEKLY.* November 14. *www.citylimits.org.*

Mink, Gwendolyn. 1995. *The Wages of Motherhood: Inequality in the Welfare State, 1917–1942.* Ithaca, NY: Cornell University Press.

———. 2002. *Welfare's End.* Rev. ed. Ithaca, NY: Cornell University Press.

Mollenkopf, John H., and Manuel Castells, eds. 1991. *Dual City: Restructuring New York.* New York: Russell Sage Foundation.

Morgen, Sandra. 2001. The Agency of Welfare Workers: Negotiating Devolution, Privatization, and the Meaning of Self-Sufficiency. *American Anthropologist* 103(3):747–61.

Moynihan, Daniel P. 1965. *The Negro Family: The Case for National Action.* March. Washington DC: Office of Policy Planning and Research, United States Department of Labor.

Mullings, Leith, and Alaka Wali. 2001. *Stress and Resilience: The Social Context of Reproduction in Central Harlem.* New York: Kluwer Academic/Plenum.

Munger, Frank, ed. 2002. *Laboring below the Line: The New Ethnography of Poverty, Low-Wage Work, and Survival in the Global Economy.* New York: Russell Sage Foundation.

Murray, Charles. 1984. *Losing Ground: American Social Policy, 1950–1980.* New York: Basic Books.

Nash, June C. 1989. *From Tank Town to High Tech: The Clash of Community and Industrial Cycles.* Albany: State University of New York Press.

National Low Income Housing Coalition. 2004. *Out of Reach 2004.* Washington, DC: National Low Income Housing Coalition. *www.nlihc.org.*

———. 2005. *Out of Reach 2005.* Washington, DC: National Low Income Housing Coalition. *www.nlihc.org.*

Neubeck, Kenneth J., and Noel A. Cazenave. 2001. *Welfare Racism: Playing the Race Card against America's Poor.* New York: Routledge.

New York State Assembly. 2004. *Memorandum in Support of Legislation.* Bill Number A10097. March 2. *public.leginfo.state.ny.us.*

New York State Constitution, Article XVII. November 8, 1938. As Amended and in Force Since January 1, 2009. Albany, NY: Provided by the Department of State, Division of Administrative Rules. *www.dos.state.ny.us/info/constitution.htm.*

New York State Department of Labor, Workforce New York. 2006. *Employment Prospects to 2012. www.labor.state.ny.us.*

New York State Office of Temporary and Disability Assistance. 2000. *Welfare Reform Community Organization Resource Guide.* Albany, NY: Produced by the New York State Office of Temporary and Disability Assistance. *www.otda.state.ny.us* (no longer on website.)

———. 2002a. *What You Should Know About Social Services Programs.* New York State: LDSS-4148B (Rev. 11/02).

———. 2002b. *New York State Plan and Executive Certification.* Administration of the Block Grant for Temporary Assistance for Needy Families. Submitted by the New York State Office of Temporary and Disability Assistance. Robert Doar, Commissioner. Effective November 1, 2002–November 30, 2005. *www.otda.state.ny.us* (accessed April 22, 2005).

———. 2003. *Application For: Temporary Assistance (TA)—Medical Assistance (MA)—Medicare Savings Program (MSP)—Food Stamp Benefits (FS)—Services (S), including Foster Care (FC)—Child Care Assistance (CC).* New York State: LDSS-2921 Statewide (Rev. 7/03).

———. 2005a. Proposed Rule Making. Application for Safety Net Assistance. *NYS Register,* October 19, 28–30. *www.dos.state.ny.us.*

———. 2005b. *Temporary Assistance Source Book. www.otda.state.ny.us* (accessed February 2005).

———. 2007. *Policy Directives. www.otda.state.ny.us.*

———. n.d.a. *NYS OTDA Domestic Violence/Family Violence Option. www.otda.state.ny.us* (accessed September 16, 2005; no longer on website).

———. n.d.b. *What Is a Fair Hearing? www.otda.state.ny.us* (accessed January 12, 2006; no longer on website).

New York State Senate. 2004. *Introducer's Memorandum in Support.* Bill Number S6358. March 4. *public.leginfo.state.ny.us.*

Newman, Katherine S. 1999. *No Shame in My Game: The Working Poor in the Inner City.* New York: Knopf and the Russell Sage Foundation.

———. 2006. *Chutes and Ladders: Navigating the Low-Wage Labor Market.* New York: Russell Sage Foundation.

Niman, Michael I. 2000. Incarceration Nation: The US Is the World's Leading Jailer. *Buffalo Beat,* January 4. *www.mediastudy.com.*

Obama, Barack. 2009a. *President Barack Obama's Inaugural Address.* January 21. Washington, DC: The White House, President Barack Obama. *www.whitehouse.gov.*

———. 2009b. *Remarks of President Barack Obama—Address to Joint Session of Congress.* February 24. Washington, DC: The White House, President Barack Obama. *www.whitehouse.gov.*

———. 2009c. President's Message. In *A New Era of Responsibility: Renewing America's Promise.* February 26. Washington, DC: The White House, President Barack Obama. Office of Management and Budget. *www.gpo.gov.*

Pappas, Gregory. 1989. *The Magic City: Unemployment in a Working-Class Community.* Ithaca, NY: Cornell University Press.

Parrott, Sharon. 2009. *Despite Critics' Over-Heated Rhetoric, the Economic Recovery Bill Does Not Undermine Welfare Reform.* February 17. Washington, DC: Center on Budget and Policy Priorities. *www.cbpp.org.*

Parrott, Sharon, and Liz Schott. 2009. *Overview of the TANF Provisions in the Economic Recovery Act.* February 26. Washington, DC: Center on Budget and Policy Priorities. *www.cbpp.org.*

Parrott, Sharon, Liz Schott, Eileen Sweeney, Allegra Baider, Evelyn Ganzglass, Mark Greenberg, Elizabeth Lower-Basch, Elisa Minoff, and Vicki Turetsky. 2007. *Implementing the TANF Changes in the Deficit Reduction Act: "Win-Win" Solutions for Families and States.* 2nd ed., February. Washington, DC: Center on Budget and Policy Priorities, and Center for Law and Social Policy. *www.cbpp.org.*

Passaro, Joanne. 1996. *The Unequal Homeless: Men on the Streets, Women in Their Place.* New York: Routledge.

Pavetti, LaDonna, Michelle K. Derr, Gretchen Kirby, Robert G. Wood, and Melissa A. Clark. 2004. *The Use of TANF Work-Oriented Sanctions in Illinois, New Jersey, and South Carolina.* April 30. Washington, DC: Mathematica Policy Research. *www.mathematica-mpr.com.*

Pearce, Diana. 2004. *The Self Sufficiency Standard for the City of New York 2004.* November. Prepared for Women's Center of Education and Career Advancement in conjunction with Wider Opportunities for Women's Family Economic Self-Sufficiency Project. *www.sixstrategies.org.*

Pearce, Diana, with Jennifer Brooks. 2000. *The Self Sufficiency Standard for New York.*

September. Diana Pearce and New York State Self-Sufficiency Standard Steering Committee. *www.sixstrategies.org.*

Peck, Jamie. 2001. *Workfare States.* New York: Guilford.

Piven, Frances Fox. 1998. Welfare Reform and the Economic and Cultural Reconstruction of Low Wage Labor Markets. *City and Society.* 21–36.

Piven, Frances Fox, and Richard A. Cloward. 1979. *Poor People's Movements: Why They Succeed, How They Fail.* New York: Vintage Books.

———. 1993. *Regulating the Poor: The Functions of Public Welfare.* Updated ed. New York: Vintage Books (Orig. pub. 1971).

Polakow, Valerie, Sandra S. Butler, Luisa Stormer Deprez, and Peggy Kahn, eds. 2004. *Shut Out: Low Income Mothers and Higher Education in Post-Welfare America.* Albany: State University of New York Press.

Price, Charles, and Tracy Steffy, with Tracy McFarlane. 2003. *Continuing a Commitment to the Higher Education Option: Model State Legislation, College Programs, and Advocacy Organizations that Support Access to Post-Secondary Education for Public Assistance Recipients.* April. New York: Howard Samuels State Management and Policy Center, City University of New York Graduate Center. *www.howardsamuelscenter.org.*

Quadagno, Jill. 1994. *The Color of Welfare: How Racism Undermined the War on Poverty.* New York: Oxford University Press.

Renwick, Trudi. 2005. *Testimony Presented at the New York State Legislature's Joint Budget Hearing on Human Services.* Testimony of Trudi Renwick, Ph.D., Senior Economist, Fiscal Policy Institute, before the Senate Finance and Assembly Ways and Means Committees, Joint Public Hearings on Human Services, February 7. Latham, NY: Fiscal Policy Institute. *www.fiscalpolicy.org.*

———. 2006. *The Impact of Federal TANF Reauthorization in New York.* March 2. Latham, NY: Fiscal Policy Institute. *www.fiscalpolicy.org.*

Republican Members of the House of Representatives. 1994. *Republican Contract with America.* United States House of Representatives. *www.house.gov/house.*

Roberts, Dorothy. 2002. *Shattered Bonds: The Color of Child Welfare.* New York: Basic Civitas Books.

Rogers-Dillon, Robin H. 2004. *The Welfare Experiments: Politics and Policy Evaluation.* Stanford: Stanford University Press.

Rowe, Gretchen, with Jeffrey Versteeg. 2005. *Welfare Rules Databook: State TANF Policies as of July 2003.* April. Washington, DC: Urban Institute. *www.urban.org.*

Schram, Sanford F. 2000. *After Welfare: The Culture of Postindustrial Social Policy.* New York: New York University Press.

Shostak, Marjorie. 1983. *Nisa: The Life and Words of a !Kung Woman.* First Vintage Books ed. New York: Vintage Books.

Sidel, Ruth. 1996. The Enemy Within: A Commentary on the Demonization of Difference. *American Journal of Orthopsychiatry* 66(4):490–95.

Silverman, Sydel F. 1975. The Life Crisis as a Clue to Social Function: The Case of

Italy. In *Toward an Anthropology of Women*, ed. Rayna R. Reiter, 309–21. New York: Monthly Review Press.

Stack, Carol B. 1974. *All Our Kin: Strategies for Survival in a Black Community.* New York: Harper and Row.

Street, Paul. 2001. Color Bind: Prisons and the New American Racism. *Dissent*, Summer, 49–54.

Susser, Ida. 1982. *Norman Street: Poverty and Politics in an Urban Neighborhood.* New York: Oxford University Press.

———. 1991. The Separation of Mothers and Children. In *Dual City: Restructuring New York*, ed. John H. Mollenkopf and Manuel Castells, 207–24. New York: Russell Sage Foundation.

———. 1996. The Construction of Poverty and Homelessness in US Cities. *Annual Review of Anthropology* 25:411–35.

———. 1997. The Flexible Woman: Regendering Labor in the Informational Society. *Critique of Anthropology* 17(4):389–402.

Susser, Ida, and John Kreniske. 1987. The Welfare Trap: a Public Policy for Deprivation. In *Cities of the United States: Studies in Urban Anthropology*, ed. Leith Mullings, 51–68. New York: Columbia University Press.

U.S. Bureau of the Census. P007. Detailed Race – Universe: Persons. Data Set: 1990 Summary Tape File 1 (STF 1)—100 Percent Data. American FactFinder. *www.factfinder.census.gov.*

———. 2000a. *Census 2000 Demographic Profile Highlights.* American FactFinder. *www.factfinder.census.gov.*

———. 2000b. *Poverty: 2000 Highlights.* Revised May 13, 2005. *www.census.gov.*

———. 2004a. *Counties within United States: R2001. Median Household Income (In 2004 Inflation-Adjusted Dollars): 2004.* Universe: Households. Data Set: 2004 American Community Survey. *www.factfinder.census.gov.*

———. 2004b. *Westchester County, New York. Selected Housing Characteristics: 2004.* Data Set: 2004 American Community Survey. *www.factfinder.census.gov.*

———. 2006. *Poverty: Historic Poverty Tables. www.census.gov/hhes/www/poverty/histpov/hstpov2.html.*

U.S. Congress. 1996. *Personal Responsibility and Work Opportunity Reconciliation Act of 1996. Public Law 104–193—August 22, 1996.* HR 3734. 104th Cong. *wdr.doleta.gov/readroom/legislation/pdf/104–193.pdf.*

U.S. Department of Agriculture, Food and Nutrition Service. *Supplemental Nutrition Assistance Program: Number of Persons Participating (Data as of February 27, 2009).* Washington, DC: USDA. *www.fns.usda.gov.*

U.S. Department of Health and Human Services, Administration for Children and Families. 2000. *Statistics. Temporary Assistance for Needy Families (TANF) Percent of Total U.S Population, 1960–1999. www.acf.hhs.gov* (accessed October 14, 2005).

———. 2004à. *Total Number of TANF Families and Recipients: Fiscal Year 2004 as of 7/31/04. www.acf.hhs.gov* (accessed October 23, 2004).

———. 2004b. News Release. *Welfare Rolls Fall under Two Million: 1st Quarter Data for 2004 Shows Another Decline in Caseloads.* October 7. Washington DC: AFC Press Office. *www.acf.hhs.gov.*

———. 2006a. 45 CFR Parts 261, et al. Reauthorization of the Temporary Assistance for Needy Families Program; Interim Final Rule. *Federal Register,* June 29. 71(125):37453–83. Washington, DC: GPO. *www.gpoaccess.gov.*

———. 2006b. [TANF] *Fact Sheet.* Updated October. *www.acf.hhs.gov.*

———. 2008. 45 CRF Parts 261, 262, 263, and 265 Reauthorization of the Temporary Assistance for Needy Families (TANF) Program; Final Rule. *Federal Register.* February 5. 73(24):6771–6828. Washington, DC: GPO. *www.gpoaccess.gov.*

———. n.d. *Fact Sheet. Welfare Reform: Deficit Reduction Act of 2005. www.acf.hhs.gov* (accessed July 27, 2007; no longer on website).

U.S. Department of Labor, Bureau of Labor Statistics. 2007. *Labor Force Statistics from the Current Population Survey. data.bls.gov* (data extracted March 15, 2007).

———. 2009. Economic News Release, Employment Situation Summary. February 6. *data.bls.gov.*

U.S. House of Representatives, Committee on Ways and Means. 1998. *1998 Green Book: Background Material and Data on Programs Within the Jurisdiction of the Committee on Ways and Means.* Washington, DC: GPO. *www.gpoaccess.gov.*

Valentine, Bettylou. 1983. Women on Welfare: Public Policy and Institutional Racism (1981). In *Class, Race, and Sex: The Dynamics of Control,* ed. Amy Swerdlow and Hanna Lessinger, 276–87. Boston: G. K. Hall.

Valentine, Charles A. 1968. *Culture and Poverty: Critique and Counter-Proposals.* Chicago: University of Chicago Press.

Waldron, Tom, Brandon Roberts, and Andrew Reamer, with Assistance from Sara Rab and Steve Ressler. 2004. *Working Hard, Falling Short: America's Working Families and the Pursuit of Economic Security.* October. Annie E. Casey Foundation, Ford Foundation, and Rockefeller Foundation. *www.aecf.org.*

Weeden, Kim A. 2005. Is There a Flexiglass Ceiling? Flexible Work Arrangements and Wages in the United States. *Social Science Research* 34:454–82.

Weil, Alan, and Kenneth Finegold. 2002. Introduction. In *Welfare Reform: The Next Act,* ed. Alan Weil and Kenneth Finegold, xi–xxxi. Washington, DC: Urban Institute Press.

Weiner, Annette B. 1976. *Women of Value, Men of Renown: New Perspectives in Trobriand Exchange.* Austin: University of Texas Press.

West, Guida. 1981. *The National Welfare Rights Movement: The Social Protest of Poor Women.* New York: Praeger.

Williams, Lucy A. 1995. Race, Rat Bites and Unfit Mothers: How Media Discourse Informs Welfare Legislation Debate. *Fordham Urban Law Journal* 22:1159–96.

Index